The Basics of Speech Communication

Scott McLean

Arizona Western College

Boston   New York   San Francisco
Mexico City   Montreal   Toronto   London   Madrid   Munich   Paris
Hong Kong   Singapore   Tokyo   Cape Town   Sydney

For Lisa, my wife, and our children, Mackenzie, John, and Katherine.

Vice President, Editor-in Chief: *Karen Hanson*
Senior Editor: *Karon Bowers*
Editorial Assistant: *Jennifer Trebby*
Marketing Manager: *Mandee Eckersley*
Production Editor: *Christine Tridente*
Editorial Production Service: *Modern Graphics, Inc.*
Composition Buyer: *Linda Cox*
Manufacturing Buyer: *Chris Marson*
Cover Administrator: *Kristina Mose-Libon*
Electronic Composition: *Modern Graphics, Inc.*

For related titles and support materials, visit our online catalog at
www.ablongman.com.

Between the time Website information is gathered and then published, it is not
unusual for some sites to have closed. Also, the transcription of URLs can result in
unintended typographical errors. The publisher would appreciate notification
where these errors occur so that they may be corrected in subsequent editions.

Library of Congress Cataloging-in-Publication Data

McLean, Scott. 1969–
 The basics of speech communication / Scott McLean.
  p. cm.
 Includes bibliographical references and index.
 ISBN 0-205-33528-4
 1. Oral communication. I. Title.
P95 .M4 2002
302.2'242—dc21

2001056078

Printed in the United States of America

10 9 8 7 6 5 4 3 2 1   08 07 06 04 03 02

Contents

6 *Intrapersonal and Interpersonal Communication*   **113**

Preface

Goal of the Text

The Basics of Speech Communication is designed to deliver what the title states, a clear and concise introduction to the basics of speech communication. This text is designed clearly with the student taking his or her first communication course in mind and assumes no prior academic preparation in the field. It does not, however, underestimate the vast knowledge and experience base that each student brings with him or her into the classroom setting. This text presents these basic concepts, vocabulary, theories, and exercises in a readily accessible manner, incorporating current pedagogy to enhance the learning process.

This text:

1. Focuses on key concepts, class tested to improve clarity.
2. Provides clear chapter objectives at the beginning of each chapter.
3. Features chapter opening class activities to introduce concepts and spark curiosity.
4. Provides a view of communication from the student's perspective, with clear connections between abstract concepts and real-world examples.
5. Focuses on skills and active applications.

Universities and community and vocational colleges often state as their mission to serve the needs of the community, from running start high school students completing college transfer courses to returning non–traditional age students seeking enrichment. Students may be returning to school after time working or raising a family, currently employed and balancing academic and work activities. Students who have not had significant success in other academic environments are often attracted to open admission institutions with classes held in the evenings and on weekends. For an increasing percentage of students, English is not their first or only language. To meet this diverse range of needs, many community colleges and universities design hybrid courses to meet expectations efficiently and effectively.

This text is designed to introduce the basics of speech communication in a clear, concise, and engaging way. Activities to enhance learning featured in this text include first-day-of-class activities, role-playing exercises, journal writings, case studies, mapping exercises, pair and small-group activities, games, and self-assessment questionnaires. In addition, study skills such as note taking and step by step outlining are provided.

Organization

This text is organized in a straightforward, practical, and workable approach to teaching the fundamentals of speech communication.

Each chapter features learning objectives and introductory exercises. The learning objectives communicate clearly the goals of each chapter, and the exercises stimulate curiosity while providing a common reference for analysis.

In addition, each chapter includes boxed features to reinforce, highlight, and expand on information in the text. Case study features go more in depth on a point, example, or theory. Intercultural communication features provide examples of how culture, language, race, and ethnicity are part of the communication process. Computer-mediated communication features provide examples of communication in this context drawn from real-world experiences.

Each chapter concludes with notes about additional information for further research and features four types of questions to use in class or for student-driven learning. Factual questions underline specific concepts or terms, whereas interpretative questions require more application and critical-thinking skills. Evaluative questions encourage students and instructors to go beyond the text, and application questions reinforce key concepts.

Here is a brief summary of each chapter and an overview of how they relate and build on one another.

Chapter	Description
1	Discusses why we need to study communication, its basic elements and principles, models, and importance in our lives.
2	Discusses perception and listening theory and skills, both fundamental to the comprehension and application of subsequent chapters. It features exercises, puzzles, and examples to reinforce learning.
3	Discusses verbal communication, principles of language, the nature of language and perception, and language-based obstacles to communication.
4	Discusses nonverbal communication, detailing the characteristics, types, and function.
5	Introduces the fascinating study of intercultural communication, expanding on information presented in Chapters 3 and 4.
6	Begins the discussion of communication in context, addressing intrapersonal and interpersonal communication. This chapter outlines

interpersonal needs, self-concept, and theories associated with the motivation to communicate.

7   Discusses group communication, group development and life cycles, leadership styles, and conflict resolution.

8   Builds on both group communication and interpersonal communication to discuss communication at work, including research, interviewing, and meetings in personal and electronic settings.

9   Discusses mass communication, which combines aspects of all of the previous chapters, provides a brief history of several types of mass media, and focuses on ways to be a critical media consumer.

10   Discusses how to select a topic, conduct research, organize information, and prepare for a speech or oral presentation.

11   Discusses speech delivery, use of voice, body language and movement, visual aids, and the importance of ethics in communication.

Note to Student

This text was designed with your success in mind. It should prove itself to be accessible to read and you should be able to locate information you need to understand and implement key concepts and skills. You are asked to re-flect, take notes, and complete exercises on your own or in groups through-out the text. Like many things in life, you get out of something what you put into it. Read this text with an open mind and draw on your years of making sense of your world, your relationships with yourself and others, and your own talent and skills as a communicator. You have been doing it all your life, and now this text and this class will help you understand this dynamic and interactive process better.

In addition, please note that the cost of this text is relatively low for a reason. Communication is an important part of all our lives, and the degree to which we can understand its basic principles and effect positive changes in our lives, from performing more effectively in a job interview setting to forming and maintaining positive relationships, has an impact beyond ourselves. Taking a communication course is an excellent first step, and being able to afford the text is important.

Note to Instructor

This text was also designed with your success in mind. Students juggle work, relationships, and other courses outside of our classrooms. The text can serve as a stand-alone, low-cost, "nuts-and-bolts" survey text of communication, providing your students with the opportunity to prepare for classroom discussion by completing reading and note-taking assignments, and giving you a solid foundation to build on, adapt, and/or complement with additional material depending on your individual instruction methods, goals, or objectives. Please feel free to arrange the material presented in the order that works for you. The speech preparation and speech presentation chapters are placed after the fundamentals and contexts, but you may choose to introduce them early in the quarter or semester.

In addition, this text is accompanied by an Instructor's Manual that contains "zero preparation" exercises, clear connections between interactive activities and concepts, assessment forms, and answer keys.

Acknowledgments

I would like to extend my thanks to all my friends and colleagues, particularly Karen Spencer at Arizona Western College, for their encouragement and support. Karon Bowers at Allyn & Bacon also deserves many thanks as she worked step by step with me through this process, always keeping in mind our goal of a concise, clear, and affordable text well suited to students and instructors of the basic hybrid communication course.

To my students I owe a debt of gratitude as you have taught me how to be more creative in the instruction of this knowledge, and your constructive feedback has contributed to the production of the text you now hold in your hands.

I appreciate all the specific feedback that led to significant improvements in the text. Additionally, I want to thank the following reviewers: Barbara Laughlin Adler, Concordia College; Rusalyn Andrews, Cottey College; Edd Applegate, Middle Tennessee State University; Leonard Assante, Volunteer State Community College; Virginia Chapman, Anderson University; Hank Flick, Mississippi State University; and Thomas E. Ruddick, Edison Community College.

Finally, I would like to acknowledge the significant contributions made to the text by my partner and wife, Lisa. Your "so what's," "can't you make this clearer," and "if I were your student I wouldn't get this concept as it's written," challenged me to improve the text for everyone.

Scott McLean

Why Study Communication?

Chapter Objectives

After completing this chapter, you should be able to:

1. Understand the importance of communication.
2. Define communication.
3. Describe communication as a process.
4. Identify and describe four models of communication.
5. Identify and describe eight essential components of communication.
6. Identify and describe five types of communication contexts.
7. Describe five key principles of communication.

Introductory Exercise 1.1

Have you ever considered how we use communication in the workplace? Is communication important to our success? Is it something we just do, or is it a skill that can be learned? Using these three questions, ask yourself how communication is used where you work. Compare your notes with those of other people in your class.

Introductory Exercise 1.2

Have you ever thought about how much or how often you communicate in a day? How about how often people communicate with you? How often do you watch television, listen to the radio, or read a newspaper or magazine? How often do you spend time on the Internet? Where do you get your information? For one day, try to take notes on all the ways you communicate and how often. You may be amazed at what you find!

*I know that you believe that you understood what you think I said, but I
am not sure you realize that what you heard is not what I meant.*

— Robert McCloskey, State Department Spokesman

Why Study Communication?

What was the common theme in the first introductory exercise? If you said
communication is the key to success, you got it right! Employers around the
world consistently include good communication skills in their list of top
requirements for most, if not all, positions. Why is communication the key
to success at work? Work is all about relationships, with co-workers, supervisors, clients and customers, suppliers, and producers.

Exercise

Make a short list of what you value most in life. How many relate to communication?

Many people indicate family, loved ones, relationships, work, and hobbies
as what they value most in life. In each instance, communication is central
to what they consider important. If what you value most in life, from your
family to your partner or co-workers, involves communication, wouldn't
you want to be good at it?

Have you ever thought about the power communication has in our
lives? Communication is all around us. We send ourselves messages all
the time, and we share them with others through body language and
words. Sometimes we need to speak in public, and other times we need to
get the word out to everyone. Finally, stop to consider the media and its impact on your life. Do you watch television? Listen to the radio? Read a
newspaper or magazine? What were your results in the second exercise?
How we communicate with others makes an impact on our lives, and our
ability to understand that dynamic process can further our ability to communicate effectively. This book is designed to do exactly that: to give you
the understanding of key concepts in communication using exercises and
thought-provoking examples that can translate into an improvement in
your communication skills.

Now you may ask, "How do I improve my communication skills?"
One way is to get out there and just do it! Trial and error. Is this the *best* way
to prepare yourself for life? Communication is all around us, but it is hardly
perfect. One positive way to improve communication skills is to take a communication class.

Have you ever had a miscommunication happen at work? With
someone you care about? Perhaps an e-mail that got the facts across but of-
fended the person it was sent to caused friction, or interrupting someone in

a meeting took their turn away, so they did not get to share the information they prepared. Failure to have face-to-face communication, with all the nonverbal signals present, or neglecting to respect each other while competing for attention, can often contribute to miscommunication. Your knowledge of the communication process, and of how to pay attention to all the communication cues, can help prevent miscommunication.

Communicating what you want to say is a difficult task, and people who can do this well are often rewarded. In business, the ability to communicate effectively is highly prized. In a 1997 survey, executives who work for Fortune 500 companies indicated that they want workers who know how to speak, listen, and think effectively; who work well with people from diverse backgrounds; and who can make good decisions on their own and in groups (Seiler & Beall, 2000).

Can you think of a time when you did not communicate? When you awoke this morning you may have remembered the dream you had last night. You probably got yourself ready for the day and left for work or school. When you arrived you may have heard people in conversation. You may have made observations to yourself, or saw someone you knew and said "hi," starting a conversation. If you cannot think of a time when you are not communicating with yourself or others, you are right. Communication is everywhere. Now take a look at the beginning of this chapter again. The theme runs throughout life—good communication skills are necessary to be successful.

In this text you will learn communication skills that can improve your life and the lives of those around you. By learning the basics of communication, you will be able to feel more confident in your abilities as a communicator. People use their communication skills every day to try to share their needs and wants, hopes and dreams. This text will help prepare you to be a better communicator.

Exercise

Ask someone who is not in your class:

1. When was the last time you had a miscommunication with someone?

2. Describe what happened.

Compare your notes with those of other students in the next class session.

Definition of Communication

Communicare is the root of *communication.*

Communicare means to share, or to make common, in Latin. (Weekley, 1967, p. 338)

Communication is defined as the process of understanding and sharing meaning. (Pearson
& Nelson, 2000, p. 6)

Let's take a look at the definition. First comes the word *process.* A **process**
is a dynamic activity that is hard to describe because it changes (Pearson &
Nelson, 2000). Imagine you are alone in your room, thinking to yourself.
Someone you know enters your room and you talk briefly. What has
changed? Now imagine that the first person who entered your room is
joined by someone else, someone you do not know. What has changed?
Does the situation change depending on who enters the room? When they
enter the room? If they knock or enter without knocking on the door?
When we interact, all of these factors and many more influence the process
of communication.

The second key word is ***understanding***. To understand is to perceive, to
interpret, and to relate our perception and interpretation to what we already
know. If someone shares with you that he or she fell off his or her bike, what
image comes to mind? Now he or she points out the window and you see a
motorcycle lying on the ground. Understanding the words and understanding the shared meaning are important in the communication process.

Next comes the word ***sharing***. Sharing is when you give someone a
gift, or they spend time with you, or you decide to spend time with yourself,
relaxing and making sense of the day. Your exchange of your thoughts,
ideas, or insights with others or yourself is key to communication.

Finally, ***meaning*** is what we share through interaction. The word
"bike" represents both a bicycle and a motorcycle. By looking at the context
in which the word is used, and by asking questions, we can discover the
shared meaning of the word and understand the message.

Definition: **Communication** is defined as *the process of understanding and sharing
meaning.* (Pearson & Nelson, 2000, p. 6)

Models of Communication

Exercise _____

Draw what you think communication looks like. Share with another student.

In a Bell Telephone Company laboratory, shortly after World War II, two researchers gave this observation some consideration. Claude Shannon and
Warren Weaver wanted to know how to control communication in order to
communicate effectively and efficiently the maximum amount of information. One way they did this was by drawing a picture of what they thought
communication looked like, adapting their model from an earlier one
(Laswell, 1948). This model is called the *linear* model of communication

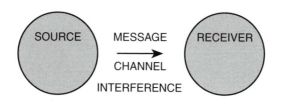

FIGURE 1.1 *Linear Model of Communication*

(Figure 1.1). The source sends the message to the receiver (Shannon & Weaver, 1949). Although this emphasis on three key components of the communication process may, at first, seem simple, it set the stage for an understanding of the exchange of information that became fundamental to computer and communication technologies to come.

As the study of communication evolved, the way people viewed communication changed. The focus shifted from a linear perspective, in which communication occurs in a set sequence, to how the source and receiver are *interactive*, sending messages back and forth in a more dynamic way (Figure 1.2).

Researchers observed that the source and the receiver send messages at the same time, often overlapping. Rather than looking at the source sending a message and someone receiving it as two distinct acts, researchers came to view communication as a *transactional* process, with actions often happening at the same time (Figure 1.3).

Finally, researchers examined the idea that we all construct our own interpretations of the message. Like Robert McCloskey said at the beginning of the chapter, what I said and what you heard may be different. In the *constructivist* model, we focus on the negotiated meaning, or common ground, when trying to describe communication (Cronen & Pearce, 1982; Pearce & Cronen, 1980). Imagine you go to Atlanta, Georgia, and go out to dinner. When asked if you want a "Coke," you may reply "sure." The waiter may then ask you again, "What kind?" and you may reply, "Coke is fine." The waiter then may ask a third time, "What kind of soft drink would you like?"

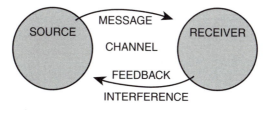

FIGURE 1.2 *Interactional Model of Communication*

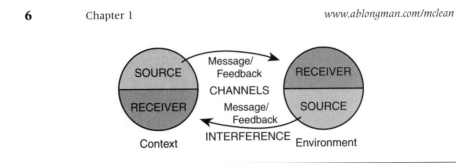

FIGURE 1.3 *Transactional Model of Communication*

The misunderstanding in this example is that, in the home of Coca-Cola, most soft drinks are generically referred to as "Coke." You then need to specify what type, even if it is not a cola beverage or even made by the Coca-Cola company. To someone from other regions of the United States, they may expect to hear "pop" or "soda pop," but not necessarily the brand "Coke" to describe most soft drinks. In this example, both you and the waiter understand the word "Coke," but you both understand it to mean different things. To communicate, you both must establish common ground and what the term means to each other to fully understand the request or provide an answer. Because we carry the multiple meanings of words, gestures, and ideas within us, we can use a dictionary to guide us, but we will still need to negotiate meaning.

Look at Figure 1.4 and see if you can identify parts of the communication process. Look for parts of the process we have not discussed yet.

Essential Components of Communication

As you can see from the models, the communication process becomes more complicated the closer you examine it. The source is sending a message across channels at the same time the receiver is giving feedback across channels. For example, if a speaker observes that an audience member is yawning, he or she may decide to change the presentation to make it more

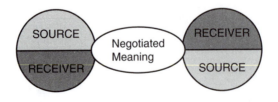

FIGURE 1.4 *Constructivist Model of Communication*

exciting. An audience member may ask a question about a point that is not clear. Through nonverbal communication (or body language) and verbal communication, both speaker and audience receive and send messages.

To better understand the communication process, the models we use to represent this dynamic process are composed of components. Each component plays an integral function in the overall process. Now let's examine the eight components that compose the communication process.

1. Source

The **source** creates and sends the message. In a speech, the source conveys the message (that they are confident and knowledgeable about the subject) through their presentation by sharing new information with the audience. The source also conveys the message (of confidence) through their choice of clothes, their enthusiasm, and body language. The source does this by first determining the message—what they want to say and how they want to say it. The next step involves encoding the message by choosing just the right order or the perfect word to convey the intended meaning. The third step is to present the information, sending the information to the receiver or audience. Finally, the source perceives how well the audience received the message, by watching for their reaction, and responds with clarification or supporting information.

2. Message

The **message** is the stimulus or meaning produced by the source for the receiver or audience. At first the message may seem to be only the words you choose to convey the meaning of the message. But that is just the beginning. The words are brought together with grammar and organization. You may choose to save the most important point for last. The message also consists of the way you say it, with your body, your tone of voice, and your appearance. Finally, part of the message may be the environment or context you present in and any noise that may make your message hard to hear or see.

3. Channel

The **channel** is the way in which a message or messages travel between source and receiver. For example, think of your television. How many channels do you have on your television? Each channel takes up some space in the cable or in the signal that brings the message of each channel to your home. Television brings together an audio signal you hear with a visual signal you see. Together they convey the message to the receiver or audience. Turn off the volume on your television. Can you still understand what is happening? Many times you can, because the body language conveys part of the message of the show. Now turn up the volume but turn around so that you cannot see the television. You can hear the discussion and still follow the story line. When a speaker presents, he or she uses channels such as voice, dress, and body language to carry the message to the audience.

4. Receiver

The **receiver** receives the message from the source, analyzing and interpreting the message in ways both intended and unintended by the source. To better understand this component, think of a receiver on a football team. The quarterback throws the message (football) to a receiver, who must see and interpret where to catch the football. The quarterback may intend the receiver to "catch" his message in one way, but the receiver may see things differently and miss the football, or intended meaning, altogether.

As a receiver, you listen, see, touch, smell, and/or taste to receive a message. Take for example an ice cream cone. You can see the color, touch the cone, smell and taste the flavor, and hear the server's voice say, "Your cone is ready." You respond to the ice cream vendor while he or she is making the cone—one scoop, two scoops, and which flavor. You also respond as you try the ice cream for the first time, making a face because it is too cold or smiling with joy at the rich flavor. The source is sending you messages and perceiving your response. So are you. All of this happens at the same time, illustrating why and how communication is always changing.

5. Feedback

When you respond to the source, you are giving feedback. **Feedback**, by definition, is the messages the receiver sends back to the source. You give feedback through your voice and your eyes as you point with your hand to which flavor. All of these signals in response to the source are called feedback. Feedback is a very important part of communication. It allows the source to see how well his or her message was received, and gives the receiver or audience the opportunity to ask for clarification, to disagree, or to indicate that the speaker could make the subject more interesting. One study found that as the amount of feedback increases, including spoken and unspoken responses, the accuracy of communication also increases (Leavitt and Mueller, 1951).

6. Environment

The **environment** is the atmosphere, physical and psychological, where you send and receive messages. The environment can include the tables, chairs, lighting, and sound equipment that are in the room. The environment can also include psychological factors, such as whether a discussion is open and caring or more professional and formal. People may be more likely to have an intimate conversation when they are physically close to each other and less likely when they can only see each other from across the room.

7. Context

The **context** of the communication interaction, unlike the chairs, tables, or lighting of the environment, involves the setting, scene, and expectations of the individuals involved. A professional context may involve business suits, but it also involves expectations of language and behavior.

A presentation or discussion does not take place as an isolated event. When you came to class you came from somewhere. So did the person seated next to you, as did the instructor. The degree to which the environment is formal or informal depends on the context. A wedding may be a formal event, where there is a time for open, free discussion and a time for silence as the bride walks down the aisle. In a business meeting, who speaks first? That probably has some relation to the position and role each person has outside of the meeting. Context plays a very important role in communication, particularly across cultures (Intercultural Communication 1.1).

8. Interference

The last part of the communication process that plays an important role is interference. Interference, also referred to as noise, can come from any source. **Interference** is anything that interferes with or changes the source's intended meaning of the message. If you drove a car to work or school, chances are you were surrounded by noise. Car horns, billboards, or perhaps the radio in your own car interrupted your thoughts, or your conversation

---

INTERCULTURAL COMMUNICATION 1.1 • *Cultural Context*

Cultural context involves the rules and customs, values and beliefs that are carried from one generation to the next. The communicator has his or her own cultural context, gained through a lifetime of experience, that guides how he or she communicates a message. In some cultures, children are taught to look at their parents when speaking or being spoken to. In other cultures, direct eye contact is a sign of disrespect. What is the expectation for eye contact where you come from?

with a passenger. Psychological noise, or your own thoughts in response to someone's comments, based on your own experiences or expectations, can prevent you from listening completely to their whole message. Preparing your own response and listening to yourself while failing to listen can interfere with the communication process. Perhaps you are hungry, and your attention to your own situation interferes with your ability to listen. Maybe the classroom is hot and muggy. How could this impact your ability to listen and participate?

Noise interferes with normal encoding and decoding of the message carried by the channel between source and receiver. Not all noise is bad, but noise by definition can interfere with the communication process.

Look at Computer-Mediated Communication 1.1 and see if you can identify all of the parts of the communication model.

COMPUTER-MEDIATED COMMUNICATION 1.1 • *Model of Communication*

The Shannon and Weaver Model of Communication could never have anticipated the dynamic environment of computer-mediated communication (CMC). In the diagram, the traditional transactional model of communication is set within a CMC framework. Examine how the technology affects the process of encoding and decoding information. One computer sends a message through a server to a satellite dish, where it is sent to a satellite that relays the message to another satellite dish that sends it to a server and on to the destination computer. On the surface, this may seem similar to the use of a telephone. When you take a closer look, you see that the development environment for each message may be different. Like languages, computers use code in different programming languages, such as HTML, XML, Java, and ActiveX. To be able to communicate with each other, the computers require an integrated development environment that supports more than one programming language. In the model, can you identify all eight elements of communication? Can you identify points where transferred information may experience interference? Can you describe then different kinds of interference?

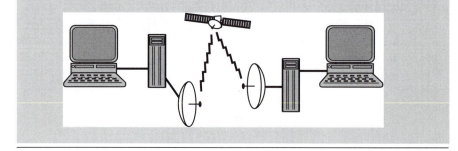

Communication in Context

Now that we have examined the eight components of communication, let's examine this in context. Is a quiet dinner conversation with someone you care about the same experience as a discussion in class or giving a speech? Each context impacts the communication process, and they can overlap and interrelate, creating an even more dynamic process.

Intrapersonal Communication

Have you ever had a conversation in which, after it was over, you came up with a great comeback? Have you ever been thinking about what you are going to say as someone is talking to you? Finally, have you ever told yourself how you did after a test or speech? As you "talk with yourself," you are engaged in intrapersonal communication (Figure 1.5).

FIGURE 1.5 *Intrapersonal communication*

Intrapersonal communication involves one person and is often called "self-talk" (Wood, 1997, p. 22). Donna Vocate's (1994) book on intrapersonal communication explains how, as we use language to reflect on our own experiences, we talk ourselves through situations. For example, think of it as that voice within you that tells you "Keep on going! You can DO IT!" as you exercise or says "That speech went pretty good." Your intrapersonal communication can be positive or negative, and it directly influences how you perceive and react to situations and communication with others.

It is also important to note that what you perceive in communication with others is influenced by your culture and upbringing. Habermas (1984) wrote, "Every process of reaching understanding takes place against the background of a culturally ingrained preunderstanding" (p. 100). You may have certain expectations of time and punctuality, a need for specific rules, or a desire for freedom to complete a project in your own way, and your background plays an important part of intrapersonal communication.

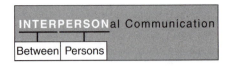

FIGURE 1.6 *Interpersonal communication*

Interpersonal Communication

The second major context within the field of communication is interpersonal communication, or communication that involves two people (Figure 1.6). Within the context of communication between people, there is considerable range, from intimate and very personal to formal and impersonal. You may carry on a conversation with a loved one, sharing the experiences of the day and your hopes for the future. The next day at work you may have a casual conversation with a sales agent from another organization, or communication with the clerk at the grocery store on your way home. Both examples qualify as interpersonal communication but differ in terms of depth and levels of intimacy. The first example implies previous knowledge, understanding, and trust established over time between two caring individuals. The second example implies a lack of previous knowledge, little need for understanding, and trust only to the extent that the meeting or purchase is completed.

Group Communication

So if two is company, what is three? A crowd. Have you ever noticed how a conversation with someone, one on one, is changed when someone else comes along? It can be awkward, or it can make the conversation even better, as you share new ideas and listen to new stories.

Group communication is a dynamic process in which a small group of people engage in a conversation. Group communication generally involves three to eight people, and the more people in the group, the harder it is to pay attention to any individual, unless one speaker steps forward and the group actively listens.

Public Communication

In a public-speaking situation, one person speaks to a group of people. The speaker may ask questions, and engage the audience in a discussion, but the dynamics of the conversation are distinct from group communication, where different rules apply. In a public-speaking situation, the group usually defers to the speaker. One person speaks to everyone, and the group or crowd listens.

Exercise

Recall a time when you gave a speech in front of a group. How did you feel? What was your experience? What did you learn from your experience?

Mass Communication

How do you tell everyone on campus where and when all the classes are held? A schedule that lists all classes. How do you let everyone know there is a sale in your store, or that your new product will meet their needs, or that your position on the issues is the same as that of your constituents? You send a message to as many people as you can through mass communication. Does everyone receive it the same way they might receive a phone call? Not likely. Some people receive mass mailings, such as offers to subscribe to magazines, that do not meet their needs and they throw away what they consider to be "junk mail." Others choose to tune out and not pay attention to a television advertisement. Mass media is a powerful force in modern society and our daily lives and is adapting rapidly to new technologies. Mass communication allows us to communicate our message to a large number of people, but we are limited in our ability to tailor our message to specific audiences, groups, or individuals.

Principles of Communication

Exercise

Learning to listen to yourself is as important as listening to others. What do you say to yourself when something goes right? Goes wrong? Write down when you notice what you say and bring it to class for discussion.

1. Communication Is Constant

There is no moment when you are not in the process of communication. This may first sound impossible, but let's look at a few examples. You are communicating whether you are talking or not. Your body language displays signals that express what you are thinking and feeling. Your face, your posture, your type of clothing, and even your choice of friends can send nonverbal messages that are open to interpretation. When you speak, the tone of your voice, when you take a breath, and your pitch and volume all contribute to the message, combining to form expressions that attempt to convey your message. When you listen, to yourself or others, your internal monologue or self-talk comments on what you see, hear, think, and/or feel. Within the context of interpersonal relationships or small group discussions, communication is always occurring; you cannot *not* communicate (Watzlawick, 1993).

In other contexts, the state of constant communication with self and others is less prevalent, and in some cases, such as a patient under anesthesia, communication may cease. The point is, communication is constantly occurring, intentional or unintentional, in a range of contexts. Becoming aware of communication in these contexts will contribute to a better understanding of the dynamic nature of the process of communication.

2. Communication Is Transactional

Think of yourself in a situation in which you were bargaining over the price of an item. Perhaps it was at a garage sale, or in a marketplace in a foreign country. You and the seller negotiated a price, which is another way of saying that you came to an agreement on the value of the item. You might have offered a low price, whereas the seller insisted on a higher price, but as you negotiated the price, you came to define in a certain sense what the item meant to each of you.

This example highlights another way of looking at the communication process. In the linear model, the source sends a message to the receiver and it arrives relatively intact. For Shannon and Weaver, the model of communication for telephones had its roots in the earlier telegraph, where Morse code was sent in a series of long and short beeps and pauses to a receiver, where the results were translated using an established code book. The message often retained its integrity, with the message staying exactly the same from source to receiver.

The interactional model builds on this model, as we have seen previously, incorporating feedback and showing a two-way, often overlapping communication process. The transactional model of communication takes this model an additional step, establishing that meaning and interpretation are part of the individual. Where did you grow up? What language(s) did you learn? What did you learn to value? All of these factors and many more contribute to your interpretation of the message and your response to it.

One good example of transactional communication is the phenomena of **understood meaning**. Understood meaning occurs when two or more people have in some way negotiated a common meaning for a word or phrase. Have you ever known two people who have been together for a long period of time? Could they finish each other's sentences? Did they have their own "words?" Their vocabulary held meanings they understood, drawn from years of experience together. An outsider might only guess at what they were talking about. The words themselves were only part of the picture. To fully grasp the understood meaning of the message you would have to have been part of the experience that led to the shared meaning.

Families and groups often create their own catch phrases that come from common experiences. Perhaps a family had an awful vacation at

Yellowstone National Park, where everything that could go wrong did. The next year when the family discusses where to go for a vacation, someone replies, "Not to Yellowstone," which gets everyone laughing. To the casual outsider, the natural question would be "What's wrong with Yellowstone?" but they would be missing the understood meaning. "Not to Yellowstone?" refers to the awful experiences they all shared rather than to the specific geographic location.

Exercise

Can you think of words that have special meanings in your family or group of friends or with someone you have known? Write down the words and their special definitions.

Outside of a small, close-knit group, do you think this process occurs on a wider scale? As we discussed previously, if you travel from one part of the United States to another, do all of the words and phrases have the same meaning? Not necessarily. To order a soft drink in one corner of the country you might ask for a soda, in another a pop, and in yet another a "Coke." Where you come from influences the words you use with others. To understand the meaning of the words, we need more than just the words themselves.

3. Communication Is a Process

> No one can step twice into the same river, nor touch mortal substance twice in the same condition. By the speed of its change, it scatters and gathers again.
>
> —Heraclitus, Greek Philosopher

A river is a dynamic process, where water gathers and pools, forming streams that join together in a river only to be absorbed by the sea. Heraclitus (544–483 BC) noted that it is never the same river twice. The water changes, the conditions change, and, over time, even the course changes. Communication is a dynamic process, where people come together, mingle, and then part. When you come together again, it is in a new context with a new set of conditions. It is not the same. Like a river, communication is a dynamic process. Could you give the same speech to two groups? Certainly. Is it the same speech? No. The context has changed since the first time you gave the speech, the audience is new, and even you yourself are different. You may find that something works in one situation, but may not work in the next. We, like an audience or the river, are constantly changing.

4. Communication Is Irreversible

Have you ever said something you wish you could take back? We have all learned the hard way that once something is expressed, it cannot be taken back. The children's rhyme "sticks and stones may break my bones but words will never hurt me" does not hold true. Words and gestures can make an impact, and their impact can be felt for a lifetime. Whether they are meant to be positive or negative is up to you. You can make positive statements that contribute to your relationships, or make negative ones that undermine those relationships. Who has not heard the words "You can't play with us" as a child and not felt rejected? Who has heard the words "You did wonderful" and not felt reaffirmed? We never know how a message will be received, or which messages will make a mark that will not fade with time. By taking an active role in our communication with others, and recognizing that communication is irreversible, we can take a proactive approach to the words and gestures we use.

5. Communication Is Learned

Although there is some debate as to the universal nature of language across cultures, most researchers conclude that our knowledge of communication is learned through interaction with others (Case Study 1.1). Smiles and laughter may cross the language barrier, but words and many gestures require an understanding of the culture and context. From the time of birth until around six months of age, babies make similar sounds and gestures re-

CASE STUDY 1.1 • *Children Raised in the Wilderness*

Like the fictional characters Tarzan and Mowgli, feral (or wild) children have been discovered abandoned in the wild throughout history. These children lack the ability to use language or to reason intellectually, and they give us some insight into how we learn to communicate.

There are more than 35 recorded cases of children either found wandering alone or discovered being brought up by animals as varied as bears, wolves, monkeys, leopards, and even gazelles (McCrone, 1993). According to McCrone, some of these stories are exaggerated and have been enhanced with time, but a few are well documented and provide considerable insight.

The first reports of feral children were recorded by German monks in the fourteenth century. In 1341, a seven-year-old boy was found in the woods of Hesse, and three years later, a twelve-year-old was found in Wetterau. Both children were described as wild, with an apparent immunity to cold temperatures, and neither could speak beyond grunts.

In the story of the wild boy of Aveyron, Victor (as he was later called) was found running wild in the forests and mountains of Southern France in 1800. He was twelve years old at the time and was found naked. He often walked on all four limbs, could not speak, and could not relate to humans. Many attempts were made to "civilize" him and teach him words, but he learned only simple tasks and less than ten words in his lifetime.

In India, there have been several documented cases of children raised by wolves. Amala and Kamala, like Victor, were discovered living with wolves in 1926, when they were approximately ages three and five years. They acted like wolves, ate like wolves, and did not communicate in a human sense. Kamala did learn about 40 words before her death from typhoid in 1929, but she remained markedly "wild." Another child, called "Ghadya Ka Bacha," or the wolf boy, was found outside a hospital in Balrampur in 1954. He too acted like a wolf and showed no interest in humans (Shattuck, 1980).

Jean-Jacques Rousseau (1712–1788), a French philosopher, believed that human beings were innately wise and generous, and in his day, it was generally accepted that humans possessed the innate gift of speech. Do we possess an in-born gift of speech? What happens when we grow up without language and culture? Discuss your answers with another student.

gardless of the language of their primary caregiver. Between six and nine months, babies start to imitate the vocalizations of their caregiver and start on a path toward using the language. At around one year, a child often uses his or her first word, and "book" sounds different than "libro." In addition to the use of words, the gestures and customs that are part of a culture are also learned as a child develops. In Chile, for example, a child would learn to give a light kiss on the cheek to a family friend or neighbor after saying "hola." In the United States, a child learns to extend a hand for a handshake as he or she says "hello."

Summary

In Chapter 1, we discussed how important communication is in our lives. Employers prefer job candidates who have good communication skills. Relationships can be healthier when the participants actively work at good communication. In addition, we looked at a definition of communication, and how process, understanding, and sharing relate to the definition. In our discussion of four models of communication, we examined how they incorporate the eight components of communication and become increasing complex in their representation of the communication process. We also examined the range of contexts in which communication occurs, from intrapersonal communication to mass communication. Finally, we discussed five principles of communication and how we learn to communicate. In the next chapter, we'll examine the concept of perspective, how we listen, and how these elements impact our communication with ourselves and others.

For More Information

On communication as a discipline, go to:

National Communication Association: http://www.natcom.org/

Heraclitus:

http://dir.yahoo.com/Arts/Humanities/Philosophy/Philosophers/Heraclitus_c_544_483BC

Children raised in the wild:

http://www.btinternet.com/~neuronaut/webtwo_features_feral_kids.htm

Review Questions

1. Factual Questions
   a. What is the definition of communication presented in this text?
   b. What are four models of communication presented in this text?
   c. What are five principles of communication?

2. Interpretative Questions
   a. What assumptions are present in the Shannon and Weaver model of communication? What assumptions are present in later models?
   b. Do the principles of communication apply in all cases?
   c. How does our native language or culture influence our communication?

3. Evaluative Questions
   a. Does the definition of communication given work in all instances of communication? What might be a better or more accurate definition? Where does this definition place emphasis, and what does it leave out?
   b. Do the models of communication accurately present this dynamic process? What could improve these models?
   c. Can the cases of "wild" children be compared with one another? What problems do individual accounts of these cases present?

4. Application Questions
   a. Observe two people talking. Can you draw a model of their communication?
   b. Can you find an example of a model of communication where you work?
   c. Can you find an example of one principle of communication?

Works Cited

Cronen, V. & Pearce, W. B. (1982). The coordinated management of meaning: A theory of communication. In F. E. X. Dance (Ed.), *Human communication theory* (pp. 61–89). New York: Harper & Row.

Habermas, J. (1984). *The theory of communicative action* (Vol. 1). Boston: Beacon Press.

Laswell, H. (1948). The stucture and function of communication in society. In L. Bryson (Ed.), *The communication of ideas*. New York: Harper & Row.

Leavitt, H. J. & Mueller, R. (1951). Some effects of feedback on communication. *Human Relations, 4,* 401–410.

McCrone, J. (1993). *The myth of irrationality: The science of the mind from Plato to Star Trek.* London: Macmillan.

Pearce, W. B. & Cronen, V. (1980). *Communication, action, and meaning: The creation of social realities.* New York: Praeger.

Pearson, J. & Nelson, P. (2000). *An introduction to human communication: Understanding and sharing* (8th ed.). Dubuque, IL: McGraw-Hill.

Seiler, W. & Beall, M. (2000). *Communication: Making connections* (4th ed.). Boston: Allyn & Bacon.

Shannon, C. & Weaver, W. (1949). *The mathematical theory of communication.* Urbana: University of Illinois Press.

Shattuck, T. (1980). *The forbidden experiment: The story of the wild boy of Aveyron.* New York: Farrar, Straus, and Giroux.

Vocate, D. (Ed.) (1994). *Intrapersonal communication: Different voices, different minds.* Hillsdale, NJ: Lawrence Erlbaum.

Watzlawick, P. (1993). *The language of change: Elements of therapeutic communication.* New York: W.W. Norton.

Weekley, E. (1967). *An etymological dictionary of modern English* (Vol. 1). New York: Dover Publications.

Wood, J. (1997). *Communication in our lives.* Boston: Wadsworth.

2

Perception and Listening

Chapter Objectives _____

After completing this chapter, you should be able to:

1. Describe the relationship between perception and the communication process.
2. Describe the process of perception.
3. Understand how perception differs between people.
4. Understand the relationship between perception and self-concept.
5. Identify the key components of self-concept.
6. Understand the importance of listening skills.
7. Describe the difference between passive, active, critical, and empathetic listening.
8. Identify and describe the stages of the listening process.
9. Identify and describe three key barriers to listening.
10. Identify and describe ways to improve listening.

Introductory Exercise 2.1 _____

Please read the story and see if you can find the miscommunication(s).

Andres:	How was your test?
Gabby:	Fine, I guess … I thought I was prepared, but now I'm not so sure.
Andres:	Oh, I'm sure you did fine. So, where do you want to go to lunch?
Gabby:	Oh, I dunno, wherever. I thought I knew the answers …
Andres:	Are you hungry for a burger, maybe Chinese?
Gabby:	Whatever's easiest. There was this one question …
Andres:	I hear that new Greek restaurant is really good, what do ya think?
Gabby:	You aren't listening to me.
Andres:	What? I thought we were talking about lunch.

Introductory Exercise 2.2 _____

Please find the hidden message(s):

E	E	P	M	E	P	A	O	E	E	T
V	P	W	O	L	E	G	O	G	M	D
I	S	E	R	B	H	N	L	A	S	A
T	R	N	F	O	T	I	Y	S	I	E
C	E	A	M	R	T	K	B	S	H	R

Introductory Exercise 2.3 _____

Please connect the dots with four straight lines, making sure you do not lift your pen or pencil from the paper or retrace lines.

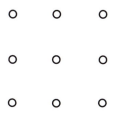

Did you find the miscommunication in the first exercise? Gabby had just completed a test and she was unsure of her performance. She wanted to talk about it, and Andres was not completely listening. He heard at first that she had completed the test, told her she must have done well, and then changed the subject to what he wanted to talk about. Gabby, however, was not ready to change the subject and only gave token responses to his questions while returning to her topic. Gabby's agenda was to talk about her test. Andres's agenda was to go to lunch. They missed each other because they were not completely aware of each other's agenda. Awareness is a complicated and fascinating area of study. The way we take in information, give it order, and assign it meaning has long interested researchers from disciplines such as sociology, anthropology, and psychology.

In the first chapter we learned about the basic models of communication and how the elements come together as a dynamic process. Throughout this book we examine this process from different perspectives, reinforcing more than one point of view, to help you become aware of how each element contributes to the process. For you to take advantage of the material in this book, you will need to keep an open mind. Some of this material may seem very familiar. You may miss something that can offer new insight if you glance over passages you think you understand. Choose to be open to the material as we look at this dynamic process from distinct and fascinating perspectives, and you will be amazed at how it changes the way you view your communication with yourself and others.

Your mind is like a parachute. It works best when it's open.

—Anonymous

Did you solve the second exercise? If so, how did you solve it? By accident, or did you use a pattern, looking for common letter combinations or odd letter pairs. There are many ways to solve this puzzle but only one right answer. Reading from right to left, not left to right, and bottom to top, not top to bottom, the puzzle reads: READ THIS MESSAGE BY LOOKING AT THE PROBLEM FROM A DIFFERENT PERSPECTIVE.

English-speakers learn to read from left to right, top to bottom. People who read and write Arabic learn from right to left, and people who learn to read and write Japanese and/or Chinese learn from left to right, top to bottom, in rows. Beyond the direction we learn to read or write, we use different characters to represent different sounds and distinct words and concepts, in many diverse ways. This exercise helps illustrate what Habermas (1984) calls "preunderstanding." We often enter a new situation, or solve a new problem, with a set of expectations, drawn from our experiences, already present to help guide us to our goal. Within our own community, language group, or culture, these expectations can facilitate communication with a common reference base as a resource. However, as we come into contact with groups, cultures, and puzzles that require different expectations and viewpoints, our ability to adapt to alternate perspectives becomes a key resource.

Finally, did you solve the third exercise? This exercise requires you to think outside of the "box." Looking at the solution, can you see how you had to go outside of the margins to solve the challenge? This puzzle, like the second exercise, requires you to explore alternate perspectives to discover a solution.

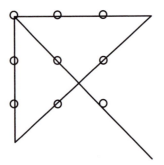

These three exercises illustrate the importance of perspective, and how when you change your perspective, things change. Have you ever been frustrated or even angry over something you later found out to be a miscommunication? Have you ever played the game of rumors, where one person tells a story to another who tells it to another? By the time the story goes through the group, it has transformed from its original form into a new story. This game helps illustrate how we select, organize, and interpret information, assigning importance or meaning to some words or phrases and neglecting or forgetting others.

> *In third grade I was a Girl Scout. We made tie-dye shirts, swam at the community pool, camped out, and made S'mores. But the activity I remember the most occurred one rainy night when we had to be indoors. There were about 25 girls in our troop. Our leader had us sit in a large circle, and then our leader whispered a short story into the ear of the first Girl Scout so only she could hear. Then the girl whispered the story into the ear of the next girl in the circle, and the story was soon whispered around the room. To this day I don't recall what the story was about, but I know the original story was nothing like the story that was told at the end of the circle. I will never forget this lesson about listening and getting the "real story."*
>
> Julie Warnick

We all have different interests and experiences, and we don't all pay attention to the same things. In this chapter we examine how our individual perspectives and listening skills impact our communication.

Why Don't We All See Things the Same Way?

As Julie's example illustrates, we remember things differently. What is important to you, I might not pay attention to, and vice versa. Why is this? One reason is we choose to select different aspects of a message on which to focus our attention based on what interests us or what is familiar. Another reason that is often overlooked is that, for many of us, our listening skills could use improvement. We spend considerable effort thinking about a message and how to deliver it. After we have said it, we spend time thinking about how we said it. How much time do you spend thinking about how to best listen to what other people are saying? To better understand perception and the listening process, we will examine how you choose to pay attention, remember, and interpret messages within the communication process.

First we examine how you select, organize, and interpret communication, noting characteristics that influence your perception. Next we examine how your self-concept is formed and how communication with others helps form your image of how you see yourself. Finally, we examine the process of listening, identifying key barriers and ways to overcome them.

Exercise _____

With friends, turn the volume off on a television show or movie and watch a couple of scenes. Now turn off the television and tell each other what you saw. You may want to repeat the exercise, but leave the sound on, and again compare your notes.

Perception and Awareness

Everyone hears only what he understands.

—Goethe

Take for example the following scenarios:

1. You come home after a long day at work and have just picked up your children from school and everyone is hungry. You enter the house and set down your bag and move toward the answering machine while the children go around the corner and down the hall. You listen to the messages while moving toward the refrigerator, yelling to the children, "Who wants milk?" and only half listening to the response. The doorbell rings, and as you move toward the door the phone rings. The children come down the hall and look for the milk. You handle it all like a pro.
2. You are studying for a test at the same time your roommate is talking on the phone with a friend. The television is loud and the room down the hall has the stereo blaring with music that is definitely not your favorite. You write notes on each vocabulary word and are able to recall the discussion in class. You stay focused and are getting the job done.

Do these scenarios sound familiar? For some people they may sound very familiar, but for others, they may not. Why? Because we all have different interests, goals, backgrounds, and responsibilities that require us to focus our attention on specific sounds, people, and issues. The children did not focus on the answering machine, but you did. Your roommate paid no attention to your studying, but you were, in fact, getting a lot done. Your interests were different and depended on your age, responsibilities, and goals. It is impossible to perceive, remember, process, and respond to every action, smell, sound, picture, or word we see, hear, smell, taste, or touch. Because we cannot pay attention to everything at once, we choose to pay attention to what seems to be the most relevant for us. This action of sorting competing messages, or choosing stimuli, is called **selection.**

Selection is one very important part of perception and awareness. You select what to pay attention to based on what is important to you, or what you value, and that is different for each person. Take, for example, the proverbial remote control for the television. Have you ever known someone who loves to constantly change television channels? Have you ever known someone else who says, "Just pick something and leave it there"?

One person is selecting a channel based on what interests him or her. The second person values any program over a cascade of constantly changing channels. Both individuals are involved in selecting what they want to watch based on their own interests and whatever catches their eye. The act of choosing one program over another is an example of the selection process.

Selection has three main parts: exposure, attention, and retention (Klopf, 1995). **Selective exposure** is both information we choose to pay attention to and information that either is not available to us or we choose to ignore. For example, you may choose to read the sports page in the newspaper but to ignore the classified section. You may, however, choose to pay attention to the classified advertisements if you are shopping for something such as a car or house. If, however, your newspaper is missing the sports page or classifieds, you do not have that information available to you. **Selective attention** is when you focus on one stimulus, such as the television, and tune out a competing stimulus, such as the radio playing in the same room. **Selective retention** is when you choose to remember one stimulus over another. Say we talk about the television program you were watching. What was it about? Who were the main characters? What was the plot? You may be able to answer all of these questions easily. Now you are asked to recall the songs on the radio that was playing in the same room. Even if you recall that the radio was playing, you may have a hard time remembering what songs you heard. Although you may have *heard* them in the background, you may not have chosen to *listen* to them. Listening implies you actively listened to the songs, processing the sounds, making it easier for you to recall.

Organization, the second step in the perception process, is when we sort and categorize information in ways that make sense to us. As the term implies, we organize what we perceive into categories based on what we have perceived previously. When you were younger and did not know the difference between a square and a circle, you saw little difference. As you grew, you learned the difference and saw squares and circles everywhere. Then you learned the difference between squares and rectangles. As an adult, you follow the same process you did as a child. You come across a situation in which you are in unfamiliar surroundings, so you use clues to make sense of where you are and find your way home. You are in a conversation with someone and hear something presented in class. You connect what you learned in class to this new conversation and have insight to offer. Your ability to organize information, taking information that you know and remember and applying it to new information, helps you make sense of your world and is key to communication.

Two examples of this facet of organization are called figure and ground and closure. **Figure and ground organization** is the act of organizing stimuli into categories that receive extra emphasis, becoming more pronounced,

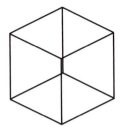

FIGURE 2.1   *Cube*

while other categories are neglected, becoming less noticeable. In Figure 2.1, take a look at the cube. What do you see? Which part of the cube is closest to you? Can you see the underside of the cube or are you looking down on it, viewing the top?

This illustrates the concept of figure and ground. If you look at it one way, one part of the cube becomes the foreground, closest to you. If you look at it another way, a different part of the cube is closest to you. What changes? Your perception of the cube. The box itself does not change. Figure and ground refers to the idea that as you pay selective attention to one part of the box, other parts of it blend into the background.

Closure is our perceptual ability to fill in the gaps and connect the dots. Have you ever been in a conversation with someone when something nearby drowns out some of his or her words? You might have automatically filled in the words if you anticipated what was going to be said next. Did you guess right? See Intercultural Communication 2.1.

INTERCULTURAL COMMUNICATION 2.1 • *New Words and Languages: Making Sense of it All*

Have you ever been to a new place such as a city, a region, or a country? Did you find making sense of the way people talked a challenge? The difference between the English of someone from the United States and that of someone from New Zealand, Australia, or the United Kingdom can be quite significant. Look at the Australian words below. Do any of them make sense to you? (Answers at the end.)

- agro   (ag'RO)
- arvo   (ar'VO)
- drongo   (dron'GO)
- dunny   (dun' E)
- footy   (foot' E)

INTERCULTURAL COMMUNICATION 2.1 • *Continued*

Within the United States it can also be quite a challenge to be understood. Ask for a "Coke" in Chicago and you'll receive a "soda pop" called Coke. Ask for a "Coke" in Texas and they'll ask you what kind (orange, root beer, lemon-lime, etc.).

When you are learning to speak a new language, you often listen for the words you know. Once you hear a couple of words you know, you start to guess at the general meaning of the sentence. Combined with a conscious effort to think about the context of the conversation and your environment, you can sometimes make reasonable guesses, and by asking for more information or repetition, you can often get the general idea. This follows the same principle of filling in the gaps.

You may enjoy playing Australian rules football, American football, rugby, or soccer (*footy*), but if you play in the hot savannah sun in the afternoon (*arvo*), you may wind up aggravated (*agro*), sick, or even in the need of a toilet (*dunny*) break. Then the local Australians will call you an idiot (*drongo*).

Source: Newsweek, September 4, 2000, p.8

Look at Figure 2.2. Do you see a ring of "Pac-Man"–like circles? Do you see anything else?

What image(s) does the ring of "Pac-Man" circles form? Do you see a star? Why?

The ability to mentally fill in the gaps, creating the perception that the shape of a star exists, is an example of closure. This ability is advantageous but can lead us to false conclusions. If we connect the dots incorrectly, or take a few words and interpret their overall meaning to be something other than it is, then our ability to close the gaps between information has steered us in the wrong direction. It can, however, help us make associations and solve problems every day. If we know where Twenty-Fifth Street is and read

FIGURE 2.2 *Pac-Man/Star*

that there is a new restaurant on Twenty-Sixth Street, our ability to build on what we know can help. Be aware of how you connect the dots and seek good information.

We also selectively select, organize, and interpret information based on how physically close things are or to what degree things resemble one another. **Proximity** is the perceptual organization of information based on physical space between objects. In the "Pac-Man/star" example, which illustrated closure, the physical proximity of each circle to one another contributed to the perception of the star. We perceive, intentionally or unintentionally, that if images, words, or shapes occur close to one another they must be somehow related. We also tend to perceive that similar objects, ideas, and images are related. **Similarity** is the perceptual organization of information based on perceived points of similarity across distinct items. For example, a zebra is like a horse, and we may perceive them as similar. We can rationally understand that this tendency to group items physically close to one another or that resemble each other, like figure and ground and closure, can lead us to false conclusions.

Each way of perceiving information highlights your ability to take what you perceive, together with what you know, and apply it to new situations. We always try to make sense of our world, and as a general rule, we hardly ever have all the information necessary at one time. We often make decisions based on incomplete information, taking what we know and applying it to new and uncertain situations. How did you select this class? Your academic counselor may have recommended it as part of your degree program. Your friend may have taken the class from the instructor last semester. Perhaps the course description in the catalog sounded interesting. You made a decision to take the class but could not know what it was really like until you actually started the first class.

The third step in the perception process is called interpretation. **Interpretation** occurs when you assign meaning and value to what you perceive. Let's say you want to buy a car. You know you need to get from point A to point B, but you want to do it in style. You may value style over other features like mechanical reliability when you choose a sports car. You assign meaning and value to the car beyond its transportation usage.

Perceptual Differences

So why do we perceive things differently? There is no easy answer. As we've discussed previously, we all select what to pay attention to and remember differently, organize what we perceive in different ways, and interpret what we perceive based on our individual experiences. Our individual differences combine to influence our perception and our responses. Individual differences include:

- Physical characteristics
- Psychological state
- Cultural background
- Gender
- Media
- Perceptual set

First let's look at **physical characteristics.** Some people are tall, others short. Some have excellent hearing (and some might say they have eyes in the back of their head), whereas others are hard of hearing. These individual differences greatly influence our perspective and how we view stimuli. One example might be the door overhang. If I am short, going through doors is a matter of routine. If I am tall, it is part of my routine to watch out for overhangs so I don't hit my head. If I hear within a normal range, I may not factor in my hearing ability when I choose where I sit in a classroom. A person with hearing impairment may choose to consider this an important factor when selecting a seat in relation to the instructor.

Psychological characteristics also influence perception. Are you happy to be in class? Are you distracted by something that happened before class? Are you frustrated? Your emotional state directly influences how you perceive your world. If you are in a good mood and something goes wrong, you are more likely to view it as a momentary setback (Covey, 1989). If you are sad or depressed, you may view the setback as more serious, even as a defeating blow.

Cultural background includes more than just your nationality, race, or ethnicity. Did you grow up in a small town? A large city? Do you come from a large family? A small one? Is religion a part of your life? Do you speak more than one language? Cultural differences are expressed in many shades and are hard to define. They can, however, be observed, and their influence on communication has been clearly documented (Gage & Berliner, 1998).

Gender is another important factor that influences perception and awareness. Gender concerns your sex role and what you perceive that role to be, as opposed to your sex, which is either male or female. Gender comes into play when people have certain expectations for themselves and others. Who is going to fix the light? Who is going to make dinner? Who is going to stay home to take care of the baby? If you watched television shows in the 1950s, or caught them on many of the channels that feature "classic" programming, you observed that there were definite gender roles. For example, in a classic program entitled *Leave it to Beaver,* Ward Cleaver went off to work while June, his wife, stayed home. Their activities, experiences, roles, and responsibilities were clearly defined. Does television depict the 1950s accurately? No more than to say that as a cultural generalization, in the post-World War II United States gender roles were more rigidly defined than we see today (Case Study 2.1). Gender roles, like all roles in societies,

CASE STUDY 2.1 • *Working Women in World War II*

During World War II, American women responded in record numbers to government encouragement to enter the heavy war production industry and meet the need for workers. Women, previously working in "pink-collar jobs," or in

lower-paying women's quickly made the move work and the opportu- skills while making the end of the war ment reversed the pro- vacancies for the re- time to go home," pro- ments, and women up their jobs.

industrial jobs, to war production nity to learn new higher wages. When came, the govern- paganda to make turning soldiers. "It's claimed the advertise- were expected to give

"Rosie the Riveter" known poster from the woman showing her sleeve and exclaims Advertisements soon

is featured in a well- time, featuring a bicep as she rolls up a "We can do it!" changed to portray

women at home, preparing for the return of the soldiers by making sure every surface was clean. How did this change in the portrayal of women affect their lives? Research this fascinating time online and in the library. Share your information and relate the information to the concepts of self-image and self-esteem.

are part of a constant, dynamic change. As people's individual perceptions and preferences change, so do expectations, and television has sometimes captured these societal changes. Popular programs like *Ally McBeal* or *Friends* reflect different societal and cultural expectations than programs produced 20 or 40 years ago.

Media, from radio to television and newspapers to the Internet, also contributes to the way we see the world. How much television do you watch? What kind of television do you watch? Do you read a newspaper? How often? How about the radio? The Internet? Chat rooms? What you consume in terms of information through the media influences how you see the world. In many ways, "you are what you eat" holds true. You may be well informed through television or the Internet and be able to contribute insightful opinions in conversations. You may also consume the media equivalent of fast food and grow large on quantity but lack quality, losing time for other activities. What you choose to watch, listen to, log on to, or read influences how you perceive the world. In the chapter on mass communication we will examine how mass media is created, controlled, and manipulated for the audience, including you.

Finally, **perceptual set** is when we use a fixed perspective to view the world. One way to think of it is to imagine that you are always wearing sunglasses. Your sunglasses are formed from your past experiences and from all the characteristics we've discussed previously. Our use of just one set of "sunglasses" to view events, people, or objects, without taking into account how the glasses themselves color and shade the way we perceive the world, can limit or distort our perceptions. A common example is stereotyping, where we categorize events, people, or objects without taking into account individual or unique differences. "All pit bull dogs are mean." This is a stereotype that generalizes an entire breed of dogs in one way without taking into account individual differences in training or temperament.

Now that we have examined the many ways and reasons why we perceive the world in different ways, let's look inside at how we view ourselves. We look in the mirror and see one facet of ourselves, but we also recognize that there is more to us than other people, or even ourselves, know about us. People treat us in distinct ways, and we respond to them, and ourselves, through communication. This process over time contributes to our self-concept, or how we perceive ourselves. How we see ourselves plays an important role in what we expect from ourselves, and what we expect others to expect from us. Let's examine self-concept, how it is formed, and how it influences our communication with ourselves and others.

Self-Concept

Our self-concept is what we perceive ourselves to be. This involves the mental picture you have for yourself, and how you judge yourself. How you see yourself, to a large extent, is based on how you think others see you. You gather a sense of how others see you through communication, interacting with others.

Exercise

How do people "treat" you? How do you think that affects the way you see yourself? Draw yourself as you see yourself and list ten attributes you feel you possess. What attributes do you think others seem to know about you? What attributes do you think others do not know about you? If you could express one attribute that you think most people do not know about you, what would it be?

Your self-concept combines two main components: self-image and self-esteem.

Self-concept = Self-image + Self-esteem

Your **self-image** is just like it sounds—the image you have of yourself. **Self-esteem,** however, has to do with how you feel about yourself and your attributes. Have you ever known someone who has an eating disorder? These deadly diseases have everything to do with self-image and self-esteem. If someone's image of himself or herself is one of being overweight, and he or she feels that is negative and wants to change, he or she may exercise more and control his or her diet. If someone who is already thin sees himself or herself as fat and feels bad about their body image, he or she may also diet and exercise even though they might be below their ideal weight or body mass. Anorexia and bulimia are two eating disorders that involve a self-concept that reinforces dangerous behaviors, which can have life-threatening results. Being aware of your self-concept, and how you form that concept of yourself, is very important.

Self-concept is a process by which what we sense in communication with others becomes internalized. From the time we are born, or even in the womb, we hear others. In our first year of life we learn the faces of those who are close to us and start to imitate sounds. By our second year of life we are using some words and many gestures to communicate our needs and wants. We develop communication skills by doing as we grow, trying new words and phrases, participating in conversations with people our own age or different ages. As we broaden our communication skills, we also reflect more on how others communicate with us. We spend more time noticing what others wear, how they present themselves, and how we fit into groups. We all have different talents, and depending on how people celebrate them or put them down has a significant impact on our self-concept as we grow and develop. This process continues throughout our lives.

Statements that reinforce positive self-concept:	Statements that contribute to negative self-concept:
• You are so smart!	• You are so stupid!
• You are my best friend.	• You can't play with us.
• Could you help with this—you're so good at it!	• Can't you ever do anything right!

When people encourage you, it affects the way you see yourself and how well you perform. In a well-known study, teachers were told that specific students were expected to do quite well because of their intelligence, whereas other students were described to the teachers as "late bloomers," or developmentally delayed. Researchers observed the students during the course of the school year, and the students who were expected to do well actually did. Those who were expected not to do as well also lived up to the expectation. The students were chosen at random at the beginning of the study, so there was, in fact, no reason to expect that students would demonstrate either better than average or worse than average academic abilities (Insel & Jacobson, 1975; Rosenthal & Jacobson, 1968). According to the researchers, the differences probably came from the teacher's expectations of the students, the extra attention, and the communication—nonverbal as well as verbal—of those expectations. Have you ever lived up to someone's expectations of you? How about your expectations of yourself? Write down one example of each situation. See Computer-Mediated Communication 2.1.

The Pygmalion effect, otherwise known as a self-fulfilling prophecy, is quite powerful. As Ovid (43 BC–17 AD), a Roman philosopher and poet, told the story in the tenth book of *Metamorphoses,* the sculptor Pygmalion,

COMPUTER-MEDIATED COMMUNICATION 2.1 • *Chat Groups: Perception of Identity*

When you walk into a room where everyone is talking, you can see the conversation participants and make observations about them. In a "virtual" room, where a chat session takes place, you can only observe what the conversation participants want you to observe. Within a real-time chat room, created by connecting computer users to each other, you can see only scrolling text on a monitor. People invent names for themselves, and some do not stop there. Since you can't see the people you are talking with, they can change their age, their occupation, and even their gender.

Some people, however, use the virtual space to their advantage, creating space for the discussion of topics that create community. To establish identity, group norms, and common ground, people sometimes choose to establish their identity in cyberspace through their affiliation with ethnic and racial groups.

Researcher Gary W. Larson (1999, p.12) found while studying identity formation online that "The creation of racial space on IRC (Internet Relay Channel) should be seen as symptomatic of something lacking in our physical culture. The traditional role of black churches as meeting places, lecture halls, protest sites, and spaces of joyous worship has been diminished." Larson makes the case that just as physical spaces used to help us come together as a community, now computer-mediated communication environments like chat groups and online conversations help us feel connected to one another.

a prince of Cyprus, sought to create an ivory statue of the ideal woman. He named the statue Galatea. She was so beautiful that Pygmalion fell hopelessly in love with his own creation. He prayed to the goddess Venus to bring Galatea to life, and she did. The couple lived happily ever after. In George Bernard Shaw's play *Pygmalion*, later popularized as the classic 1964 film starring Audrey Hepburn entitled *My Fair Lady*, a character named Professor Henry Higgins takes a peasant flower girl and transforms her into a formal duchess. Eliza Doolittle, the peasant girl, says to Higgins' friend Pickering:

> "You see, really and truly, apart from the things anyone can pick up (the dressing and the proper way of speaking and so on), the difference between a lady and a flower girl is not how she behaves, but how she's treated. I shall always be a flower girl to Professor Higgins, because he always treats me as a flower girl, and always will, but I know I can be a lady to you because you always treat me as a lady, and always will."

From Ovid to Henry Higgins, we can see how people have expressed an interest in this effect for a very long time. Can you think of a similar story from a television show or movie? What was necessary for the effect to work? See Case Study 2.2.

To summarize the process of self-fulfilling prophecies, let's examine four key principals that Robert Rosenthal (Rosnow & Rosenthal, 1999), a professor of social psychology at Harvard, has observed while studying this effect:

1. We form certain expectations of people or events.
2. We communicate those expectations with various cues, verbal and nonverbal.
3. People tend to respond to these cues by adjusting their behavior to match the expectations.
4. The outcome is that the original expectation becomes true.

Next, let's examine how we learn values, beliefs, and attitudes as we grow and adapt to our environment. As discussed previously, we communicate with others and ourselves to learn what we like and what we don't like. We assign meaning to things we value and that we notice other people value. As we grow, this process of assigning meaning helps us form our core values.

We learn from our parents or caregivers, for example, the meaning of the golden rule: treat other people as you yourself would like to be treated. We learn to value relationships, ideas, places, and people. **Values** are generally the ideals we wish to see in others and ourselves, like

CASE STUDY 2.2 • *Clever Hans*

In 1911, two researchers named Stumpt and Pfungst conducted an investigation on a famous horse named Clever Hans. Hans could apparently add, subtract, multiply, divide, spell, and solve problems. While trained animals had to be cued by their trainers, Clever Hans had a mind of his own. Clever Hans would run through his routine even when his owner, a German mathematician named Von Osten, was not with him. In fact, Clever Hans would answer questions for almost anybody.

Robert Strom, in his 1971 text entitled *Teachers and the Learning Process,* describes how Stumpt and Pfungst discovered the secret. They noticed first that if Hans could not see the person asking the question, he couldn't answer the question. They then focused on the questioner and observed that when the question was asked, the questioner leaned forward. A forward inclination of the head of the questioner would start Hans tapping. As Hans neared the answer, the questioner would start to straighten up, and he would stop tapping. According to Strom, Stumpt and Pfungst also found that more subtle clues, like the raising of the eyebrows or the dilation of the questioner's nostrils, were a cue for Hans to stop tapping. People were giving the horse the message to stop by communicating their expectations to him through physical signals and body language. Hans was perceptive and able to pick up on those nonverbal signals.

honesty or the value of commitment. If you were raised in an environment in which family is very important, and everything was done together as a group, then you may value family and relationships. If you were raised in an environment in which family members were more independent, and independence was a dominant value, you in turn may also value independence. These values, to a certain extent, help guide our actions and behaviors. They serve as goals of what we would like to be and see in others.

Our **beliefs** also form over time but hold less of a core position in our self-concept. Beliefs are based on our view of the world but do not necessarily have the support of proof. We may believe in something or someone but cannot produce tangible evidence to support that belief. You may believe your team is going to win this weekend, but your conviction or belief is not based on just hard evidence. It also involves an element of faith.

Attitudes are similar to values and beliefs in that they are an expression of what is important to you, but they are much more focused and hardly permanent. You may like a certain brand of soft drink, and years from now you won't even remember you like it. Today you may think your new shirt is great, but as fashions and your opinions change with time, that shirt loses its appeal to you.

VALUES	Ideals that guide our behavior and are generally long lasting.	Education is important.
BELIEFS	Convictions or expressions of confidence that can change over time.	This class is important because I may use the skills I'm learning someday.
ATTITUDES	Your immediate disposition; can change easily and frequently.	I liked the game in class today.

We learn our values, beliefs, and attitudes through our interactions with others. By listening to others, we learn what is important to us. See Intercultural Communication 2.2.

INTERCULTURAL COMMUNICATION 2.2 • *Short Story: Cultural Backgrounds*

While in Chile, a traveler from the United States tried to take a shower. Both faucets produced cold water. He called a repairman and asked him to take a look at the hot water tank. The repairman expressed he didn't know what the man was talking about. The repairman took the expatriate downstairs and showed him how to light the *calefont*, a gas-powered heater that directly heats the water as it passes through the copper pipe. The traveler had never seen such a device. The repairman thought the idea of constantly keeping water hot in a tank, when it might be only used for morning showers and washing the dishes in the evening, was a wasteful use of energy. Both men came from distinct cultural backgrounds, which influenced what they considered "normal" and how they related to the world. Can you think of a similar story?

Perception is influenced by prior experience and expectations, and in this example, there were two sets of expectations that influenced communication. In Chile, where most of the electricity is generated by hydroelectric power, if there is a dry season in which there is little rain or snow, the coming year is predictably short on electricity. To address this issue, alternative forms of energy and the use of that energy to heat water or light buildings are explored. In the United States, which uses proportionally more energy, we are now exploring more efficient ways to generate and use energy. Can you think of recent examples, most notably in California, where people with different cultural backgrounds but with similar challenges can learn from one another?

Ears

Eyes

Heart

FIGURE 2.3 *Listen*

Eyes, Ears, Heart

When you hear, you passively receive sound. When you listen, you actively focus on receiving and interpreting aural (heard) stimuli. According to the Chinese character for listening, when you listen you use your eyes, ears and heart (Figure 2.3). With your eyes you may pay attention to nonverbal cues, like Clever Hans. With your ears, you may pay attention to not only the words but the tone of voice, pitch, rate of speech, and degree of fluidity of the words spoken. With your heart, you may pay attention to the emotional state of the speaker and observe the context in which the message is spoken. Listening is an important skill, and we will examine the kinds of listening and ways to improve your skills.

Importance of Listening

> *If speaking is silver, then listening is gold.*
>
> —Turkish Proverb

Why is listening so important? As examined previously in this chapter, your communication with others directly affects how you feel about and perceive yourself. Your ability to actively listen to the messages that are directed to you gives you the ability to control what you receive and how you interpret it.

Another reason why listening is important is the simple fact that you spend a considerable amount of your time engaging in listening activities. One of the first studies on listening behavior found that people are involved in listening activities, person to person or listening to mass media for example, around 40% of the time (Pearson & Nelson, 2000). Werner (1975), for example, found that people spend 55% of their time listening.

Kinds of Listening

As stated previously, it is important to make the distinction between hearing and listening. Hearing is the passive reception of sounds, whereas listening is the act of actively focusing on specific sounds with a purpose (Barker, 1971). The difference is easy to remember:

HEAR: You hear sounds all around you simply because they are here.

LISTEN: You make a list of exactly what you choose to hear when you listen.

There are three different kinds of listening: **active, empathic,** and **critical.** Each kind of listening, as each title implies, has a specific focus. We will examine the focus of each type of listening and then see how they relate to common listening barriers.

In **active listening,** you want to hear something. While the radio plays in the background, someone asks you a question. You want to hear that person, so you selectively attend to them, trying to listen to what they have to say. You want to give the person **feedback,** letting him or her know you are interested. If you nod to the person, he or she may understand that you have heard them. This is called **positive feedback,** and reinforces the listener's interest to the speaker. If you hold your hand to your ear and move your head back and forth, as in "no," you are indicating that you did not receive the message. This is also positive feedback, because you are still showing your interest. **Negative feedback** indicates that you did hear the message but that you don't like what you heard. Perhaps you show this negative feedback by glancing away or frowning. Your message to the speaker is one of frustration, or lack of interest, and it communicates an interest in not continuing the conversation.

In **empathic listening,** you take one more step. First, you listen with a purpose, wanting to hear the message. Second, you listen with the intent to understand the other person's point of view. In empathic listening, you pay attention not only to the words and nonverbal gestures but also to the context, previous information that pertains to the present situation, and the speaker's emotional state. Are they excited? Angry? Why are they so worked up? You attempt to gain insight into where the message comes from and why it is expressed in a particular way.

In **critical listening,** you listen with attention to detail, listening for clear support of the statements and trying to identify any inconsistencies. A salesperson may say, "This is our most exclusive (expensive) product—it is the best." They are using a logical shortcut that people often use: if it costs a lot, it must be good. Does this assertion hold up in all cases all the time? Of course not. It is up to you, the critical listener, to evaluate information for its accuracy and utility and to decide whether you can use it. This is called **critical thinking.** Where does someone get their information to support what they say? Do they have a financial interest in your decision? Examine what is said closely, paying attention to nonverbal as well as verbal cues. Examine even closer that which is not said, because without all the information, your decision may be based on partial truths. As a critical listener and a critical thinker, your goal is to actively listen and decide whether the message gives you the information you need.

Active listening	1. Choose to listen
Empathic listening	1. Choose to listen
	2. Try to understand speaker's point of view
Critical listening	1. Choose to listen
	2. Try to understand speaker's point of view or agenda
	3. Pay particular attention to detail

Stages of Listening

Now that we've discussed the importance of listening, let's examine the eight steps in the listening process (Figure 2.4). These may seem familiar to you

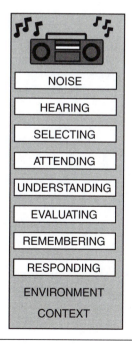

FIGURE 2.4 *The Listening Process*

because you use them all the time, often without even thinking about it. Let's pretend you want to listen to the radio. You turn the power on, and out of the speaker comes **noise.** The static that you **hear** tells you that you need to find a radio station signal. You tune the radio into a station and **select** the music coming out of the speakers rather than noise. You then choose to **attend to,** or focus on, the music to see if you can **understand** which group is playing the music or determine the song. You then **evaluate** the music, deciding whether you like it or not by **remembering** if you have heard it before or by determining that the new song sounds interesting. Finally, you **respond** to the music, either choosing to listen to it or by changing the channel.

1. Noise   External interference
2. Hearing   Registering sound
3. Selecting   Choosing stimuli
4. Attending   Focusing
5. Understanding   Assigning meaning
6. Evaluating   Analyzing and judging
7. Remembering   Recall and thinking
8. Responding   Listener responds to message

In addition to the eight steps in the listening process, we need to keep in mind two important factors that influence this process. As we discussed in the basic elements of the communication process, **environment** and **context** play an important role. If the environment in which you listen to the radio is quiet, then you may not need much volume to listen. If it is already filled with other sounds, like another radio, a television, or people talking, you may need to reduce the noise level to hear the radio. In terms of context, are you listening to the music by yourself? Then you can choose to listen to your favorite music, regardless whether it is rap or hard rock. If you share the space with other people, or they are trying to study, you might need to take this into account when you select the music. See Intercultural Communication 2.3.

Barriers to Listening

Barriers to listening are exactly what they sound like: things that get in the way of you hearing the message. The environment may be full of noise that makes a message hard to hear. Or it might be right after lunch, when you've had a full meal, and you are feeling a little sleepy. Beyond environmental and contextual distractions, there are four key barriers to listening that can contribute to a failure to listen.

INTERCULTURAL COMMUNICATION 2.3 • *How Do You Show That You Are Listening?*

- You are the teacher. You are speaking to a student about a problem behavior you want him to change. The student looks at his feet.
- You are a student. Your teacher is talking to you about a problem behavior she wants you to change. You look her in the eyes as she speaks.

What is the difference? If you are a member of many Native American tribes or from many of the countries in Latin America, you learned to show respect by not establishing eye contact with an authority figure. In Native American cultures, eyes are often considered windows to the soul and not to be shared casually. If you were raised in the United States, you may have heard the phrase "Look me in the eye when I am talking to you!" This phrase underlines the importance of maintaining eye contact with an authority figure to signal attention. How people show they are listening, and how people have chosen, through social custom or ritual, to speak varies around the world. Across cultures, however, the importance of showing you are listening, in a culturally appropriate way, is universal. Here are a few tips to help you if you find yourself in a new place, where people communicate in ways that are new to you.

1. Check your perceptions
It is necessary to ask if what you think the other person said is accurate or if that which happens between you has the same meaning for him or her it has for you. Wait until the other person has clearly finished speaking, and wait an extra second to be sure.

2. Look for feedback
Remember to ask for more than a simple yes or no answer. In some cultures it is impolite to say no.

3. Don't judge
Reserving judgment while listening allows you to be more open to another's message and point of view, reducing defensiveness in intercultural communication.

4. Be self-aware
Be conscious of the way you behave, your verbal and nonverbal communication style, and your values, beliefs, and attitudes. Intercultural communication can be challenging. Start with examining your own cultural background.

1. Lack of Interest

If you are not interested in what the speaker has to say, you are less likely to listen. In addition, if the speaker is not interested in what they are presenting, and fail to show enthusiasm for the topic, the speaker's lack of interest may influence your decision to listen. Try to find one thing about the message that interests you or look for something within the speech that may come in handy later.

2. Dislike the Speaker, Disregard the Message

If you do not like the speaker because of his or her choice of clothes, manner of speaking, or other personal attributes, you may fail to listen to the speaker and lose the message. Aristotle discusses the importance of **ethos,** or credibility and proof of character, as an integral part of any speech (Covino & Joliffe, 1995). If the audience isn't receptive to the messenger, they won't receive the message. You also may make a spot judgment about a person and decide that whatever he or she has to say does not interest you. The saying "never judge a book by its cover" holds true when it comes to listening. You never know where the person is coming from until you listen, and you never know what they may share if you tune them out.

3. Can't See the Forest Through the Trees

You may focus on the details within the message (trees), and lose sight of the larger picture (the forest). Perspective is important, and attention to detail is as well. In critical listening as part of critical thinking, attention to detail can have a large impact on your ability to understand the message and its value to you. The key to critical listening, and not getting lost, is to take notes. Actively listen for points you find interesting or ideas and issues you want to address later. In order not to get distracted by thinking (internal monologue) about one detail and missing countless others, take a note and then actively listen to the speaker, letting go of the point you recorded. Imagine that sometimes you have the perspective of a mouse, low and close to the ground, where small things can be easily seen. Other times have the perspective of the hawk, with its precise eyesight from high above, where you can take in the larger picture. Both perspectives have value, and you need both to listen actively.

4. Faking Attention

Have you ever been listening to someone and seen them talking but your mind is thousands of miles away. They ask you a question, and you are not listening. To answer the question, you have to ask them to repeat what they said. Faking attention is dangerous because the other person may not get that you missed what they were saying, and without checking, assume that you will use the information to get something done. Let's say a health care provider instructs a nurse to administer a shot to a patient, an important shot that contains medicine that the patient will need throughout the day. If the nurse fakes attention, how will he or she know which drug to use? Perhaps he or she can go to the chart and check, and perhaps not. People depend on each other, emotionally and professionally, and more than feelings can get hurt. Try to quiet your own "inner" voice and be there for the speaker. Wood (1997) relates this ability to quiet your own voice to the Zen Buddhist concept of mindfulness, of being fully engaged in listening (and not thinking about what you need to do next or what your response will be).

Improving Listening Skills

Now that we've discussed how important listening is as a part of the communication process, let's look at a brief list of some ways to improve listening skills (adapted from Galanes et al., 2000).

- Be silent. Let the other person speak and wait until you are sure that he or she is finished before you respond.
- Acknowledge understanding. Clearly communicate to the other person that you have heard and understood what he or she is saying.
- Take turns. Balancing the time between speaking and listening allows each person to take a turn.
- Don't interrupt. Interrupting may prevent something from ever being said.
- Communicate acceptance. Be open to what your partner is communicating. Being open and accepting to communication does not mean that you have to agree with what they say.
- Confirm understanding. Make sure you understand what your partner is communicating. If you don't understand, say so and check for meaning.
- Be attentive. Focus on the words, the message, the ideas, the body language, the context, and the speaker's emotions as he or she communicates with you.
- Make time. It is important to take time to listen. Plan on it. If you know you will spend some of your time listening beforehand, it will help take the pressure off to move on to the next activity. Also consider a special time for listening, for people you care about or have a relationship with, for communicating when you will not be disturbed or interrupted. Taking the time needed to get yourself understood and hearing the other person's thoughts, ideas, and hopes will keep you connected and your relationship will grow stronger.

Now that we've discussed several ways to improve your listening skills, let's leave our discussion on perception and listening with a reminder to practice active listening. Hearing is a passive activity, but active listening requires your time and attention. At the beginning of this text we discussed the importance of communication and how much time you spend communicating throughout your lifetime. Communication is a powerful force in our lives, and active listening is a critical part of the process. Here is a short list of helpful hints to encourage you to practice active listening.

- Give positive eye contact
- Smile and nod your head gently to give positive nonverbal feedback
- Restate the speaker's main ideas when you take your turn to speak
- Ask clarifying questions to better comprehend the message
- Let go of resentments, issues, and your own agenda
- Create environments to share feelings
- Turn off your own internal monologue, refraining from "preparing" your response before the speaker has finished speaking

Summary

We've examined the concept of perception, how our perspective is personal and how it impacts our communication with others. We've also examined how our self-concept is formed and the differences between values, beliefs, and attitudes. We've discussed the importance of listening, looked at three kinds of listening, examined the eight stages in the listening process, and identified four key barriers to listening. Improving our communication skills can be both challenging and rewarding, in terms of new relationships, understanding new concepts, and making sense of our world.

> To listen well is as powerful a means of communication and influence as to talk well.
>
> —John Marshall

For More Information _____

Perception: http://www.perceptionweb.com/

Rosie the Riveter: http://www.library.csi.cuny.edu/dept/history/lavender/rosie.html

Academic Survival Tips, provided by Edinboro University of Pennsylvania: http://www.edinboro.edu/cwis/acaff/suppserv/tips/tipsmenu.html

Review Questions _____

1. Factual Questions
   a. What are the three types of listening?
   b. What are the eight stages in the listening process?
   c. What are the four barriers to listening?

2. Interpretative Questions
   a. What is perception and how does it limit/expand our understanding?
   b. How does our self-concept impact our interaction with others?
   c. Do people hold similar values across cultures?

3. Evaluative Questions
   a. Is it really important to always listen?
   b. Can some listening cause harm to the listener?
   c. How do we account for hate speech or abusive language when stating it is important to listen?

4. Application Questions
   a. What do people value? Create a survey, identify a target sample size, conduct your survey, and compare the results.
   b. What laws pertain to the freedom of speech? Are there limitations and in which cases? Investigate the issue and share your findings.
   c. What does the field of psychology say about self-concept? Can you find one example of how self-concept impacts individual behavior? Compare the results.

Works Cited

Barker, L. (1971). *Listening behavior.* Englewood Cliffs, NJ: Prentice Hall.

Covey, S. (1989). *The seven habits of highly effective people.* New York: Simon and Schuster.

Covino, W. & Joliffe, D. (1995). *Rhetoric.* Boston: Allyn & Bacon.

Gage, N. & Berliner, D. (1998). *Educational psychology* (6th ed.). Boston: Houghton Mifflin, p. 151.

Galanes, G., Adams, K. & Brilhart, J. (2000). *Communicating in groups: Applications and skills* (4th ed.). Boston: McGraw-Hill.

Habermas, J. (1984). *The theory of communicative action* (Vol.1) Boston: Beacon Press.

Insel, P. & Jacobson, L. (1975). *What do you expect? An inquiry into self-fulfilling prophecies.* Menlo Park, CA: Cummings.

Klopf, D. (1995). *Intercultural encounters: The fundamentals of intercultural communication.* Englewood, CA: Morton.

Larson, G. (1999). *Building racial identity through discourse in a computer-mediated environment.* Unpublished doctoral thesis, Elliot School of Communication, Wichita State University.

Pearson, J. & Nelson, P. (2000). *An introduction to human communication: Understanding and sharing* (8th ed.). Boston: McGraw-Hill.

Rosenthal, R. & Jacobson, L. (1968). *Pygmalion in the classroom.* New York: Holt, Rinehart, and Winston.

Rosnow, R. & Rosenthal, R. (1999). *Beginning behavioral research: A conceptual primer* (3rd ed.). Upper Saddle River, NJ: Prentice Hall.

Strom, R. (1971). *Teachers and the learning process.* Englewood Cliffs, NJ: Prentice Hall.

Werner, E. (1975). *A study of communication time.* Unpublished master's thesis, University of Maryland.

Wood, J. (1997). *Communication in our lives.* Belmont, CA: Wadsworth.

Verbal Communication

Chapter Objectives

After completing this chapter, you should be able to:

1. Describe language and its role in perception and the communication process.
2. Identify and describe five key principles of verbal communication.
3. Identify and describe nine ways language can be an obstacle to communication.
4. Identify and describe three barriers to communication.
5. Identify and describe six ways to improve verbal communication.

Introductory Exercise 3.1

What does the mystery word mean?

Sometimes you just have to have a mysurp. You think to yourself, after a long, hard day at work or school, that it's time to reward yourself, and what comes to mind? A mysurp! Your muscles let go of the tension of the day, your frustrations peel away from you, and what's left? A mysurp! Get your mysurp today! You deserve it!

Introductory Exercise 3.2

What do you perceive in Figure 3.1?

How do you communicate? How do you think? Philosophers and researchers alike have asked these questions for a very long time. This chapter discusses the importance of verbal communication and examines how the characteristics of lan-

FIGURE 3.1 *Frame of Reference #1*

Source: Adapted from Sinha, P. & Adelson, E.'s exercise as featured in Steven Pinker's *How the Mind Works* (1997, p. 6,7).

guage interact in ways that can both improve and diminish effective communication. We will examine how language plays a significant role in how we perceive and interact with the world and how culture, language, education, gender, race, and ethnicity all influence this dynamic process. Finally, we will look at ways to improve your awareness of miscommunication and focus on constructive ways to decrease barriers to communication.

What Is Language?

Right now you are reading this sentence. Hopefully it makes sense to you. You are reading by assigning meaning to each individual letter that is part of a specific grouping, called a word, brought together by a set of rules called syntax or grammar. How do you know what each word means? You know the code. The family, group, or society in which you were raised taught you the code, called language. Does that mean everyone knows our code? Probably not. People are raised in different cultures, with different languages, values, and beliefs, every day. Even people with similar languages, like speakers of English in the United States, Australia, or New Zealand, speak and interact using their own distinct code words.

The words we exchange every day are directly and indirectly shaped by what we mean them to represent, and the person that receives them may miss our meaning entirely. This can be intentional and unintentional, and we'll look at how intentional manipulation of words and their meanings can be an obstacle to good communication later in this chapter. Languages have borrowed words and ways to organize them forever. Does the word "rodeo" make sense to you? It makes sense to a Spanish speaker as well. English adopted the word to express sporting events that involve horses, riders, and obstacles because there wasn't a word to describe these events. The letters come together to form an arbitrary word that refers to the thought or idea of the thing in "the semantic triangle" (Figure 3.2).

This triangle illustrates how the combination of five letters refers to the thought, which then refers to the thing or event itself. Who decides that "R O D E O" means the sporting event? Each letter stands for a sound, and when they come together in a specific way, the sounds they represent, when spoken, express the "word" that symbolizes the event. The key word is "symbolizes." The word stands in for the actual event. Words allow us to talk about something that isn't right in front of us. The word stands in place of the event, representing it.

Principles of Verbal Communication

Verbal communication, through language, has certain basic principles. In this section, we'll refer to examples we have discussed previously, highlight the principles of verbal communication, and look forward to how knowledge of these principles can help us improve our communication.

1. Language Has Rules

> *Language is a code, a collection of symbols, letters, or words with arbitrary meanings that are arranged according to the rules of syntax and are used to communicate.*
>
> —Pearson and Nelson, 2000, p. 54

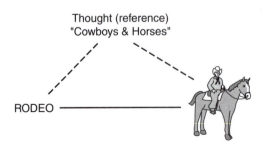

FIGURE 3.2 *The Semantic Triangle*

Source: Adapted from Ogden and Richards (1932).

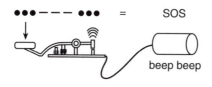

FIGURE 3.3 *Morse Code*

In the second exercise, what did you think "mysurp" was? Did you think it was something you ate or drank? A stuffed animal to be cuddled with? A television program? It could have been anything you wanted it to be. Did the word itself make sense to you? The organization of the letters followed standard rules for English, so it probably looked like English, rather than a word from a foreign language used in an English sentence. As language users, we know the rules so well that we hardly ever think of them, except for when we need to learn a new language. Can you read and write Morse Code? At one time Morse Code was the primary way of exchanging information across long distances. This system was eventually replaced by the telephone. In the late 1800s and early 1900s, even throughout World War II, Morse Code allowed people to communicate ideas by sending and receiving sounds that represented letters that formed words and eventually sentences. Short sounds (dots) and long sounds (dashes) represent sounds and pauses to form a code that both sender and receiver recognize.

Figure 3.3 features a World War II–era Morse sender and receiver, with the series of dots and dashes that represent "SOS," or "Save Our Souls," commonly interpreted as a distress signal. See also Intercultural Communication 3.1.

There are three types of rules that govern or control our use of words, when we use certain words, and how to interpret these words when used. You probably use these rules all the time but may not have given it any thought. Can you think of a word that is ok to use sometimes and not others? How about a word your friends understand, but other people do not?

Syntactic rules	These are the rules that govern where words come in a sentence. In English you would say "a happy person," but in Spanish you would say "una persona contenta."
Semantic rules	These are the rules that govern the meaning of words and guidelines on how to interpret them. We agree "rodeo" means a sporting event featuring riders, horses, and cattle. If we didn't agree, we would all be making our words mean whatever we want them to when we say them, and communication would be impossible.

INTERCULTURAL COMMUNICATION 3.1 • *Navajo Code Used in World War II*

An elite group of Native American soldiers serving on Iwo Jima during World War II developed a code within their native language that enemy intelligence never broke. From their native Navajo, they used words like "egg" to represent "bomb" and "hawk" to represent "dive bomber." Their code finally totaled more than 400 words, and their ability to communicate in an oral language that had never been written down allowed them to exchange information efficiently and accurately.

For more information, visit the DEPARTMENT OF THE NAVY—NAVAL HISTORICAL CENTER at http://www.history.navy.mil/faqs/faq61-2.htm

To listen to the Navajo language in song, visit:

http://www.tandem-music.com/newreleases.htm

Song: Navajo Healing Song, From the album "Heart Of ... Wolf" (mono, 43 sec)
Contact: www.tandem-music.com

Contextual rules   These are the rules that govern meaning and word choice according to context and social custom. The word "no" can mean many things, whether it is spoken by a judge, an instructor, or a two-year-old child.

In this section we examined how language has rules and how even though we know the rules, we still may not get the correct meaning. Words represent the ideas we want to communicate but often require us to negotiate their meaning, creating a common vocabulary.

2. Our Reality Is Shaped by Our Language

Have you ever thought of what it would be like if you were raised in China? Or Greece? Or Spain? You would have learned a language other than English, and your world would have been different. You would have eaten different foods, celebrated holidays that came from your religion or social customs, and perceived the world through your experiences.

Two researchers, Benjamin Lee Whorf and Edward Sapir, were among the first to investigate the nature of perception through language and culture. Whorf, employed by the Hartford Fire Insurance Company, found the conflict between science and religion fascinating. He started taking classes at Yale University, and he studied the Hopi language under the supervision of Edward Sapir. Whorf explored the world of linguistics and formulated what later became known as the Whorf/Sapir hypothesis. By relating culture and actions to language, he formulated the concept that states, "Our perception of reality is determined by our thought process and our thought processes are limited by language and, therefore, language shapes our reality" (Whorf, 1956). Whorf died young and did not have time to fully support his ideas, but his idea is well supported by most linguists, and his writings are the source of continuing debate.

European scholars, often referred to as "post-modern," such as Jacques Derrida (1974) and Michel Foucault (1980) take as a basic assumption that language creates reality and extend their application to the deconstruction of ideas, breaking them down to their elemental levels, to increase understanding. Others, like Jean Piaget, whose ideas contributed to our understanding of how people learn, or, more currently, Steven Pinker, director of the Center for Cognitive Neuroscience at the Massachusetts Institute of Technology, take the Whorf/Sapir hypothesis to task. There is a list of sources for further investigation at the end of this chapter.

Look back at Introductory Exercise 3.2 at the beginning of this chapter. What did you see? Now look at Figure 3.4. Notice any similarities?

They are the same, with one key difference. The dark border, which partially blocked your view, has been removed. Have you ever been in a situation where things looked one way but later, after you had more or new information, they looked another? This exercise illustrates the effect of perception, and, in this case, a two-dimensional picture becomes three-

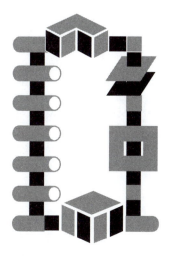

FIGURE 3.4 *Frame of Reference #2*

dimensional when fully viewed. This exercise also gives just one view of the "solution." It illustrates the importance of perspective and context.

Look back in Chapter 2 at the "star," or the circle of "Pac-Mans." Do you see how it can be seen more than one way? Our experiences become like sunglasses, tinting the way we see the world, or some might picture them as blinders, like on a horse, that create tunnel vision. To walk a mile in another person's shoes is an expression that asks you to put yourself in another person's perspective.

Hall (1966) also underlines this point when discussing the importance of context. The situation in which a conversation occurs provides a lot of meaning and understanding for the participants in some cultures. In Japan, for example, the context, such as a business setting, says a great deal about the conversation and the meaning of the words and expressions within that context. In the United States, however, the concept of a workplace or a business meeting is less structured, and the context offers less meaning and understanding. Cultures that value context highly are aptly called **high-context cultures.** Those that value context to a lesser degree are call **low-context cultures.** This ability to understand perspective and context is key to good communication, and one we will examine throughout the text.

3. Language Is Arbitrary and Symbolic

As we have seen in the Morse code example, language is symbolic. Words, by themselves, do not have any inherent meaning. We give meaning to them. The arbitrary symbols (letters, numbers, and punctuation marks, for example) stand for sounds and concepts in our experience. The letter "S" has a sound associated with it. The letter could just have easily have been reversed, or a different character entirely, when the alphabet was created. Once it was created, it became a character we referred to as representing a sound, or in combination with other letters, a word that represents an idea or concept (Hayakawa, 1978). Can you think of where our agreed-on vocabulary is documented, for us to refer to as we need to clarify meanings or words and phrases? See Intercultural Communication 3.2.

Once we have an agreed-on vocabulary, often stored in a dictionary, it is then possible to interpret words and refer to the denotative meaning. The **denotative meaning** is the dictionary meaning or common meaning that is generally agreed on. Does everyone always agree on the meaning of words? Of course not. Take the word "cool," for example. At first it referred to temperature, as seen in a scale from cold to hot, or to describe a color, as in paintings from Picasso's Blue Period are often called "cool."

After World War II, the Beat Generation of the 1950s used the word cool to mean hip or fashionable. Mainstream society still used the standard dictionary meaning and had disdain for the slang meaning. Over time, the beat meaning came to be generally accepted, and now it is in common

INTERCULTURAL COMMUNICATION 3.2 • *Names*

Names are symbolic representations of us. For example, the surname (last name) "Nancucheo" means "strong like the swift, flightless bird." If you speak Huilliche, a Native South American language spoken on the Chilean island of Chiloe, you would understand the meaning, but without knowledge of the local language and culture, the meaning is lost. "Nan" is from "Nandu," the name for a small ostrich-like bird, and "cucheo" means strong like (the Nandu). Do you know where your name comes from? What does it mean? What language and culture does it come from? Does it refer to someone within your family or come from the environment around you? Document the origins of your name and share with other students.

usage. Once, only a small group of "nontraditional" people used cool to refer to hip, but now aging "Boomers" and Dot.com CEOs alike use the word without fear of embarrassment. Take a moment and create a list of words that have a variety of meanings.

This example shows how a word can go from its denotative (dictionary) meaning to a **connotative meaning,** one that has meaning to an individual or group, and how that special meaning became common. Connotative meanings can also refer to emotions associated with words, but the association between the word and the emotion is an individual or personal one and not held by larger society.

4. Language Is Abstract

Words represent things and ideas in our environment. They simplify otherwise complex concepts. "Horse" can represent the four-legged animal without signifying the group of biological systems, from a system of muscles and bones to a well-developed respiratory system, which combined make a "horse." A "horse" for one person may mean recreation, but for another it may mean the standard form of transportation or power for farm implements. This ability to simplify concepts makes it easier to communicate, but we sometimes lose the specific meaning of what we are trying to say through abstraction. Take a look at the ladder of abstraction (Figure 3.5). Do you see how at one level, "Horse" can mean a concrete concept but at another the concept is abstract and removed from the original "Horse."

We can see how, at the extreme level of abstraction, the horse is like any other living creature. We can also see how, at the base level where the concept is most concrete, "Silver," the name given to the horse in the classic "Lone Ranger" television series, is a specific animal, with specific markings, size, shape, and coloring.

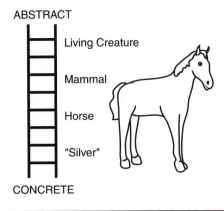

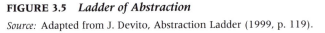

FIGURE 3.5 *Ladder of Abstraction*

Source: Adapted from J. Devito, Abstraction Ladder (1999, p. 119).

5. Language Organizes and Classifies Reality

Who wears the black cowboy hat? The white one? How do we distinguish between Luke Skywalker and Darth Vader? Our language organizes and classifies our realities in ways we may not normally notice. As discussed previously, we select, organize, and interpret information as we communicate. We tend to group words, concepts, shapes, and images, for example, by their physical proximity and/or their similarity to one another. Our ability to organize is handy, but we need to recognize that we impose categories on our world to make sense of it. Sometimes our categorizations can become habitual, without thought, or even unjustified. Western culture often reinforces the concept of opposites, such as good and evil, white and black, work and play, and the English language in particular lends itself to this dualism. For example, Robert Moore (1998, pp. 465–466) notes how the use of black and white polarizes, or creates two extremes, in our everyday language.

> Some may blackly (angrily) accuse me of trying to blacken (defame) the English language, to give it a black eye (a mark of shame) by writing such black words (hostile). They may denigrate (to cast aspersions; to darken) me by accusing me of being black hearted (malevolent), of having a black outlook (pessimistic, dismal) on life … —which would certainly be a black mark (detrimental fact) against me.
>
> …
>
> I challenge the purity and innocence (white) of the English language. I don't see things in black or white (entirely bad or entirely good).

In this excerpt of Moore's essay entitled *Racism in the English Language,* can you see how he uses language to illustrate the way black has been associated with bad and white with good? Have you ever noticed this, or any type of classification in language that creates a superior and inferior group? Sometimes this classification is done by physical characteristics such as tall, short, or large, small, to create classifications. Sometimes classification, the organization of individuals into groups, happens on the basis of sex or religion. Can you think of an example when people choose to classify themselves according to a common characteristic? Can you think of an example in which someone has imposed a classification on you or a friend without your consent? Organization and classification are natural parts of our daily lives. We relate what we don't know to what we do know, using lessons learned from the past to negotiate new situations. When we fail to question previous lessons learned or assumptions in light of new information or situations, we run the risk of making quick judgments that may not be fair to ourselves or others.

Language as an Obstacle to Communication

Now we have discussed the principles of verbal communication and examined how we use language to make sense of our world. You can probably see how many of the principles of communication can be a double-edged sword, meaning the principles can work both for and against you. Let's look at nine general ways language can be an obstacle to effective communication, and then find ways to turn the negatives into positives, making our communication even more effective.

1. Speech Is Not Like Written Language

Many people write well, but when it comes to speaking, they make all sorts of errors. These errors are often grammatical or involve semantics, the way words are put together, or involve word choice. Technically speaking, you are not supposed to say "Can I go to the bathroom" to your teacher because the automatic answer is "I don't know, can you?" This response captures the "are you able to do something" sense of the word rather than the intended meaning, a request for permission. A more correct request would use the word "may." Although the technical merit of which word to use may be the subject of debate, the intended meaning is clear. If the receiver/cocommunicator focuses on the words, he or she misses, or chooses to miss, the intended meaning, creating an obstacle to communication. This may call to mind one of the basic principles of communication. Look back at Chapter 1 and see if you can make the connection.

In terms of grammar and semantics, sometimes "incorrect" grammar is actually correct within the regional dialect or comes from an adaptation in the language. Take, for example, the case of the Gullah language (Intercultural Communication 3.3).

2. Slang

We are all familiar to some extent with slang, or words that mean something to us and the people we associate with but may not be understood by people outside of our group. We discussed previously the word "cool" and how it transformed from a word among friends to one in everyday conversations across the nation. In addition to slang, **regionalisms,** or words and phrases that pertain to a particular area, can also create obstacles to effective communication. If you are a new student at Washington State University, one of the first phrases you learn is "on the hill." You hear students saying, "See you on the hill" or "I'm heading up the hill." In both cases, the "hill" is understood to be the hill that the University is located on, but to an outsider, the automatic response is often, "Which hill?"

INTERCULTURAL COMMUNICATION 3.3 • *Gullah*

There is an island off the coast of South Carolina where a group of families speak a distinct variation of English. It wasn't until a linguist discovered, through a detailed examination of slave records from dealers, that their origins were in Sierra Leone in West Africa. Comparison of the native language of Sierra Leone to the type of English spoken by the Gullahs revealed striking similarities across grammar and syntax, blending African language patterns and words with English. Curiously, the language did not change much because they were left alone. The original Gullahs had a high resistance to malaria, ever present on the island, whereas the slave owners fell victim to the disease.

From Psalm 19:10,11

Gawd Wodmo sweeta den honey ...
Wen A do wa E tell me fa do,
Gawd sen me great blessin.   *The Sea Island (Gullah) Version*

God's Words are sweeter than honey ...
And in keeping of them there is great
    reward.   *The King James Version of the Bible*

Source: Afrika, L.O. (1990). *The Gullah.* Beaufort, SC: Llaila Olela Afrika.

3. Jargon

Jargon is a profession-specific language used by professionals. You probably speak some sort of jargon when you go to work or are aware of when others, in a field that is not your own, speak in their own language. Familiar television programs often use jargon to create the illusion of authenticity. On television shows that take place in a health care environment, for example, they speak medical-eze, discussing health conditions, procedures, and medications with jargon that makes it look like they know what they are talking about. Every field has its own terms and phrases that refer to specific concepts that group members understand. This can lead to the trainee in the field feeling lost while established people in the industry communicate effortlessly. Jargon can be used to communicate about technical or specific concepts quickly and accurately and can also be used strategically to separate an outsider from a group. One phrase often heard in business, which speaks to this point, is "Knowledge is power. If you don't share, it's a problem for everyone." If the trainee missed a key point, and the established workers thought he or she "got it," the resulting mistake can be costly. See Computer-Mediated Communication 3.1.

4. Sexist and Racist Language

As we discussed in the section on how language organizes and classifies, language that creates a power position where one group is included or elevated and the other group is excluded or subordinated can be a serious obstacle to effective communication. Sexist language uses a person's gender identity as the discriminating factor.

> *Blue for boys, pink for girls. Boys are made from snails and puppy dog tails, girls from sugar and spice and everything nice.*

These phrases from childhood rhymes speak to classification based on gender from an early age. Boys are perceived, in the context of the passage, as dirty and adventurous, whereas girls are placed at the other extreme, as clean and proper. Classification in language carries over to adulthood, where policeman, once used for both male and female police officers, presumes the officer is masculine by default. Language is changing, and the title, for example, of police officer replaces policeman. Being aware of sexist language can prevent it from becoming an obstacle to shared discussions and effective communication.

In addition to sexist language, racist language is part of the tradition of the English language. Obvious racial references, used in a negative sense to create a subordinate group, include "spook," "chink," "spic," and "wetback." Each term creates a classification, grouping people of similar racial and/or

COMPUTER-MEDIATED COMMUNICATION 3.1 • *Language*

The ability to chat with another person in real-time communication changes the way we use language. Rather than write "by the way," BTW is a common abbreviation. Here are a few "e-breviations":

What I meant was	WIMW	Have you heard	HYH
Face to face	F2F	ta ta for now	TTFN
In my opinion	IMO	Laughing out loud	LOL

Like any new environment, the problem comes when the outsider doesn't know the meaning of the words the insiders use to communicate.

Real-time computer-mediated communication has also facilitated new types of communication, including process writing, active collaboration, and less logical linear writing. In process writing, the conversation participants engage in a James Joyce–like stream of consciousness, where spelling and grammar mean less than content and insight. In active collaboration, more than one person joins in the stream, and the collaboration can produce new and fascinating results. Finally, because the writing has no introduction, middle, or conclusion, and the point at which participants join in and depart varies, the writing loses its linear properties.

Have you ever participated in a chat room where process writing was used? How do you think active collaboration around a loosely formed topic engages the participants in new ways. Do these ways of communication empower people? How do they change the language?

---

ethnic characteristic in a negative context. **Color symbolism,** as Robert Moore highlights in his essay on "Black" and "White" in the English Language, creates a good/bad classification that segregates people.

By extension, **ethnocentrism** is the viewpoint that one's own culture is the "ruler" by which all other cultures are measured and all fall short. Ethnocentrism creates a context in which the dominant group views itself positively, and other groups are viewed in relation to the dominant group, often negatively. The dominant group becomes the "norm," and other groups are evaluated in terms of their level of conformity. When you hear groups discussed as marginal or on the fringe, you see how, through language, they are viewed as removed or far from the "normal" or majority.

Beyond ethnocentrism, other terms create divisions based on class and privilege. The use of the term "third world" in reference to developing nations presumes a first world that the third world could become. Development has, by its very nature, good and bad consequences, from the transformation of ecosystems to the change in social structures and interpersonal relationships. The ethnocentric viewpoint that industrial or information age infrastructure is the high point of human development is the source of considerable debate.

Finally, words can be used to segregate people from their humanity. When we replace someone's name with a pronoun like *he, she,* or *it,* we begin abstracting the idea of that individual person. When we talk about *them,* and traits *they* have, we separate ourselves from other people into *us* and *them.* We can further replace their identity with language that confuses rather than clarifies, such as "collateral damage" for civilians killed in wartime. This separation of people from our connection to them or a sense of humanity has contributed to war crimes and tortures and has made some experiments on "subjects" sound almost respectable.

In Case Study 3.1, people were not referred to as humans but as objects or things. The word "subjects" distances the speaker from personal involvement with the person he or she is discussing, viewing them in a more abstract context than a concrete one. The dehumanization of the people in this study led to serious consequences and changed the oversight and guidelines for US research protocols forever.

5. Small Talk

Every day we say things like "how are you?" and respond to similar question with "Oh fine, and you?" Are we really inquiring about each other's health or state of well-being? Of course not, we're just engaging in small talk, sometimes called "phatic communion" (Malinowski, 1935). In **small talk,** the meanings of the words are not literal, but understood, and the emphasis in the communication is on the interaction, not necessarily the content or information. It's a social custom, where we acknowledge each other's presence. To someone raised outside of Western culture, this may seem strange, but most cultures have similar rituals for greeting that focus on the context rather than on literal meaning that people can relate to.

Colloquialisms are like small talk in that words and phrases are used in social contexts as part of a ritual. When someone says, "Have a nice day," they are often not communicating their genuine wish that you indeed have a pleasant day, but instead using the phrase to signal the close of a conversation or exchange of information. See Computer-Mediated Communication 3.2.

6. Cliché

You may have heard the phrase "The early bird gets the worm." What does it mean? That people who take the initiative get the reward? Yes, but does the idea carry much weight or power? Probably not. Why? To answer the question, ask yourself: Do you know anyone who uses a phrase or word repeatedly? Does the frequent use of the word or phrase make it more powerful and impacting? For most people, words and phrases that are frequently used lose their originality and effectiveness, making the listener

CASE STUDY 3.1 • *Tuskegee Syphilis Study*

A joint study between the US Public Health Service (PHS) and the Julius Rosenwald Fund was conducted to consider ways to improve the health of African Americans in the South. The Great Depression hit, and the Rosenwald Fund withdrew its financial support, leaving the PHS unable to treat the patients.

Dr. Taliaferro Clark of the PHS suggested that the project could be partially "saved" by conducting a study on the effects of untreated syphilis on living "subjects." His suggestion was approved by the PHS, and the study continued with the focus on syphilis.

The PHS used the support of the local Tuskegee Institute to enroll participants in the study. At the time, many African Americans had almost no access to medical care. For many people, the examination by the PHS physician combined with the free food and transportation made participation attractive. Even though study participants received medical examinations, none were told that they were infected with syphilis. They either were not treated or were treated at a level that was judged to be insufficient to cure the disease, and PHS officials prevented other agencies from supplying treatment.

In 1943, while the study was ongoing, the PHS began to administer penicillin to patients with syphilis as a standard treatment nationwide. Tuskegee study subjects did not receive penicillin treatments, and their symptoms were observed and recorded as they got worse. The study was stopped in 1972 when Peter Buxton, a venereal disease interviewer and investigator for the PHS, told an Associated Press reporter, who wrote a front-page story. Congressional subcommittee meetings were held in early 1973 by Senator Edward Kennedy that resulted in a complete change in laws, policies, and the code of conduct for researchers and in a class action settlement.

The Tuskegee Syphilis Study stands as an extreme example of the effects of dehumanization of US citizens and violates basic ethical principles established for prisoners of war. Among Heller's remarks were: "The men's status did not warrant ethical debate. They were subjects, not patients; clinical material, not sick people" (p. 179).

Source: Jones, J. (1981). *Bad blood: The Tuskegee syphilis experiment: A tragedy of race and medicine.* New York: The Free Press.

tune them out or ignore them. A **cliché** is a phrase that, through overuse, has lost its impact. Can you think of an example?

7. Profanity

Words that offend can create obstacles to effective communication, and when they are abusive or vulgar, they are called **profanity.** In Latin

COMPUTER-MEDIATED COMMUNICATION 3.2 • *Netiquette*

Social customs and rules of conduct help guide our communication every day. We know what to say when we greet each other and what behavior is expected at a wedding, for example. In the new world of computer-mediated communication, new rules, called **netiquette,** are used to guide communication and our conduct. Here is a summary of netiquette rules:

Rule 1: Remember the human
Virginia Shea, in her book *Netiquette* (1994), reminds us we should never forget the person behind the words that appear on the monitor. Keep in mind that on the other end of the communication is a person, not an argument to be defeated or an object to be ignored.

Rule 2: Treat other people like you want to be treated
The golden rule applies in cyberspace. If you want to be treated well online, then take the first step and treat others that way.

Rule 3: Learn the language and customs
Before you jump into deep water you need to learn to swim. Before you get involved with an online debate, learn the rules and customs. Words in capital letters are generally considered SHOUTING and therefore rude. Emoticons [; -)] can be cute, but there is a time and a place for everything. Watch how others interact, and read the frequently asked questions (FAQs) before you take your turn.

Source: Shea, V. (1994). *Netiquette.* New York: Albion Books.

Post. P. & Post, P. (2000). *The etiquette advantage in business: Personal skills for professional success.* New York: Harper Resource.

"pro" means *before* or *outside,* and "fanum" means *temple,* which became "profane" or profanity as it is commonly known. Profane refers to "outside the temple," implying a sacred space and a place outside of that sacredness. In modern day, certain words are considered outside the boundary of good, civil taste for normal or professional conversation and are therefore considered profane. Use of words, which could be potentially offensive to the receiver or audience, can create an obstacle to clear communication and create a hostile climate where listening breaks down.

8. Euphemisms

When you go to a funeral, do people say the person has died or passed away? When someone needs to eliminate personal waste, do the say they have to urinate or that they have to go to the bathroom? In each case, the second option is more socially acceptable than the first. People often prefer to refer to something perceived as unpleasant by using a euphemism. A **euphemism** substitutes a more polite term or phrase for one that is blunt or insensitive.

9. Doublespeak

Doublespeak is an extension of the concept of a euphemism but implies the intentional misleading of the listener. **Doublespeak** is language that is intentionally ambiguous or misleading. By saying "downsizing," the listener is not asked to contemplate the workers who are losing their jobs. By saying "collateral damage," the listener is not asked to contemplate the civilians who were killed alongside soldiers. Sometimes we use words to communicate an unpleasant idea in a more socially acceptable way, but doublespeak involves an intentional abstraction from a concrete reality that the speaker does not want the listener to think about. Books such as *1984*, by George Orwell, and *Fahrenheit 451*, by Ray Bradbury, both address this intentional manipulation and control of language to create an inaccurate sense of reality.

Together we can observe how each of these nine obstacles to communication can create walls rather than bridges. If we are aware of each obstacle, we can successfully negotiate the conversation away from words and phrases that will distract the listener or audience to a negative point and focus instead on using clear, concrete terms that further mutual understanding.

Barriers to Communication

William Seiler and Melissa Beall (2000), in the book entitled *Communication: Making Connections,* note three key barriers to communication that combine elements of the obstacles we have discussed but also offer unique insight to habits that act as barriers to effective communication.

1. Bypassing

Bypassing happens when "what is meant by a speaker and what is heard and understood by the listener are often different (Seiler & Beall, 2000, p. 93). From Seiler and Beall (2000) comes a classic example of "what I said wasn't what you heard."

> "A motorist was driving down a highway when her engine suddenly stalled. She quickly determined that her battery was dead and managed to stop another driver who consented to push her car with his own to get it started.

"My car has an automatic transmission," she explained, "so you'll have to get the speed up to 15 or 20 miles an hour to get me started."

The man smiled and walked back to his car. The motorist climbed into her own and waited for him to line up his car behind hers. She kept waiting. Finally, she looked up and into the rear-view mirror to what was taking so long, only to see his car coming at hers at 15 to 20 miles an hour. The damage to her car came to over $1,000!"

What she said and what he heard were two different things. Has that ever happened to you?

2. Indiscrimination

Indiscrimination occurs when we emphasize or focus on similarities but neglect or fail to acknowledge differences, considering all things similar essentially the same (Seiler and Beall, 2000). When we ignore differences, and lump things together, we fail to discriminate and discern key differences. Sometimes it can be relatively harmless. "Fords are better than Chevys!" "Chevys are better than Fords!" There can be times when ignoring individual characteristics, differences, or qualities can be harmful and even dangerous.

Racial profiling is the marking of a person based on their race or ethnicity within a specific context, say driving a Porsche® in a nice neighborhood, as a potential suspect. Although studies may show that some crimes in certain communities may feature certain ethnic or racial groups with a certain degree of frequency, by targeting all members of these racial or ethnic groups, indiscrimination occurs. When the police officers pull the driver over because he or she failed to signal a turn, did they notice the infraction because of the violation? Or was the car "marked" by the police officers because of the driver's individual characteristics, and the infraction is an opportunity to learn more about the situation and to see whether the vehicle is stolen? This is a complex issue that involves the effects of indiscrimination.

3. Polarization

The concept of **polarization,** which we visited in Moore's essay on black and white previously, is the tendency to view issues, ideas, and the world around us in extremes. She is rich, he is poor. He is thin, she is fat. I am right, you are wrong. This view of the situation in absolute terms leaves little room for increased understanding and leads to conflict and debate. We do this naturally to save the mental effort of having to evaluate every little thing during the course of the day. For example, "We like our laundry detergent. They have a new product. It's by the same manufacturer? Oh, it must be good." or if you have to decide between two products, "Oh, I know this brand. I'll choose it," or finally, another mental shortcut, "If it costs more it must be better." All of the strategies can help us make decisions, but without reevaluation periodically, we may fall into habits that have no basis or our assumptions may be old and outdated.

The phrase "I am right and you are wrong" features polarization where rather than being open to another's point of view, or new evidence to support their opinion, you stay with your "I'm right" attitude. The is called the **pendulum effect,** where like a pendulum in a grandfather clock, you are off to one extreme, rather than in the middle, where you can see both sides. Aristotle said the mark of an educated person was his or her ability to see, and be able to argue for, both sides of an issue.

Exercise

Can you think of three examples from your own experiences where bypassing, indiscrimination, or polarization led to miscommunication? Discuss with a classmate or friend and compare notes on their experiences.

> *Good communication is as stimulating as black coffee and just as hard to sleep after.*
> —Anne Morrow Lindbergh

Improving Verbal Communication

Now let's take a look at six ways we can use our knowledge of the obstacles to communication to improve it.

1. Actively Listen to the Speaker

This means when someone is speaking to you, listen to what they are saying and how they say it. Don't listen to yourself thinking about your response to what's being said.

2. Check Your Understanding

"Did you mean ___ by saying this _____," "What I heard you say was you are concerned about _____, " or "What do you mean by _____?" are all phrases that check meaning. You may think you "got it" the first time, but by checking your understanding of what's been said, you reduce the possibility of miscommunication.

3. Define Your Terms

"By this, I mean _____." Make sure the person or persons you are speaking to understand your meaning of the word before you use it. We all may understand the denotative (dictionary) meaning of the word, but the connotative meaning varies and it is better to clarify terms up front than to define and redefine terms later.

4. Use Concrete Words

"Silver" is a horse, but he was a specific horse within a specific context. Black Beauty is also a specific horse, but the context is different. If you have not watched *"The Lone Ranger"* television program, or read Anna Sewell's book *Black Beauty* (or seen the movie), the use of concrete words about each horse can give meaning and understanding to your discussion of horses in general. You or your audience may not be familiar with "Silver" or "Black Beauty," so discussion in detail with concrete terms will improve everyone's understanding of your examples.

5. Know the Difference Between Objectivity and Subjectivity

Objectivity is "just the facts," documenting just what is observed. Subjectivity is recording not only the facts but also your interpretation of the facts. For example, let's say you are involved in a car accident. The law enforcement officer will listen to both drivers and write down what each person states as objectively as possible. This is called a statement. Then the officer will compare the drivers' stories to the visible signs of the accident, the damage, and the tire marks and interview witnesses to the accident. All of this information, collected and recorded as objectively as possible, helps the officer make a fair report of who is at fault in the accident and what contributing factors, if any, were present; this report will be an important part of the insurance claim process.

You would expect that the officer would hear both drivers out fairly and equally. You would hope that difference in the style, make, and model of your car would not influence perceptions. If you were driving an expensive car while the other car was built in 1974 and is three shades of rust, you would hope that the officer would not assume you could afford to pay for the accident when considering your degree of fault. Being objective is difficult, but critical thinking requires the ability to stand back and look at all the details before making an assessment or decision.

As we saw in the discussion on language and how it influences our perception of reality, it is challenging to be objective. At the same time, recognizing that objectivity is a goal and not a state easily achieved lends itself to the critical evaluation of information and its source. If conclusions are already provided in the discussion of information, who made these conclusions and why? Were they right? Did they have all the facts? Would I make the same decision? All of these questions apply as ways we can improve communication through critical thinking and examining what is said and heard for misunderstandings and errors. Jumping to the wrong conclusion leads you down the wrong path, but the well-placed question and the information it elicits may steer you down the right one.

Summary

In this chapter we examined how language influences our perception of the world and the verbal principles of communication. Building on each of these principles, we examined nine obstacles to effective communication and discussed six ways to improve communication. Throughout the chapter we visited examples and stories that highlight the importance of verbal communication. To end the chapter we need to remember how language can be used to enlighten or deceive, encourage or discourage, empower or destroy. Recognizing the power of verbal communication is the first step to understanding its role and impact on the communication process.

The editorial "The Environment of Language," which first appeared in the *Saturday Review*, stated this well when it said language:

> ... has much to do with philosophical and political conditioning of a society as geography or climate ... people in Western cultures do not realize the extent to which their racial attitudes have been conditioned since early childhood by the power of words to ennoble or condemn, augment or detract, glorify or demean. Negative language infects the subconscious of most ... people from the time they first learn to speak. Prejudice is not merely imparted or superimposed. It is metabolized in the blood stream of society. What is needed is not so much a change in language as an awareness of the power to condition attitudes. If we can at least recognize the underpinnings of prejudice, we may be in a position to deal with the effects.

Source: "The Environment of Language," *Saturday Review*, April 8, 1967, as reprinted in R. Moore's essay *Racism in the English Language*.

For More Information _____

On B. L. Whorf, visit: http://grail.cba.csuohio.edu/~somos/whorf.html

On J. Piaget, visit: http://www.piaget.org/

Steven Pinker's books on the subject include:

Language Learnability & Language Development

How the Mind Works

The Language Instinct

Review Questions

1. Factual Questions
   a. What is language?
   b. What are the principles of communication?
   c. How can language be an obstacle to effective communication?
   d. What is one way language can be used to improve communication?

2. Interpretative Questions
   a. From your viewpoint, how do you think that thought influences the use of language?
   b. Does Robert Moore accurately capture the nature the English Language?
   c. What does the author mean by conditioned in the phrase "people in Western cultures do not realize the extent to which their racial attitudes have been conditioned since early childhood by the power of words to ennoble or condemn, augment or detract, glorify or demean?"

3. Evaluative Questions
   a. To what extent does language help us communicate?
   b. To what extent does verbal communication limit communication?
   c. Who controls or regulates verbal communication?

4. Application Questions
   a. How does language change over time? Interview someone older than you, and younger than you, and identify words that have changed.
   b. How does language affect self-concept? Explore and research your answer, finding examples that can serve as case studies.
   c. Can people readily identify the barriers to communication? Survey ten individuals and see if they accurately identify at least one barrier, even if they use a different term or word.

Works Cited

Derrida, J. (1974). *Of grammatology* (G. Spivak, Trans.). Baltimore: Johns Hopkins Press.

Devito, J. (1999). *Messages: Building interpersonal communication skills* (4th ed.). New York: Addison, Wesley, Longman.

Foucalt, M. (1980). *Power/knowledge: Selected interviews and other writings: 1972/1977* (C. Gordon, Ed.). Brighton, UK: Harvester.

Hall, E. (1966). *The hidden dimension.* New York: Doubleday.

Hayakawa, S. I. (1978). *Language in thought and action.* Orlando, FL: Harcourt Brace Jovanovich.

Malinowski, B. (1935). *The language and magic of gardening.* London: Allen & Unwin.

Moore, R. (1998). Racism in the English language. In P. Rothenburg (Ed.), *Race, class, and gender in the United States* (4th ed.). New York: St. Martin's Press.

Ogden, C. & Richards, I. (1932). *The meaning of meaning: A study of the influence of language upon thought and of the science of symbolism.* New York: Harcourt Brace and World.

Pearson, J., & Nelson, P. (2000). *An introduction to human communication: Understanding and sharing* (8th ed.). Boston: McGraw-Hill.

Pinker, S. (1997). *How the mind works* (pp. 6–7). New York: W.W. Norton & Company.

Seiler, W., & Beall, M. (2000). *Communication: Making connections.* (4th ed.). Boston: Allyn & Bacon.

Whorf, B. L. (1956). *Science and linguistics.* In J. B. Carroll (Ed.), Language, thought, and reality (pp. 207–219). Cambridge, MA: MIT Press.

Nonverbal Communication

Chapter Objectives

After completing this chapter, you should be able to:

1. Describe nonverbal communication and its role in the communication process.
2. Identify and describe six principles of nonverbal communication.
3. Identify and describe eight types of nonverbal communication.
4. Identify and describe three ways to improve nonverbal communication.

Introductory Exercise 4.1

Watch a movie or television show without sound.

Have you ever watched a silent movie, like one with Charlie Chaplin? You'll notice you understand most of the jokes because the humor is largely physical (falling down, pants dropping). In today's movies and television shows, actors may rely on the audio part of the program to create the mood, but they still have to show the audience what they are feeling. Pick a program you do not normally watch or a new movie. Watch it without the sound. Record the major plot points (who does what to whom, when, why, and how is it resolved?) Record how you can tell. Record what you think of each character, and why you think that. Describe the relationships between the characters, and note how you arrived at your conclusions. Compare with another student (watch the same program but keep separate notes, for example) and notice any patterns.

Introductory Exercise 4.2

Play with Space.

Have you ever felt uncomfortable because someone has "invaded" your space? Or felt awkward because someone was "just too close." Sometime we don't even notice how important space is to communication, and it produces some interesting results. As an objective observer, pick three friends or relatives and make a conscious effort to notice how far apart they stand from people when they talk. Record the results (approximations are fine and you don't have to tell people you are watching them to observe space). Are there differences in male/female conversations? Are there differences in same-sex conversations? Are there generational (age) differences. Discuss your results with another student and see if together you can see any patterns.

If you enjoyed this exercise, repeat the process, this time focusing on touching in conversation, noting how often and where people touch each other while in conversation.

> *Communication is something so simple and difficult that we can never put it in simple words.*
>
> —T.S. Matthews

What Is Nonverbal Communication?

To arrive at a definition, let's first examine what happened in the first exercise. Did you understand the program? Could you figure out how the characters were related? Could you tell who liked and disliked each other? How? You couldn't hear a word they said. "Body language," or more technically "nonverbal communication," was the key to your understanding.

You are already aware to some extent of how we communicate our thoughts, hopes, ideas, and feeling in ways other than words. People cry in pain and cry for joy. They hold both arms up in victory after winning a sporting event. We can tell what they are communicating through their nonverbal communication. So, like the term itself implies, **nonverbal communication** is communication that is not verbal. This may sound simple, but let's examine the six principles of nonverbal communication and discover how complex it can be.

Principles of Nonverbal Communication

1. Nonverbal Communication Is Fluid

As we discussed in Chapter 1's principles of communication, communication is like a river. It keeps moving and is never the same twice. It is irreversible. Once something is said, it is out there and you can't take it back. Nonverbal communication is fluid in the sense that it is always occurring. If someone drives in front of you suddenly, your surprise and frustration is communicated, even though you might be the only person in the car, through your facial gestures, by how tightly you grip the steering wheel, and in the tenseness of your jaw. In conversation, nonverbal communication is continuous in the sense that it is always occurring, and because it is so fluid, it can be hard to determine where one nonverbal message starts and another stops. Words can be easily identified and isolated, but if we try to single out a gesture, smile, or stance without looking at how they all come together in context, we may miss the point and draw the wrong conclusion.

2. Nonverbal Communication Is Fast

As in the driving example, nonverbal communication gives away our feeling before we even complete the thought or speak a word. Wrinkled eyebrows or wide eyes, white knuckles or posture all communicate our feelings at that moment. This makes catching signals that are expressed through body language difficult, but we do it every day. Nonverbal communication contributes to the message, and, intentionally or unintentionally, it can happen quickly. We have to be alert to nonverbal communication to get the whole message.

3. Nonverbal Communication Can Add to or Replace Verbal Communication

Sometimes we want to add emphasis to what we're saying so we add nonverbal communication to reinforce our point. "Which way is the library?" "That way (with arm extended, finger pointing)." We used a nonverbal gesture called an **illustrator** to communicate our message effectively. We may also use a nonverbal gesture called an **emblem** when we signal "OK" with the OK sign after the other person has indicated comprehension of where to find the library. See Computer-Mediated Communication 4.1.

In addition to illustrators and emblematic nonverbal communication, we also use regulators, affect displays, and adaptors to communicate our messages nonverbally. **Regulators** are nonverbal messages that control, maintain, or discourage interaction. If you nod your head in agreement on important points and maintain good eye contact, you are encouraging your partner to continue speaking. You may also look at your feet when asked a question and indicate an unwillingness to respond. **Affect displays** are nonverbal communication that express emotions or feelings. If your team wins a sporting event, you may raise your arms in victory. Your arms and body language communicate your emotions. **Adaptors** are displays of nonverbal communication that help you adapt to your environment and each context, helping you feel comfortable and secure. With a **self-adaptor,** you may play with your hair or make sure it is not sticking up to meet your need for security or to feel comfortable. An **object-adaptor** is nonverbal communication with the use of an object in a way that it was not designed for.

COMPUTER-MEDIATED COMMUNICATION 4.1 •
Representations of Nonverbal Communication

In everyday communication, our nonverbal communication often expresses as much as our words. In a computer-mediated communication environment, for the most part, all we see are words. To help the reader understand the author, people often use smileys or emoticons to enhance their online writing. Here are a few commonly used references to nonverbal communication.

:)	Smiling	<:*	Kiss	:-D	Laughing	:-/	Scowling
:-O	Surprise, Shock	>:-(	Angry	:-(	Frowning	;-)	Winking
:X	Lips are sealed	O:-)	Innocent	<:-)	Dunce cap	:o)	Clowning

Source: Sanderson, D. & Sanderson, D. (1993). *Smileys.* Cambridge, MA: O'Reilly & Associates.

Tapping your pen on the tabletop communicates impatience and uses the pen in a way other than it is typically used.

Illustrators	Illustrators reinforce a verbal message	Indicating where the library is located with words and gestures
Emblems	Emblems have a specific meaning and can replace or reinforce words	The "OK" sign substituted for the word
Regulators	Regulators control, encourage, or discourage interaction	Nodding your head in agreement
Affect displays	Affect displays express emotions or feelings	Arms over your head to signal victory
Adaptors	Adaptors help us feel comfortable or indicate emotions or moods	Grooming your hair; tapping a pen on a table

These types of nonverbal communication can compliment, repeat, re-place, mask, or contradict verbal communication. In the case of the first example, indicating "that way" with your arm **compliments** the verbal message. If the person you gave directions to did not understand the first time, they might shrug their shoulders to indicate confusion. You may then state again, "That way," but this time point in the direction after your state the direction verbally. This effectively **repeats** the verbal message with a nonverbal one. As the person walks in the direction of the library, they may glance back at you for confirmation. You may then point toward the library, but say nothing. You have **replaced** your verbal message with a nonverbal one.

We also mask or even contradict our thoughts, feelings, or words with nonverbal communication. **Masking** involves the substitution of appropriate nonverbal communication for nonverbal communication you may want to display. Let's say you are working with a customer who is hard to please and you are becoming frustrated. You may mask your emotions with a calm, professional demeanor more appropriate to the work environment. If the customer picks up on your frustration, then your nonverbal communication may have been in disagreement with your spoken words. **Contradiction** is the communication of nonverbal messages that conflict with verbal communication.

Complements	Nonverbal communication that reinforces verbal communication.
Repeats	Nonverbal communication that repeats verbal communication.
Replaces	Nonverbal communication that replaces verbal communication.
Masks	Nonverbal communication that substitutes more appropriate displays for less appropriate displays.
Contradicting	Nonverbal communication that contradicts verbal communication.

4. Nonverbal Communication Is Universal

Have you ever traveled to a country other than your own, where people spoke a different language and had a distinct culture. How did you communicate? Besides having a friend who spoke the language, how did you communicate and get your needs met? Did you refer to your dictionary and try to pronounce words? Perhaps you just said one word in the local language and hoped they would understand. "Baño?" Then they point you in the direction of the bathroom. Many people who do not speak the native language find gestures and even pantomiming to get the point across quite effective. Pretending to eat shows the listener you want to eat. Rubbing your tummy and pushing your plate away indicates you are full. We all use these gestures in our daily lives, but when we are thrust into a situation where verbal communication just doesn't work, nonverbal communication often saves the day.

One word of caution, however. You will find in Chapter 5 on intercultural communication a discussion about how gestures are different in many countries. You wouldn't want to give the "OK" sign if you knew it was an insult to the local community members. Ask someone from a culture other than your own to give you an example of a gesture he or she sees used in the United States that is different from their own. Nonverbal communication itself is universal, but specific gestures vary greatly in their meaning and interpretation (Figure 4.1).

5. Nonverbal Communication Is Confusing and Contextual

Nonverbal communication can be very confusing. What one person thinks he or she is conveying may not at all be related to what the receiver or audience perceives. A gesture may have multiple meanings depending on the context in which it is used. Raising a hand in class communicates a far different message than raising your hands while being arrested. One communicates a wish to speak, the other submission or surrender. A crossing guard may raise his or her hand to indicate that traffic is to stop, or an athlete may raise his or her arms to stretch before an event. Each action is similar, but

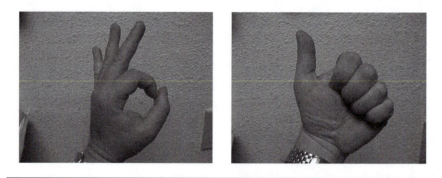

FIGURE 4.1 *Gestures* Gestures mean different things to different people, particularly if they come from different cultures, languages, or traditions (Axtell, 1991). What may mean "A-OK" to you is a serious insult to many people in Latin America, or means "zero" to someone from France. The "V" for victory sign, which has been adopted by a telecommunications company as its sign, can be an old insult to an Englishman. Years ago, the English fought with the French with bows and arrows, and to disable captured archers, the victor would cut off the middle and index fingers. The signal with two fingers upthrust came to mean triumph and the ability to fight another day. The universal thumbs-up isn't so universal. In the United States it commonly means "good going," but in many Islamic countries it's equal to the upraised middle finger. Can you think of any gestures that may be misinterpreted?

through our perception of the context, we can draw different conclusions. Is the hand raised in a classroom? Does the crossing guard have a fluorescent vest and a handheld sign? These clues help us make sense of nonverbal communication.

6. Nonverbal Communication Can Be Intentional or Unintentional

If we go back to the earlier driving example, where another car suddenly pulled in front of you, would your actions be intentional or unintentional? Your wrinkled eyebrows, white knuckles, or wide eyes may have been unintentional. Nonetheless, they clearly communicate your feelings at that moment. Someone asks you later about the incident and you shrug your shoulders and say, "No big deal." Your intentional shrugging of your shoulders contributes to your message. Can we tell when people are intentionally or unintentionally communicating nonverbally? Ask ten people this question and compare their responses. You may be surprised. It is clearly a challenge to understand nonverbal communication in action.

Now that we have discussed the general principles that apply to nonverbal communication, let's examine eight types of nonverbal communication to further understand this challenging aspect of communication.

Types of Nonverbal Communication

1. Space

What did you find as you completed Introductory Exercise 4.2? Did you notice any patterns? Were people who knew each other well standing any closer than people who were not as familiar with each other? Was gender a factor in the differences? How about age? All of these issues relate to how important space is in our everyday communication.

Edward T. Hall served in the European and South Pacific regions in the Corps of Engineers during World War II. As he traveled from one place to another, he kept a record of his observations and noticed that in different countries, people kept different distances from each other (see Intercultural Communication 4.1). In France, they stood rather close. In England, they stood farther apart. Hall wondered why that was and began to study what he called **proxemics,** or the study of the human use of space and distance in communication.

He gathered his observations and conclusions and published *The Hidden Dimension* in 1966. Hall placed the spotlight on aspects of communication that people hadn't studied in depth previously.

INTERCULTURAL COMMUNICATION 4.1 • *Space*

"Americans overseas were confronted with a variety of difficulties because of cultural differences in the handling of space. People stood "too close" during conversations, and when the Americans backed away to a comfortable conversational distance, this was taken to mean that Americans were cold, aloof, withdrawn and disinterested in the people of the country. USA housewives muttered about "waste-space" in houses in the Middle East. In England, Americans who were used to neighborliness were hurt when they discovered that their neighbors were no more accessible or friendly than other people, and in Latin America, exsuburbanites, accustomed to unfenced yards, found that the high walls there made them feel "shut out." Even in Germany, where so many of my countrymen felt at home, radically different patterns in the use of space led to unexpected tensions." (Hall, 1963, p. 422)

As you can see in Hall's observations, space can play an important role in communication across culture. Find your International Student Programs Office on campus and learn where and when international students get together. Make the effort to learn more about the importance of nonverbal communication within the context of intercultural communication, and you may be amazed at what you find!

In *The Hidden Dimension,* he indicated that there are two main aspects of space that are necessary to study it. The first is **territory.** Hall drew on anthropology, or the study of cultures, to get at the concepts of dominance and submission. People claim space all the time, but who gets the big corner office and who gets the broom closet office? The more powerful person often claims more space. Within everyday life we often establish territory as a matter of routine, and we have customs to accommodate this. When you sit at a cafeteria table your space may be established by your tray. What's on your tray is yours. Let's say the salt and pepper are to your right, and someone sits next to you on your left. They could easily reach across the table and take the salt and pepper, but their awareness (hopefully) of you and your territory means they will not reach across your tray, and your space, to get them. Instead they will ask, "May I have the salt and pepper," in which case you simply pass them to the person, respecting the boundaries you've established for yourself and reinforcing your territory.

The second main aspect of space is **personal space.** Initially this may sound like territory, but there is a key difference. Power. Territory implies the ability to control a space and to mark that space as owned by you. You may do this with fences or walls around your house or a poster on the door of your own room. This sense of ownership, or the right to control that space, is implicit in territory.

Personal space moves with you like a bubble all around you. It is the space you need to carry out your business. In a lecture hall, people often sit quite close together. In an aerobics class, people stand or dance with more distance between them. You need a little personal space in which to write in the lecture hall, but you need more personal space (so you don't hit each other) on the gym mat. Hall was a pioneer in the field of proxemics and the first to categorize the types of space used in communication.

Consider the last time you stepped into an elevator. Where did everyone look? Did people speak to one another? Typically people will give each other space by standing apart in the elevator and face forward, noting the changes in floors as they approach their destination. As more people enter the elevator, space between individuals decreases. People may be more tolerant of shoulders rubbing in this situation than in other contexts.

Exercise

Note where people sit on the first day of class, and each class session thereafter. Do students return to the same seat? If they do not attend class, do the classmates leave their seat vacant? Compare your results.

Figure 4.2 features the four main categories that of distance used in communication (Hall, 1966). **Intimate space** is generally up to eighteen inches away from you, whereas **personal space** can range from eighteen inches to four feet. **Social space** can range from four to twelve feet and can usually be found in more formal settings like workplaces. Finally, **public space** is usually more than twelve feet and can often be found in public-speaking situations in the classroom, courtroom, or church.

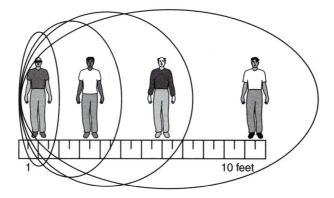

FIGURE 4.2 *Categories of Space*

2. Time

Have you ever gone to a doctor's appointment and not been seen on time? Many people wait for varying lengths of time before seeing, or gaining audience to, the doctor. Why do they wait? Because the doctor is in a position of power. Because they need the information that he or she has. Have you ever called someone who has been too busy to talk right at that moment? Have you ever talked to someone who speaks English as his or her second language? Can you see how, in each case, time is a relevant factor in the communication process? See Case Study 4.1.

The study of how we refer to and perceive time is called **chronemics.** Researchers have long found time in verbal and nonverbal communication to be an extremely important factor to consider. Tom Bruneau, of Radford University, is a pioneer in the field and has spent a lifetime investigating

CASE STUDY 4.1 • *Health Communication*

Communication is a powerful force in all our lives, and it takes on additional importance within the clinical setting. When you go to your health care provider, you want your responses to be heard and the information you provide to help lead to an effective outcome. The study of health communication is growing across the United States as we come to understand just how important effective communication is in the clinical setting.

In the article *"What You Don't Say Can Hurt You,"* Mandell (1993) discusses a case in which a mother brought her children into a rural clinic when she was concerned that they had high fevers. The mother reported to the attending nurse that she had removed two ticks from one child. The physician diagnosed measles and recommended aspirin and a dark room for the children until they recovered. Four days later one child died and another was rushed to the hospital. Rocky Mountain spotted fever claimed one life, and the nurse, who failed to pass on the report of the ticks, was found liable. Listening to both verbal and nonverbal messages is key to gathering information from patients (McLean, 1996), and failure to do so can be disastrous.

In addition to individual patient/provider communication, "Health communication is concerned with the use of ethical, persuasive means to craft and deliver campaigns and implement strategies that promote good health and prevent disease" (Ratzan, 1996, p. v). You may have seen antismoking campaign advertisements or messages promoting a designated driver in the popular media. Compare with your friends or classmates health messages you have seen or heard or experiences communicating with health care providers. How did nonverbal communication play a role in your previous communication with your health care provider?

how time interacts in communication and particularly intercultural communication (Bruneau, 1974; 1990; Bruneau and Ishii, 1988).

For example, in Western society, time is money (Intercultural Communication 4.2). The value of speed is highly prized in our society (Schwartz, 1989) and can be seen all around us in the way we buy our food (drive through or, recently, ordering it online to be delivered); the way we want faster computers, cars, and instant gratification; and the decrease in the time between access to communication devices (such as pagers, cellular/digital telephones, e-mail). Some people use all the technology to "stay in touch" and end up being "on-call" all the time. How has this need for speed affected your life or habits?

This idea about time, however, is not universal. Some Orthodox Jews observe religious days in which they use no electricity and do not work. Some Mexican American citizens say dinner is at eight, but it is understood that it really doesn't start until nine, and then goes on until after midnight. Some Native Americans, particularly elders, speak in well-measured phrases and take long pauses, not hurrying their speech or competing for their turn. Cultures have difference ways of expressing value for time.

Now consider how time and the time we give each other in communication sends a message. How long would you expect the President of the United States to give you? Would the length of time be different from that of your health care provider, or instructor, or close friend? What message does the amount of time you give someone communicate to him or her?

INTERCULTURAL COMMUNICATION 4.2 • *Time Orientations*

Edward T. Hall and Mildred Reed Hall (1987) state that **monochronic time–oriented cultures** (the United States, Germany, and Switzerland, for example) schedule one thing at a time, whereas, **polychronic time–oriented cultures** (Greece, Italy, Chile, and Saudi Arabia, to name a few) schedule many things at one time. In monochromatic time, it is one thing at a time (no interruptions), and everything has its own time. First work, then play. Polychromatic time looks a little more complicated, with business and family mixing with dinner and dancing. People in monochronic time–oriented cultures often view time seriously (time is money), whereas people in polychronic time–oriented cultures view schedules as more flexible. Understanding the value and treatment of time in different cultures can help you communicate more effectively.

3. Physical Characteristics

Have you ever heard that taller people get paid more, or that people prefer symmetrical faces (equal sides) over asymmetrical faces (unequal sides, like a broken nose or having one eye slightly higher than the other)? There is a fair amount of debate in both the popular press and the scientific community over the impact of physical characteristics on our lives. To some degree, we have control over our weight and the length of our hair, but we can't control our DNA and its expression in terms of body type, skin tone, height, or predisposition for disease or recovery from illness. Researchers indicate that people often make judgments about a person's personality or behavior based on physical characteristics. They also point out that those judgments are often inaccurate (Wells & Siegel, 1961; Cash & Kilcullen, 1985).

Exercise _____

Please fill in the blanks:

  1. Fat people are _____

  2. Thin people are _____

  3. Short people are _____

  4. Tall people are _____

If you were able to answer quickly, you may want to be careful not to make judgments based on physical characteristics.

4. Body Movements

Have you ever seen someone move their arms while giving a speech to add emphasis or emphatically point "That way!" when giving directions? Body movements are key to nonverbal communication in a variety of ways. Let's examine four distinct ways body movements compliment, repeat, regulate, and replace our verbal messages.

Body movements can complement the verbal message by reinforcing the main idea, like pointing while giving directions. They can also reinforce the message by repeating it. If you first say "take a right at the end of the street" and then motion with your hand to the right, your repetition can help make sure the listener understood your message. In addition to repeating our message, body movements can also regulate our conversations. Nodding your head to indicate you are listening may encourage the speaker to continue speaking. Drawing your hand across your throat or giving the time-out "T" sign with your hands may signal them to stop. Finally, body movements may actually substitute for verbal messages. Remember, "Which way to the library?" can be answered with just a pointing gesture.

On an interesting note, Ekman and Friesen (1967) found that when studying the communication of emotions, facial features communicate to others our feelings, but our body movements often reveal how intensely we experience those feelings. For example, if the nurse draws blood from your arm and your face shows your pain but you remain still, we could discern that although it hurt, it wasn't that bad. If, however, you pull back or, worse, try to stand up, we know that what you feel, you feel intensely.

5. Touch

Can you remember a time when someone placed a hand on your shoulder, or gave you a hug, and it meant more to you than any words could say? How long did they hold you? For many people, across cultures and language, touch is an important aspect of nonverbal communication. Seiler and Beall (2000) identify five distinct types of touch in communication, also sometimes referred to as **tactile communication** or **haptics.**

The first involves the most impersonal type, **the functional-professional touch.** This is when, e.g., a doctor touches you during an exam. The touch only serves to fulfill the professional function and is generally brief. The next level of touch is called the **social-polite touch.** We shake hands in Western society, while in other cultures they may briefly kiss each other on the cheek as a form of polite greeting. Beyond these two levels of impersonal touch comes a more familiar touch that conveys trust and familiarity. The **friendship-warmth touch,** such as a hug when greeting, is used between conversation partners that know each other. They have formed bonds of friendship and express it through a familiar touch like a hug. A more intimate type of touch, as you may guess, involves a more intense degree of relationship and is called the **love-intimacy touch.** People hold hands, hug, kiss, and caress in ways that communicate their love. Finally, the most intimate form of touch between two consenting adults is the **sexual-arousal touch.**

6. Paralanguage

"Uh-huh," "Ohhh (yawn)," and "Arrggh!" are all no doubt familiar "verbal fillers" that you hear people use all the time. "Uh-huh" may serve as an indication of agreement and encourage the speaker to continue talking, like a head nod. A yawn may show disinterest or reveal that the listener is tired. "Arrggh!" may express frustration without using words. All of these cues, both vocal and silent, are called **paralanguage.** The inflection in someone's voice may communicate that he or she is nervous or happy. If someone says "I saw him at the *store*," the emphasis on *store* gives it importance in relation to the other words. The entire meaning of the same sentence can change if we change the emphasis on one word. "I saw *him* at the store," shift the emphasis from the *store* to *him* and changes the meaning of the sentence.

Silence or vocal pauses can communicate hesitation or the need to gather thought or can serve as a sign of respect. Keith Basso (1970) quotes an anonymous source as stating "it is not the case that a man who is silent says nothing." Sometimes we learn just as much, even more, from what a person does not say as from what he or she does say. In addition, both Basso and Susan Philips found that traditional speech among Native Americans places a special emphasis on silence (Intercultural Communication 4.3).

INTERCULTURAL COMMUNICATION 4.3 • *Silence in Communication among Native Americans*

"For a stranger entering an alien society, a knowledge of when *not* to speak may be as basic to the production of culturally acceptable behavior as a knowledge of what to say." (Basso, 1970, p. 303)

The importance of silence in the traditional speech of Native Americans has long been studied. Leslie Spier (1893–1961) and Edward Sapir (1884–1939) were pioneers in the study of native languages, and their work *Wishram Ethnography* (1939), was a seminal work. In it they documented native speech from the Sahaptin and Wasco languages along the Columbia River Gorge before the dams. It now stands as one of the few remaining documents of the languages. Susan Philips built on their foundation and found in her study (1983) on the Warm Springs Indian Reservation that "there is almost no interruption of one speaker by another in Warm Springs talk....Rarely do two people begin to talk at the same time. The pause between the talk of two different speakers is typically longer than in Anglo conversation" (Philips, 1983, p. 58). A more recent study of intergenerational communication between Warm Springs elders and younger Tribal members found that whereas elders retained the traditional speech style, younger Tribal members spoke quicker and took much shorter pauses, making communication between generations at times difficult (McLean, 1998).

There are currently 516 treaty tribes and 46 nontreaty tribes, and where there was once hundreds of native languages, now few remain as elders age and their numbers decrease. Many Native American youth, into the late 1950s, were removed from their homes and put in dormitories at boarding schools by the Bureau of Indian Affairs. Teachers were under orders to reprimand students if they were caught speaking any tongue other than English on school premises. Tribal members today recall the loss of language, and with it cultural traditions, with profound grief.

Learn more about the importance of silence in traditional Native American speech, the loss of native languages nationwide, and what is being done to reverse the effects of boarding schools and to save endangered languages at the Cheyenne Language Web Site: http://www.mcn.net/~wleman/langlinks.htm

7. Artifacts

Three rings in the ear, one in the nose, and a stud through the tongue. Whereas some people find the prospect of having their bodies pierced uncomfortable, others view it as a way to express their sense of self. **Artifacts** include rings and tattoos and also things like clothes, cars, watches, briefcases, purses, and even eyeglasses. All of these objects somehow relate to the owner, and the owner uses them to project gender, role or position, class or status, personality, and group membership. When is someone expected to wear a tie? More than likely in a formal situation. Artifacts may be culturally acceptable adornments that are associated with specific contexts, like a wedding dress, or can be expressions of self and individuality. Can you find an example of an artifact that is marketed or advertised to people your age? How is it shown to make you a member of the group? Young people may pay attention to artifacts like clothing labels, and parents of children may compare notes about minivans. Artifacts serve to express individuality and group affiliation and play an important role in communication. See Case Study 4.2.

8. Environment

The physical and psychological aspects of the communication context are called **environment**. As discussed in Chapter 1, environment is an important part of the dynamic communication process. In Chapter 2, we observed how perception of one's environment influences his or her reaction to it. In

---

CASE STUDY 4.2 • *Tattoos and Body Art in the Workplace*

According to *The San Diego Union-Tribune*, body art or tattoos are more or less likely to be accepted in the workplace depending on who you interview.

- 20% of workers indicated that their body art had been held against them on the job.
- 42% of employers said that the presence of visible body art lowered their opinion of workers.
- 44% of managers surveyed have body art.
- 52% of workers surveyed have body art.
- 67% of workers cover their body art or remove piercings during work hours.

Sources: Kinsman, M. (2001, August 20). Tattoos and nose rings. *The San Diego Union-Tribune*, p. C1.

Kinsman also credited http://www.vault.com as a source.

Chapter 3, cultures that place a high degree of emphasis on context were highlighted. Our environment influences and plays a role in our communication. Within the realm of nonverbal communication, this takes on additional aspects. The type of furniture you select for your room. The type of lighting you give a space. The smells of freshly baked bread or old socks in a room. The music playing on the radio. These elements combine to form the environment in which communication occurs, and the degree of formality/informality, temperature, and even lighting can be an element in the communication process. Think about how you might change the environment where you live if you wanted a romantic evening, have a birthday party, or host a family reunion. See also Case Study 4.3.

All of these elements combine to contribute to nonverbal communication, a powerful force in the communication process. What happens when the nonverbal message and the verbal message that you receive or demonstrate do not match? Let's say we meet and I say what a pleasure it is to meet you while looking over your shoulder and gently moving away to greet someone else. Can you think of an example in which the nonverbal and verbal messages did not match? When this happens, which communication do you believe? According to Seiler and Beall (2000), most of us tend to believe the nonverbal message over the verbal message.

CASE STUDY 4.3 • *Noise Pollution*

Noise in the environment can actually contribute to hearing loss, a problem that costs Americans more than $56 billion dollars a year. Our ears hurt when noise levels reach 140 decibels, but damage can occur with much lower levels that are part of our everyday environment.

Noise	Decibels	Length of exposure necessary to cause measurable hearing loss
Jackhammer	90	8 hours
Ride in a convertible on freeway	95	4 hours
Subway train	100	2 hours
Power lawn mower	105	1 hour
Live rock concert	110	30 minutes
Car horn	120	7.5 minutes

Source: USA Weekend, October 15, 1999, p. 22.

also see: www.betterhearing.org

Improving Your Understanding

By now you are more aware of both the principles and types of nonverbal communication. Taking this one step further, apply your knowledge that you had when you started this chapter together with the insights and connections you made to the material. How can you do this? Here are three ways to examine nonverbal communication, in yourself and others, to improve communication.

1. Watch Reactions

Pretend you are a researcher. Document what you see objectively. Take detailed notes and make sure to note context and environment. Compare your results with other students. This can be done as "people watching" or may be part of a classroom exercise. You decide where and when to watch reactions, but now that you are more aware of the different types and how they work, you'll notice them in new and fascinating ways.

2. Enroll an Observer

If the goal is for you to assess your own nonverbal communication, enroll a friend to act as the objective researcher. If you prefer to see it for yourself, have a friend videotape you in conversation and then repeat Introductory Exercise 4.1 (watch your movie, this time of yourself).

3. Focus on a Specific Type of Nonverbal Communication

How do others use their hands to communicate? Does this change or differ based on a variable (gender, age, ethnicity, cultural background, context, environment, etc.)? Through observing others you will learn more about how people communicate and more about how you yourself communicate using nonverbal communication.

Summary

In this chapter we related nonverbal communication to the dynamic process of communication, the perception process and listening, and verbal communication by examining the principles of nonverbal communication and the specific types of nonverbal communication. After defining nonverbal communication, we examined the six principles and eight types of nonverbal communication. We then looked at three ways to improve our understanding, improving awareness and understanding to communicate more effectively.

For More Information _____

On Edward T. Hall, see Chapter 3.

Nonverbal Communication Research Page, Louisiana College:

http://socpsych.lacollege.edu/nonverbal.html

Review Questions _____

1. Factual Questions
   a. What is nonverbal communication?
   b. What are the principles of nonverbal communication?
   c. What are the types of nonverbal communication?

2. Interpretative Questions
   a. What are the assumptions (explicit or underlying) about nonverbal communication in this chapter?
   b. To what degree is time a relevant factor in communication in the information age?
   c. Does it limit or enhance our understanding of communication to view nonverbal communication as that which is not verbal communication?

3. Evaluative Questions
   a. Is nonverbal communication accurate?
   b. Can you effectively study nonverbal communication?
   c. Can the study of nonverbal communication be separate from the study of intercultural communication?

4. Application Questions
   a. Create a survey that addresses the issue of which people trust more, nonverbal or verbal messages. Ask an equal number of men and women, and compare your results.
   b. See how long you can go and how much you can get done during the day without verbal messages.
   c. Interview international students about nonverbal communication in their native language and culture. Compare with your local customs and traditions.

Works Cited _____

Axtell, R. (1991). *Gestures: The do's and taboos of body language around the world.* New York: John Wiley & Sons.

Basso, K. A. (1970). To give up on words: Silence in Western Apache culture. In D. Carbaugh (Ed.), *Cultural communication and intercultural contact* (pp. 301–318). Hillsdale, NJ: Erlbaum.

Bruneau, T. (1974). Time and nonverbal communication. *Journal of Popular Culture, 8,* 658–666.

Bruneau, T. (1990). Chronemics: The study of time in human interaction. In J. DeVito & M. Hecht (Eds.) *The nonverbal reader* (pp. 301–311). Prospect Heights, IL: Waveland Press.

Bruneau, T. & Ishii, S. (1988). Communicative silence: East and West. *World Communication, 17,* pp. 1–33.

Cash, T. & Kilcullen, R. (1985). The eye of the beholder: Susceptibility to sexism and beautyism in the evaluation of managerial applicants. *Journal of Applied Social Psychology, 15,* pp. 591–605.

Ekman, P. & Friesen, W. (1967). Head and body cues in the judgement of emotions: A reformulation. *Perceptual and Motor Skills, 24,* 711–724.

Hall, E. T. (1963). Proxemics: The study of man's spatial relations and boundaries. In *Man's image in medicine and anthropology* (pp. 422–445). New York: International Universities Press.

Hall, E. T. (1966). *The hidden dimension.* New York, NY: Doubleday.

Hall, E. T. & Hall, M. R. (1987). *Hidden differences: Doing business with the Japanese.* New York: Doubleday (Anchor Books).

Mandell, M. (1993). What you don't say can hurt you. *American Journal of Nursing, August,* 15–16.

McLean, S. (1996). Communication in the clinical setting: The importance of listening. *The Journal of Multicultural Nursing and Health, 2,* 4–7.

McLean, S. (1998). Turn-taking and the extended pause: A study of interpersonal communication styles across generations on the Warm Springs Indian Reservation. In K. S. Sitaram & M. Prosser (Eds.), *Civic discourse: Multiculturalism, cultural diversity, and global communication* (pp. 213–227). Stamford, CT: Ablex Publishing.

Philips, S. (1983). *The invisible culture: Communication in classroom and community on the Warm Springs Indian Reservation* (pp. 58–61). Chicago: Waveland Press.

Ratzan, S. (1996). Introduction. *The Journal of Health Communication, 1,* v.

Sanderson, D. & Sanderson, D. (1993). *Smileys.* Cambridge, MA: O'Reilly & Associates.

Seiler, W. & Beall, M. (2000). *Communication: Making connections.* Boston: Allyn & Bacon.

Schwartz, T. (1989). *Acceleration syndrome: Does everyone live in the fast lane? Utne Reader,* January/February Issue, 36–43.

Spier, L. & Sapir, E. (1939). *Wishram ethnography* (vol. 3, pp. 151–300). Seattle: University of Washington Publications in Anthropology.

Wells, W. & Siegel, B. (1961). Stereotypes somatypes. *Psychological Reports, 8,* 77–78.

Intercultural Communication

Chapter Objectives

After completing this chapter, you should be able to:

1. Understand the importance of intercultural communication and its role in the communication process.
2. Understand the need to study intercultural communication.
3. Describe the development of the historical study of intercultural communication.
4. Identify and describe eight characteristics of intercultural communication.
5. Identify and describe three barriers to intercultural communication.
6. Identify and describe six ways to improve intercultural communication.

Introductory Exercise 5.1

List all the groups you are a part of or in which you consider yourself a member. Consider your family, your job, your profession or career, and social groups.

Introductory Exercise 5.2

From the list you created in Introductory Exercise 5.1, try to create a list of the different, unique, or interesting ways you communicate in each group. For example, perhaps your family took a trip to the Grand Canyon in the state of Arizona and the trip was full of delays or problems. When you talk about vacations, perhaps the Grand Canyon means not only the place but also all those problems you experienced together. Everyone laughs when you say "anywhere but the Grand Canyon!" Another example might include your work. Do you use any words or terms in the course of work with other co-workers that someone from a different job might not understand?

Introductory Exercise 5.3 _____

Again, from the list you created in Introductory Exercise 5.1, try to list all the places that your groups have been or interact with and the locations of those places. For example, perhaps your family has roots in Spain and France, but your great-great-grandparents moved to Canada and later to the United States. Also consider all the places, including cities and states that you've visited or in which you've lived. Another example might be at work, where (perhaps) you regularly communicate with offices in other states or even other countries. Note those places.

We travel now more than ever, and the time it takes us to travel has decreased from weeks and days to hours and minutes. You have no doubt traveled to different cities, states, or even countries. Take a moment and compare your list from Introductory Exercise 5.3 with your classmates. Create a large list and see where everyone has visited or lived. If you have access to a map or globe, get it out and compare the locations and perhaps use sticky notes to mark each place. How many places are on your group list?

As you can no doubt see, we have seen, as a group, places far and wide. Now consider this: Does everyone communicate the same way in all these places? How many different languages are spoken in these places? How many different ways of speaking the same language are used in different places? Perhaps someone in your class has visited Montreal in Canada, and they saw how French is a dominant language. Someone else may have traveled to Louisiana and heard French spoken. Still another classmate may have traveled to France and heard French yet again. Are all three types of French spoken the same, using the same words and phrases? Each dialect of French is quite distinct, and if you could bring French speakers together from these three locations, they might not even be able to understand each other. Consider why French is so widely spoken, but at the same time spoken so differently in each location. Can you think of another example? Perhaps Spanish in Puerto Rico, Spanish in Mexico, and Spanish in Texas?

Now pretend you could travel to each place, all expenses paid, and imagine what you might find. An Internet search might provide information on your search. As you began to discover information about each place, you would find that people not only speak in distinct ways but also live in different ways, having distinct local customs and ways of doing things we all have in common. From the preparation of food to traditional dances, customs of dating and marriage, and times of work and celebration, different places have different cultures. Cultures and intercultural communication play an important role in determining how we see and interpret experiences in the world.

Once upon a time it was only the well-off traveler, merchant, or explorer who traveled distances and could discover new and fascinating ways of living and communicating. Now, many of us can expand our awareness of other cultures through travel, and, if we can't travel, we can learn about places we haven't visited through the Internet, live web cameras, and travelogues of other travelers on web pages. Many researchers have long predicted that our world would grow smaller, not in terms of size but in terms of our ability to interact with each other across time and distance. Marshall McLuhan, a pioneer in the field of communication, predicted what we now know as the "global village," where information and transportation technologies have reduced the time and space required to communicate with one another (McLuhan, 1964).

With the advent of increased travel came increased interaction, the study of what we now call **intercultural communication,** or communication between cultures, became an important area of research and investigation. In this chapter, we discuss intercultural communication, examine its many characteristics, and look at a few common barriers to effective communication across cultures.

Definition of Intercultural Communication

As you might imagine, as diverse and multifaceted as intercultural communication is, it is hard to define. Rogers and Steinfatt (1999) defined **intercultural communication** as the exchange of information between individuals who are "unalike culturally." This definition focuses on the interaction, an important part of the dynamic process of communication, but in order for us to grasp the definition, we must also understand what we mean by "culture." Klopf (1991, p. 31) states **culture** is "That part of the environment made by humans." This definition focuses on the concept that culture and language, like meaning and values, are created by us, and to understand intercultural communication, we must come to understand ourselves and our interactions with others.

Where does culture come from? It comes from us. When we gather in groups and communities, we form culture. Cola-Cola has a different corporate culture than IBM, which has a distinct culture from Microsoft. Washington, DC, has a culture different than Atlanta. Specific districts within the Washington, DC, area, like Georgetown, also have distinct cultures from the larger community. You will find culture wherever people come together.

Culture is part of the community in which we live and work, and often there are many cultures, or co-cultures, that coexist and interact. How can we recognize one cultural community from another? How do we come to understand which culture(s) we belong to? How do we become a member of our culture? Before we examine intercultural communication in more depth, let's examine the history of the study of intercultural communication and the key researchers who have contributed to our current base of knowledge and given us guidance for future investigations.

History of the Study of Intercultural Communication

Intercultural communication is one of the youngest fields in the discipline of communication, but it draws on lessons learned from centuries of travelers from a wide cross section of academic disciplines. You can probably recall from a history class names like Marco Polo, Captain James Cook, Christopher Columbus, or Ponce de Leon.

Each explorer investigated a part of the world already inhabited by diverse communities and civilizations. They also brought back stories of fascinating new places to their own communities, sparking interest in discovery. New maps were created that, although not technically as accurate as today's Global Positioning System–referenced maps with the resources of a satellite network perspective, were nonetheless creative in depicting how the "new" regions and even continents were perceived. Travel diaries left stories from a personal perspective about each new place the explorer visited, and, again, although not always accurate, they still captured a perspective on people, places, and customs around the time they first interacted.

This wealth of knowledge was in fact quite limited until world events and the ability to travel and communicate across distances quickly began to expand our knowledge of each other. For example, in World War II, many soldiers who had once only known their region, state, or country came into contact with people from diverse countries. Once such person was Edward T. Hall. Hall worked in the U.S. Army Corp of Engineers and, as a part of his work, traveled to many countries throughout the war. He noticed cultures and customs and kept notes that later led him to many insights into intercultural communication. As you might expect, Hall was not the only person to study culture, but he was one of the first individuals to lay the foundation for the formal study of intercultural communication. Now let's examine the history of the field before we discuss the various aspects and their implications.

According to Guo-Ming Chen and William Starosta (2000), two current researchers in the field, there are four key periods in the history of intercultural communication as an academic discipline, beginning with the burgeoning period and followed by accomplishments of each decade. In this text, we extend the analysis to include highlights of current decades, research, and activities, as well as look toward future trends.

1. The Burgeoning Period in the Study of Intercultural Communication

In the **Burgeoning Period,** Hall came to share many of his insights and earned a distinct place in the field of intercultural communication and is often considered the "father" of the field (Chen & Starosta, 2000, p. 8). His ideas provided a framework for study and sparked several other researchers' interest in investigating the field. He published *The Silent Language* in 1959, and the term "intercultural communication" came into general use. He is generally credited with eight important contributions to our understanding of intercultural communication (Chen & Starosta, 2000; Leeds-Hurwitz, 1990).

1. Comparing cultures	Hall focused on how people interact rather than studying the culture as a single, distinct way of living.
2. Shift to local perspective	Hall focused on the local level and how culture is a practical part of everyone's lives rather than on how a whole culture, from a larger perspective, interacts with other cultures.
3. You don't have to know everything to know something	Hall focused on cultural aspects like time, space, gestures, and voice as part of culture, stating that we could learn from these individual aspects without having a complete understanding of the entire culture.
4. There are rules we can learn	Hall focused on the rules people use to interact, making it possible to analyze and predict behaviors and actions.
5. Experience counts	Hall focused on how students can learn from their own experience and advocated personal experience as an important part of understanding intercultural communication.
6. Differences in perspective	Hall focused on descriptive linguistics as a model to understand intercultural communication, one the Foreign Service still uses as a base for training. The terms "etic," or studying from a general perspective, and "emic," or studying from the culture's own perspective, grew out of his model.
7. Application to international business	Hall focused on how Foreign Service training has applications to international business, and as we continue to integrate globally, training in intercultural communication is increasingly the norm for business students.

8. Integration of disciplines   Hall focused on the link between culture
                                     and communication, bringing together
                                     aspects of anthropology and communication
                                     as academic disciplines.

As we can see, Hall's contribution to the birth of the formal study of intercultural communication, the use of aspects we can study, and the focus on rules and direct experience have had a significant impact on the course and direction of formalized study of intercultural communication today.

2. The Study of Intercultural Communication in the 1960s

In the 1960s, Kluckhohn and Strodtbeck (1961) examined value orientations, or what each culture values in comparison to other cultures, which led to a great deal of investigation. They asserted that the understanding of the degree to which cultures perceive innate human nature (are we basically good or evil?), how people relate to nature, how we perceive time, what activities we devote our time to, and what is our relationship to each other are central to the understanding of intercultural communication. Bakan (1966) also studied values and focused on religions, while Adelman and Morris (1967) studied economic development.

Values significantly influence a group, community, or culture's decision-making processes. Rokeach (1973, p. 5), from the field of psychology, defines **value** as "an enduring belief that a specific mode of conduct or end-state of existence is personally or socially preferable to an opposite or converse mode of conduct or end-state of existence." When we choose to do something, do we place emphasis on what is good for ourselves or is the good of the community placed at a higher value level than our personal needs? Each culture answers this in different ways, and the study of how we make decisions based on what we value is diverse and fascinating. We will visit this area of discussion again later in the chapter.

3. The Study of Intercultural Communication in the 1970s

The 1970s saw rapid growth in the field. Stewart (1972) published *American Cultural Patterns,* which examined cultural aspects of life in the United States and provided a model of intercultural communication. Larry Samovar and Richard Porter (1973) published the first intercultural communication textbook, *Intercultural Communication: A Reader,* which provided a wide range of articles on distinct cultures and further expanded the study and discussion of the field. There were numerous other texts to follow, most notably Michael Prosser's (1973) *Intercommunication among Nations and People.* Condon and

Yousef (1975) extended Kluckhohn and Strodtbeck's (1961) model to focus on key universal problems that we all face: the relationship to ourselves, the family, the society; to human nature; to nature itself; and to the supernatural or spiritual.

It is interesting to note that the first formal class on intercultural communication was offered at the University of Pittsburgh in 1966 and the first doctoral degree in the field was awarded by Indiana University in 1973. Young researchers continued to explore the field, publish, particularly in the new *International Journal of Intercultural Relations* (1977), and expand the field throughout the 1980s.

4. The Study of Intercultural Communication in the 1980s

This time was also marked by an increase in investigations and publications. William Gudykunst and Young Yun Kim are two well-known researchers in the field who made significant contributions in this decade. With *Communicating with Strangers* (1984) Gudykunst & Kim provided an integrated analysis of a far-reaching field. Gudykunst and Kim also published *Methods of Intercultural Research* (1984) and *Theories in Intercultural Communication* (1988).

5. The Study of Intercultural Communication in the 1990s

In the 1990s, Gudykunst and Kim further expanded our knowledge of the field with revisions to their text *Communicating with Strangers: An approach to Intercultural Communication* (1984, 1992, 1997). This text examines how people interact across cultures when one is perceived as an outsider and how to distinguish an in-group member. This understanding is a key perspective in our understanding of why and how people communicate across cultures and lends insight into many miscommunications based on divergent expectations.

6. The Study of Intercultural Communication: 2001 and Beyond

In 2001 and beyond, we will no doubt continue to see the field expand as more people discover this fascinating area of study and as more people perceive the practical necessity of understanding intercultural communication in their communities, where they work, and as they travel with increasing frequency. The 2000 U.S. Census for the first time allowed people to indicate their affiliation or identification with more than one racial or ethnic category, leading to the increased understanding that we do not exist as a member of a single culture but rather as a community of cultures. As we continue to expand our understanding of this multifaceted area of study, we in many ways reinforce one of Hall's key perspectives—focusing on the local level of culture—to begin the process of understanding. See Computer-Mediated Communication 5.1.

Characteristics of Intercultural Communication

In this section, we explore how we learn, share, and interact with culture. Keep in mind that culture, like language and the communication process itself, is dynamic and ever changing. We often belong to more than one

COMPUTER-MEDIATED COMMUNICATION 5.1 •
Intercultural Communication Links on the Internet

Organizations
Intercultural Communication Institute   http://www.intercultural.org/

Japan Center for Intercultural
Communication   http://homejcic.or.jp/

The University of British Columbia,
Centre for Intercultural Communication   http://cic.cstudies.ubc.ca/

Southern States Communication Association, Intercultural Communication
http://communication.louisville.edu/intercultural/

Intercultural Communication Websites, University of Hawaii
http://www2.soc.hawaii.edu/css/dept/com/resources/intercultural/
Websites.html

Journals
Intercultural Management Quarterly   http://www.imquarterly.com/

THE EDGE The E-Journal of
Intercultural Relations   http://kumo.swcp.com/biz/theedge/

Intermundo   http://www.stephweb.com/forum/

This is a small summary of the resources available online. The Internet itself is dynamic, and at times links change or move. You can conduct an online search with the key words *intercultural communication*. Compare your results with those of a classmate.

community, organization, or cultural tradition, but we can recognize that each group has a common sense of history, customs, and traditions that reinforce its own identity and its place in the larger community. Within these complex systems we can still discuss eight common characteristics, which give us insight into various aspects of culture that can help us be more sensitive to intercultural communication.

1. Cultures Share a Common Experience of History and Tradition that We Learn

A good place to start is to consider where we come to our knowledge of cultures, both those we are a part of and those that we come to know through experience. When a child is born, he or she is not born with a sense of his or her culture, language, or customs. A child learns this as he or she grows, interacts, and becomes a member of a cultural group or a community. As a child grows, he or she comes to understand the way people interact and what is expected of them through a process called **socialization.** Socialization refers to the process by which a person comes to understand the cultural patterns to socialize or interact with other members of the community.

A **community** can be defined as a group of people who share common bonds and relationships and consider themselves a group or community. This simple definition, however, fails to capture the dynamic nature of community, changing and transforming in a process much like the communication process itself. We can say, however, that the community shares many common attributes, such as a common sense of history, values, purpose, and symbols or identity.

2. Rites of Initiation, For Example, Serve this Purpose of Socialization into the Community

Similar examples in North American culture might include the age at which a person becomes eligible to obtain a driver's license. The ritual includes the written and driving examinations, but the license itself often symbolizes more than simply the acknowledged ability to drive. It also includes connotations of freedom and the ability to participate in activities, like driving to work or school, while parents must still drive children or older friends who have not passed the driving test. Another example in North American culture might include reaching the age of eighteen, when a child becomes a legal adult, or age twenty-one, when a legal adult can purchase alcohol. Can you think of examples of rituals that recognize the passing from one phase to another in your own culture? Perhaps a quiceñera, a celebration of a young women's fifteenth birthday, when she is recognized by family and the Hispanic community as having reached adulthood.

CASE STUDY 5.1 • *Initiation and Gangs*

We can recognize the need to communicate and form communities, but some communities reinforce negative traits or behaviors that can harm the individual and the larger community. "Gangs" are groups of people who form an affiliation for a common purpose within a specific geographic region, but they can become involved with violent or criminal activities. To become a member of the gang, potential members must often submit to or commit violent acts to prove themselves to the group. Gang members often report that they joined the group to belong, for protection, or even for the thrill of activity. From a communication or sociological perspective, these gangs meet many of the same needs as traditional groups, such as families or clubs. Like other groups, they often use symbols, signs, and language to create community and distinguish themselves from the larger community. Several risk factors are associated with gang membership, including poverty, lack of supervision, problems at home, or being related to current gang members. Explore this topic through your own research, and see if you can identify communication principles that contribute to gang recruitment and activities. As a class, learn more about gangs in your area and alternatives available for youths.

From the Galveston County Sheriff's Department, here is a short list of common gang slang terms:

GANG BANGER:	An active gang member
HOME BOY or HOME GIRL:	Gang member
JUMP IN:	Gang initiation
NUT UP:	Angry
OG:	Original gang member
PACKING:	Gang member with a gun
RAG:	Color of a gang
SHOOTER:	A gang member who uses a gun
TAGGER:	Someone who uses graffiti
WANNABE:	Young person who wants to be a gang member

For more information, go to: http://www.beattheheat.com/gangs.html

Status, an important part of socialization within a culture or community, is your position or social rank in relation to others. We may discuss status in terms of what type of job you hold, what degrees you've earned, or your experience in a particular field. You may have heard of the terms "blue-collar" and "white-collar" workers. These terms refer to the shirts those people wore, which were often associated with their profession. An electrician may wear a blue shirt, but an executive would wear a white shirt, with the understanding that he or she would not have to get dirty. Beyond the color association, we can see the division into two classes, often socioeconomic, of people. The shirts serve to signal status and group affiliation. Can you think of any way people show their perception of their status?

Status within a cultural group, whether it is an organization in which you work or one that shares your ethnic, racial, or linguistic heritage, is an important part of culture. Loss of status within a cultural group, or the disenfranchisement of a minority culture by a dominant culture, can significantly impact intercultural communication. For example, in the middle to late 1800s Native American tribes that signed treaties with the U.S. government were given specific rights as tribal members in exchange for their lands. Entire communities were relocated to reservations, and although the conditions were often poor, the cultural groups retained their identities as a tribe. Less than one hundred years later, the Eisenhower Administration processed legislation to terminate tribal status. This had a disastrous effect on many tribal communities, including the Menominee and Klamath tribes. President Nixon later called for a reversal of the policy in 1971, and the Commissioner of Indian Affairs "announced abandonment of the relocation policy in favor of development on or near reservations, with greater control in the hands of the Indians themselves" (Tjerandsen, 1980, p. 71)

Before we discuss communities and cultures further, please take a moment and write down a few important points about your family. Did your family come to the United States a long time ago or recently? Has your family always lived in the Americas? Has your family moved to your current location during your lifetime? Is your family close or separated geographically? What norms would you say exist within your family that people who are not a part of your family would not necessarily know? If you have the opportunity, interview a parent or grandparent and ask them why they chose to live where they currently reside. What issues or challenges did they have to address? How has that affected your life?

Communities, like families, share a sense of common history. For example, the African American community has a common sense of history, with elements of slavery, the Civil Rights movement, and overcoming historical injustices. Communities of African Americans have shared stories of past experience through written works, such as songs and poetry.

3. We Share Cultures

The transmission of culture requires communication and interaction, and the understanding that comes through socialization is one that emphasizes group expectations rather than individual ones. A person comes to understand what the group norms are in much the same way as we discussed in the chapter on group communication. A person has basic needs, as Maslow and Schutz have outlined for us, and fitting into a group, or a culture, meets many of these basic needs.

One aspect of this awareness of group affiliation is the acknowledgement of others status as non-group members. We recognize cultures distinct from our own, and we recognize difference. Gudykunst and Kim (1997), referred to previously, offer us insight into this dynamic process in *Communicating with Strangers*. See Intercultural Communication 5.1.

INTERCULTURAL COMMUNICATION 5.1 • *Uncertainty Reduction Theory*

Have you ever met someone and not been able to "figure them out"? When we meet someone for the first time there is a degree of uncertainty, and Berger (1979) and Berger together with Calabrese (1975) developed the uncertainty reduction theory to examine the ways we come to know each other and how we reduce uncertainty as we develop relationships.

Here are their seven axioms of uncertainty reduction:

1. There is a high level of uncertainty at first. As we get to know one another, our verbal communication increases and our uncertainty begins to decrease.
2. Following verbal communication, as nonverbal communication increases, uncertainty will continue to decrease, and we will express more nonverbal displays of affiliation, like nodding one's head to express agreement.
3. When one is experiencing high levels of uncertainty, they will increase their information-seeking behavior, perhaps asking questions to gain more insight. As one's understanding increases, uncertainty decreases, as does the information-seeking behavior.
4. When one is experiencing high levels of uncertainty, the communication interaction is not as personal or intimate. As uncertainty is reduced, intimacy increases.
5. When one is experiencing high levels of uncertainty, communication will feature more reciprocity or displays of respect. As uncertainty decreases, reciprocity may diminish.
6. Differences between people increase uncertainty, whereas similarities decrease uncertainty.
7. Higher levels of uncertainty are associated with a decrease in the indication of liking the other person, whereas reductions in uncertainty are associated with liking the other person more.

Cultural communities often define themselves with borders or boundaries. Have you ever seen a gated community? How about a new subdivision? How about a section of town that has its own identity, like Harlem in New York or Watts in Los Angeles? Have you ever heard of a *barrio*? Communities often form around geographic boundaries, and features like walls or fences, streets, or railroad tracks often reinforce these boundaries. Gloria Anzaldúa explores the concept of boundaries in her book *Borderlands/La Frontera* (1987). She explores the physical borderland along the Texas and United States Southwest border with Mexico and the psychological borderlands that encompass identity, sexuality, and spirituality. In terms of the physical boundaries, she explores how a region that was once occupied by native inhabitants came to be part of Mexico and later became part of the United States. Many of the inhabitants' families have lived there for generations, and she describes in detail how the intersection of cultures, languages, traditions, and borders has impacted people. She also broadens her discussion to include personal boundaries of identity and orientation and how, like the turbulent history of the U.S. Mexican border mirrors and contrasts personal turbulence.

4. Cultures Share Common Values and Principles

We are by nature an organization that is unable to tolerate indifference.
We hope that by arousing awareness and a desire to understand,
we will also stir up indignation and stimulate action.

—Rony Brauman, MD, Former President, Médecins
Sans Frontières (also known as Doctors Without
Borders or MSF)

Doctors Without Borders or MSF was founded in 1971 by a small group of French doctors who expressed the belief that "all people have the right to medical care and that the needs of these people supersede respect for national borders, delivers emergency aid to victims of armed conflict, epidemics, and natural and man-made disasters, and to others who lack health care due to social or geographical isolation" (MSF, 2001, www.doctorswithoutborders.org).

Linked by a common sense of values and principles, medical professionals from around the world work, in many cases as volunteers, to provide emergency assistance to people in need. This community has grown to serve eighteen countries, involving more than two thousand volunteers and fifteen thousand locally hired staff to provide medical aid in more than eighty countries.

Consider your local service organizations, such as Rotary or Kiwanis, which contribute time, energy, and resources to the community. What values do they have in common, and what principles to they adhere to? Do you think the cultural norms and traditions of Doctors Without Borders are similar to other medical professionals? How might they be different?

5. Communities Share a Common Purpose and a Sense of Mission

For example, Doctors Without Borders has a two-part common purpose: to meet the health care needs of those they serve and to call attention to the underlying issues and challenges that contribute to those health care needs. Community colleges, for example, value education and have as one of their defining principles the equal access to education for everyone. Can you think of a community, group, or institution that has a common purpose? Do they have a mission statement? What does the mission statement say about the organization?

6. Cultures Have Common Symbols, Boundaries, Status, Language, and Rituals

Symbols, one way groups establish and express identity, are images, icons, and figures that represent ideas or concepts. For some groups, the symbols may involve a banner or flag, for others a logo or icon. Sometime symbols have distinct meanings for different groups. Take for example the debate over the use of the Confederate Flag. For some, the symbol is one that represents a shared history and common traditions. For others, it is a racist reminder of a past of injustice and slavery. Each group defends its right to display or call for the removal of the Confederate Flag. Each group builds a common sense of community around the symbol, but from a distinct frame of reference. This debate over the use of a symbol, with the use of mass communication to share interpretations, is fascinating from a communication perspective. The symbol itself is created from simple colors, simple patterns, and simple shapes. Its effect on communities, however, is significant and dynamic. The 1991 NAACP Confederate Flag Resolution Abhorring the Confederate Battle Flag set in motion a debate and a boycott of tourism in several states that continues in many ways today, raising issues about symbols and their appropriate use in communities. You will find several links to explore this issue further at the close of this chapter.

A similar example of how symbols serve or hinder a community can be found in your own school mascot. What does your school use as a mascot? How is it received? What is the role of a mascot? Historically mascots were taken to symbolize a value, character, or prominent figure in the community it represents. Stanford University, for example, once had a Native American as its mascot. The University, however, changed its mascot to the Cardinal in 1972.

7. Our Cultures Are Always Changing

In addition to our understanding that we learn, share, and acknowledge differences in cultural norms, languages, and traditions, we must also acknowledge that cultures are always changing. Look back to the introductory exercises. Are there any groups that you belonged to but do not now affiliate with? If you went back to your elementary school, would it be the same as when you were a student? Do you think that the conditions that were present at the time of your grandparent's or great grandparent's lives impacted or influenced where they chose to live or how they lived their lives? Economic, political, and social factors often influence cultures, and, as a result, cultures change. Within cultures, individual members or groups of members within the large community change as well.

When Martin Luther led the Reformation in 1517, cultures changed and groups formed that continue to exist today. The Hutterites, the Old German Brethern, the Amish, and the Mennonites all became communities that relocated geographically to practice their own religions. You may have seen the film *Witness*, which featured members of the Amish culture, and saw how members control their use of modern technology. For example, the Amish have traditionally limited their use of modern technology and, as a culture, have resisted use of the telephone. At first telephones were not used, and if a telephone was used, it involved a trip to town. As times changed, so have customs, and eventually telephones were located at the end of the street, but still not in individuals' homes. Currently, some Amish families have built small "outhouses" that house a telephone on their property but still maintain its separation from the home.

8. Our Cultures Are Complex

We are a part of many cultures, and cultures themselves are quite complex. Each culture has its own set of norms, customs, and traditions, which, as we have seen, change over time in response to or anticipation of changes in the environment of those who are members of the cultures.

Co-cultures

Look back at Introductory Exercise 5.1 and count how many groups you consider yourself a part of, a member in, affiliated with, or in which you are active. Are there ever times where one group you are involved with comes into contact with other groups in which you are a member or affiliated? Do your friends or fellow students ever see you at work? Do you ever interact with more than one group or community, and do the expectations and roles ever change? **Co-cultures** are groups whose beliefs, customs, or behaviors, although similar to those of the larger culture, make it distinct as its own culture. As we can see, we are often members of more than one culture.

Barriers to Intercultural Communication

Now that we have examined the eight characteristics of intercultural communication and learned about co-cultures, you should have a better understanding of this dynamic, multifaceted aspect of communication. To build on what we covered, we now examine three key barriers to intercultural communication: language, perception, and ethnocentrism.

1. Language

Language serves to both bring us together and help us reinforce our group status. Language can include both established languages, such as Spanish or French, dialects, or even subtle in-group language styles within a larger language context. Have you ever been part of a group that has its own words or phrases that have meanings that people you do not know or who are not part of the group wouldn't know? When a group communicates in its own way, it can create a sense of belonging and can reinforce your membership and place in that group.

People often tell each other stories, which often communicate a value or meaning in the culture. Perhaps you have heard of "The early bird gets the worm" saying, with its underlying meaning of the one who is prepared and ready gets the reward. In North America, this saying is common and reflects a cultural value. Diverse cultures have diverse sayings that reflect differences in values, customs, and traditions. See Intercultural Communication 5.2.

Can you imagine what it would be like to have your language taken away from you and to be punished for speaking your language? The Bureau of Indian Affairs forced many parents to send their children to dormitory schools after World War II. These boarding schools were often outside of their own community, and English was the dominant and enforced language (McNickle et al., 1964). Native American children were often punished for using their native languages or words, even on the playground or at recess (McLean, 1998). Many children of Spanish-speaking parents report similar stories on playgrounds and schools across the country. What would it be like if you couldn't speak the language you were brought up with, the language of your parents and community? How would you feel about yourself?

Classic texts such as Aldous Huxley's *Brave New World,* George Orwell's *1984,* and Ray Bradbury's *Fahrenheit 451* all examine the importance of language in building community, and each author explores how the intentional limitation and altering of language impacts community.

INTERCULTURAL COMMUNICATION 5.2 • *Kwanzaa*

Kwanzaa is an African American celebration, from December 26 to January 1, that focuses on traditional African values called Nguzo Saba, or the seven guiding principles.

Kwanzaa, or "first fruits of the harvest" in the Kiswahili language, was founded in 1966 by Dr. Maulana Karenga.

One principle is the focus for each day of the celebration (adapted from the websites *Everything About Kwanzaa* and *The Kwanzaa Information Center*) listed below:

Umoja (OO-MO-JAH) The principle of **unity** emphasizes the importance of togetherness and continuity of the family and community.

Kujichagulia (KOO-GEE-CHA-GOO-LEE-YAH) The principle of **self-determination** involves defining common interests and making decisions with the best interest of the family and community in mind.

Ujima (OO-GEE-MAH) The principle of **collective work and responsibility** reinforces the relationship of the individual to the community, society, and world, solving problems together.

Ujamaa (OO-JAH-MAH) The principle of **cooperative economics** involves collective economic strength to meet universal needs through mutual support.

Nia (NEE-YAH) The principle of **purpose** focuses on setting personal goals that benefit the community.

Kuumba (KOO-OOM-BAH) The principle of **creativity** focuses on the dedication of creative energies to build and maintain a strong and vibrant community.

Imani (EE-MAH-NEE) The principle of **faith** encompasses honoring traditions, offering the best of oneself, with the goal of developing a better life for everyone. This emphasizes overcoming challenges through perseverance and confidence.

Sources: Everything About Kwanzaa: http://www.tike.com/celeb-kw.htm and the *Kwanzaa Information Center*: http://www.melanet.com/kwanzaa/.

Judy Pearson and Paul Nelson (2000) and Devito (1986) describe four key areas of language that serve to bring us together, but because these aspects of language involve a specialized knowledge in some unique to the group or community, they can create barriers to outsiders. These are often called **co-languages** because they exist and interact with dominant language but are nonetheless distinct from it.

Argot   Argot is a secret or specialized language of a group, usually associated with criminals. Think of police or detective television programs and the specialized language of criminals.

Cant	Cant is a profession-specific language used by nonprofessionals. Think of how people in the service industry describe customers.
Jargon	Jargon is a profession-specific language used by professionals. Think of how lawyers speak to one another.
Slang	Slang is a word that takes the place of a standard or traditional word in order to add an unconventional, nonstandard, humorous, or rebellious effect. Think of the word "cool" and how it is used.

In addition to language-based barriers, there are also several factors, many of which we have visited in previous chapters, that can act as barriers to effective intercultural communication.

2. The Nature of Perception

Perception, as we explored previously, is an important part of the communication process. Your cultural value system, what you value and pay attention to, will significantly affect your intercultural communication. North American culture places an emphasis on space, with an "appropriate" distance while shaking hands, for example. If a North American travels to France, Spain, or Chile, he or she will find that a much smaller sense of personal space is the norm and may receive a "kiss" on the cheek as a greeting. If the North American is uncomfortable, the person from France may not attribute his or her uncomfortableness to personal space and may miscommunicate. Learning about other cultures can help you adapt in diverse settings and can make you more comfortable as you enter new situations where others' perceptions are different from your own.

Role identities, which involve expected social behavior, are another aspect of intercultural communication that can act as a barrier to effective communication. How does your culture expect men and women to act and behave? How about children, or elders and older citizens? The word "role" implies an expectation of how one is supposed to act and behave in certain settings and scenes, and just like in a play in a theater, each person has a culturally bound set of role expectations. Who works as a doctor, a lawyer, a nurse, or a welder? As times and cultures change, so do role identities. In business, once perceived as a profession primarily for men, women have become actively involved in starting, developing, and facilitating growth of businesses.

Goals reflect what we value and are willing to work for and vary widely across cultures. In some cultures, a siesta or afternoon lunch and resting period is the main meal of the day and a time for family. In the United States, we often have a quick lunch or even a "working lunch," with the emphasis on continuing productivity with the goal of personal and organizational achievement. The differences in values, family time versus work time, for example, establish themselves in how we lead our lives. To a European, accustomed to one month of vacation a year, the thought of someone from the United States on a few intense, 3-day power weekends hiking, skiing, or sailing might seem stressful. To a goal-oriented North American, the power weekend may be just the rejuvenation required to get "back in the game."

We have previously discussed self-concept, and you may want to revisit the section, taking a new look at how it relates to perception and intercultural communication. In this context, **self-concept** can become a barrier to effective intercultural communication. Geert Hofstede researched the concepts of individualism versus collectivism across diverse cultures. He found the United States to be the country where people perceived things primarily from their own viewpoint and how the world relates to them as individuals capable of making their own decisions, solving their own problems, and being responsible for their own actions (Hofstede, 1982). He also found many countries in Asia and South American to be much less individualistic, instead focusing on the needs of the family, community, or larger group.

In addition, there are two other systems that influence how we relate to the world that impact our intercultural communication. Carley Dodd (1998) discusses the degree to which cultures communicate rules explicitly or implicitly. In an explicit context, the rules are discussed before we hold a meeting, negotiate a contract, or even play a game.

In the United States, we want to make sure everyone knows the rules beforehand and get frustrated if people do not follow the rules. In other cultures from the Middle East and Latin American, the rules are more generally understood by everyone, and people from these cultures tend to be more accommodating to small differences and tend to be less concerned if everyone plays by the same rules. Our ability to adapt to contexts that are explicit or implicit is related to our ability to tolerate the unknown (Hofstede, 1982).

In the United States, we often look to guiding principles rather than rules for every circumstance, and we believe that with hard work, we can achieve our goals even though we do not know the outcome. In Peru, Chile, and Argentina, however, people prefer to reduce ambiguity and uncertainty and like to know exactly what is expected and what the probable outcome will be (Samovar et al., 1998).

Individualistic cultures: People value individual freedom and personal independence.

Collectivistic cultures: People value the family or community over the needs of the individual.

Explicit-rule cultures: People discuss rules and expectations clearly to be sure rules are known.

Implict-rule cultures: Rules are implied and known by everyone but not always clearly stated.

Uncertainty-accepting cultures: People often focus on principles versus rules for every circumstance and accept that the outcome is not always known.

Uncertainty-rejecting cultures: People often focus on rules for every circumstance and do not like ambiguity or not knowing what the outcome will be.

When we consider whether a culture as a whole places more emphasis on the individual or the community, we must be careful to recognize that individual members of the culture may hold beliefs or customs that do not follow a cultural norm. **Stereotypes,** defined as generalizations about a group of people that oversimplify their culture (Rogers & Steinfatt, 1999), can be one significant barrier to effective intercultural communication. Gordon Allport, a pioneer in the field of communication research, examined how and when we formulate or use stereotypes to characterize distinct groups or communities. He found that we tend to stereotype people and cultures with which we have little contact (Allport, 1958). How can you learn more about other people and cultures? Many colleges and universities have offices of international education that offer "study abroad" programs, where you can live and learn in a culture other than your own as part of your educational experience. Not only will you benefit from firsthand experience, but you will make yourself more valuable in your chosen job or profession.

In addition, your firsthand experience will provided you with an increased understanding of prejudice. **Prejudice** involves a negative preconceived judgment or opinion that guides conduct or social behavior. Within the United States, can you make a list of people or groups that may be treated with prejudice by the majority group? Your list may include specific ethnic, racial, or cultural groups that are stereotyped in the media, but it could also include socioeconomic groups or even different regions of the United States. For example, Native Americans were long treated with prejudice in early Western films. Can you imagine in other countries they may also treat groups with prejudice? In many parts of South America, indigenous people are treated poorly, and their rights as citizens are sometimes not respected. Has treatment of Native Americans changed in North America? It has also changed, and continues to change, in all of the Americas, North and South.

People who treat others with prejudice often make **assumptions** about the group or communities. As Gordon Allport illustrated for us, we often assume characteristics about groups with which we have little contact.

By extension, we can sometimes **assume similarity,** that people are all basically similar, in effect denying cultural, racial, or ethnic differences. We sometimes describe the United States as a "melting pot," where individual and cultural differences blend to become a homogeneous culture. This melting pot often denies cultural differences. The metaphor of a "salad bowl," where communities and cultures retain their distinctive characteristics or "flavor," serves as a more equitable model. In this salad bowl, we value the differences and what they contribute to the whole.

We can also run the risk of **assuming familiarity** with cultures when we attribute characteristics of one group to everyone with connections to the larger culture. For example, people may assume that we are familiar with all Native Americans if we know one tribe in our community, forgetting the distinct differences that exist between tribes and even Native Americans that live in urban areas versus on reservations.

With this discussion on stereotypes, prejudice, and assumptions, you may be anxious not to jump to quick conclusions. One positive way to learn about other cultures, as Edward T. Hall supports, is to learn firsthand. When you travel abroad to study or work, you may at first find that you experience **culture shock,** the feeling that you are overwhelmed with the differences from the new culture in contrast to your home or native culture (Oberg, 1985). Your loss of familiar patterns of how to shop, where to go for what you need, or even how to communicate, can produce anxiety and even withdrawal from the new culture. Sometimes people go home, reporting that they are homesick, without acknowledging that culture shock may be an important part of the way they feel. Once you come to understand aspects of the new culture, you will feel more comfortable and be able to explore with an increase in understanding that someone who only visits for a few days cannot appreciate. You may even, upon your return to your native culture, look at it from a whole new perspective, gained by your experience abroad.

3. Ethnocentrism

Finally, your experience may help you to not view the world and its diversity of cultures in an ethnocentric way. **Ethnocentrism** means you go beyond pride in your own culture, heritage, or background and hold the "conviction that (you) know more and are better than those of different cultures" (Seiler & Beall, 2000). This belief in the superiority of one's own group can guide individual and group behavior. If you go to a new country, and they do things differently, you would be considered ethnocentric if you consider their way the wrong way because it is not the same way "they do it back home." Groups would be considered ethnocentric if they prejudged individuals or other groups of people based on negative preconceptions.

Improving Intercultural Communication

Let's now turn our attention from the lessons learned in terms of common barriers to intercultural communication to ways in which we can improve our communication with people from distinct cultures.

Seiler and Beall (2000) offer us six ways to improve our perceptions, and therefore improve our communication, particularly in intercultural communication.

Become an active perceiver	We need to actively seek out as much information as possible. As Hall supports, placing yourself in the new culture can often expand your understanding.
Recognize that each person's frame of reference is unique	We all perceive the world differently, and although you may interact with two people from the same culture, recognize that they are individuals with their own set of experiences, values, and interests.
Recognize that people, objects, and situations change	The world is changing and so are we. Recognizing that people and cultures, like communication process itself, are dynamic and ever changing can improve your intercultural communication.
Become aware of the role perceptions play in communication	As we explored in Chapter 2, perception is an important aspect of the communication process. By understanding that our perceptions are not the only ones possible can limit ethnocentrism and improve intercultural communication.
Keep an open mind	The adage "A mind is like a parachute—it works best when open" holds true. Being open to differences can improve intercultural communication.
Check your perceptions	By learning to observe, and by acknowledging our own perceptions, we can avoid assumptions, expand our understanding, and improve our ability to communicate across cultures.

Summary

In this chapter we applied much of what we learned in previous chapters to communication across cultures. We discussed the growth of the study of intercultural communication and examined several lessons learned through research, investigation, and experience that expand our understanding. There are several principles of intercultural communication that can guide us and barriers that can limit our ability to communicate effectively. Finally, we looked at six ways we can actively improve our ability to communicate across cultures.

For More Information _____

To learn more about Doctors without Borders, go to:·
http://www.doctorswithoutborders.org/

To learn more about cultural symbols, and specifically about the debate over the confederate flag, go to:
http://fullcoverage.yahoo.com/fc/US/Confederate_Flag_Debate/

To learn more about Alex Huxley's *Brave New World*, Orson Wells' *1984*, and Ray Bradbury's *Fahrenheit 451*, conduct key word searches on the web using the author's name and title. This will yield a diversity of information, from short summaries to in-depth analyses.

To learn more about Gloria Anzaldua's exploration of borders and identities, go to:
http://www.auntlute.com/anzaldua.htm

Review Questions _____

1. Factual Questions
   a. Who is generally considered the father of intercultural communication?
   b. What eight contributions did he make to the field?
   c. What is culture shock?

2. Interpretative Questions
   a. How does perception influence intercultural communication?
   b. How does our self-concept influence intercultural communication?
   c. How might the ability to tolerate uncertainty influence communication?

3. Evaluative Questions
   a. Is it possible to completely learn enough about a culture to effectively communicate across cultures?
   b. Is it necessary to understand a culture completely to communicate effectively?
   c. Communication is a dynamic process. To what degree is the responsibility to learn to communicate interculturally shared?

4. Application Questions
   a. What do people consider their culture, heritage, or background? Create a survey, identify a target sample size, conduct your survey, and compare the results.
   b. What study abroad programs are available on your campus? Investigate the issue and share your findings.
   c. Research one culture or country that you would like to visit. Compare the results.

Works Cited

Adelman, I. & Morris, C. (1967). *Society, politics, and economic development: A quantitative approach.* Baltimore: John Hopkins Press.

Allport, G. (1958). *The nature of prejudice.* Garden City, NY: Doubleday.

Anzaldúa, G. (1987). *Borderlands/La frontera: The new Metiza.* San Francisco, CA: Aunt Lute Books.

Bakan, D. (1966). *The duality of human existence.* Chicago: Rand McNally.

Berger, C. (1979). Beyond initial interactions: Uncertainty, understanding and the development of interpersonal relationships. In H. Giles & R. St. Clair (Eds.), *Language and social psychology.* Oxford: Basil Blackwell.

Berger, C. & Calabrese, R. (1975). Some explorations in initial interactions and beyond: Toward a developmental theory of interpersonal communication. *Human Communication Research, 1,* pp. 99–112.

Chen, G. & Starosta, W. (2000). *Foundations of intercultural communication* (pp. 8–12). Boston: Allyn & Bacon.

Condon, J. & Yousef, F. (1975). *An introduction to intercultural communication.* Indianapolis, IN: Bobbs-Merrill.

Devito, J. (1986). *The communication handbook: A dictionary.* New York: Harper & Row.

Dodd, C. (1998). *Dynamics of intercultural communication* (5th ed.). New York: McGraw-Hill.

Gudykunst, W. & Kim, Y. (1984). *Methods of intercultural research.* Beverly Hills, CA: Sage.

Gudykunst, W. & Kim, Y. (1988). *Theories of intercultural communication.* Beverly Hills, CA: Sage.

Gudykunst, W. & Kim, Y. (1992, 1997). *Communicating with Strangers: An approach to intercultural communication.* New York: McGraw-Hill.

Hofstede, G. (1982). *Culture's consequences.* Newbury Park, CA: Sage.

Klopf, D. (1991). *Intercultural encounters: The fundamentals of intercultural communication* (2nd ed.). Englewood, CA: Morton.

Kluckhohn, F. & Strodtbeck, F. (1961). *Variations in value orientations.* Evanston, IL: Row, Peterson.

Leeds-Hurwitz, W. (1990). Notes in the history of intercultural communication: The foreign service institute and the mandate for intercultural training. *Quarterly Journal of Speech, 76,* 268–281.

McLean, S. (1998). Turn taking and the extended pause. In K. S. Sitaram & M. Prosser (Eds.), *Civic discourse: Multiculturalism, cultural diversity and global communication.* Stamford, CT: Ablex Publishing.

McLuhan, M. (1964). *Understanding media: The extensions of man* (2nd ed.). New York: McGraw-Hill.

McNickle, D., D'Arcy, M. & Pfrommer, V. (1964). Dinexta: A community experience. In C. Tjerandsen (Ed.), *Education for citizenship: A foundation's experience.* Santa Cruz, CA: Emil Schwarhaupt Foundation, Inc.

Oberg, K. (1985). Culture shock: Adjusting to new cultural environments. *Practicing Anthropology, 7,* 170–179.

Pearson, J. & Nelson, P. (2000). *An introduction to human communication: Understanding and sharing* (8th ed.). New York: McGraw-Hill.

Prosser, M. (1973). *Intercommunication among nations and people.* New York: Harper & Row.

Rogers, E. & Steinfatt, T. (1999). *Intercultural communication.* Prospect Heights, IL: Waveland Press.

Rokeach, M. (1973). *The nature of human values.* New York: Free Press.

Samovar, L. & Porter, R. (1973). *Intercultural communication: A reader.* Belmont, CA: Wadsworth.

Samovar, L., Porter, R. & Jain, N. (1981). *Understanding intercultural communication.* Belmont, CA: Wadsworth.

Samovar, L., Porter, R. & Stefani, L. (1998). *Communication between cultures.* (3rd ed.). Belmont, CA: Wadsworth.

Seiler, W. & Beall, M. (2000). *Communication: Making connections.* Boston: Allyn & Bacon.

Stewart, E. (1972). *American cultural patterns: A cross-cultural perspective.* La Grange Park, IL: Intercultural Network.

Tjerandsen, C. (1980). *Education for citizenship: A foundation's experience.* Santa Cruz, CA: Emil Schwarhaupt Foundation.

6

Intrapersonal and Interpersonal Communication

Chapter Objectives _____

After completing this chapter, you should be able to:

1. Understand the difference between intrapersonal communication and interpersonal communication.
2. Identify and describe interpersonal needs.
3. Understand the process of self-disclosure.
4. Identify and describe five key stages in the formation of relationships.
5. Identify and describe five key stages is the deterioration of relationships.
6. Identify and describe five ways to improve interpersonal communication.

Introductory Exercise 6.1 _____

Communication researchers have long documented the importance of trust in developing productive, healthy relationships. Within our normal range of relationships, we have different levels of trust, involvement, and commitment to the relationship. Let's establish this range as including:

Impersonal	Characterized by small talk, such as the weather, sports scores
Professional	Usually work related, to the point, about work issues
Personal	About ideas and feelings, with references to self, attitudes, and preferences
Close	About values, hopes, and dreams; you share information about yourself without fear of judgment

Think about the kinds of relationships you have with others. Think of an example from your own life that meets the criteria for each category? Write them down and share with another student or friend.

Introductory Exercise 6.2 _____

Have you ever wanted to be a fly on the wall, where you listened in on a conversation but no one knew you were there? In this exercise, you are to play the role of observer but not the role of participant. That means you will observe with an emphasis on objectivity and just the facts but not participate in the actual conversation(s).

Listen in on the conversations around you. That does not mean hold a glass to a door or eavesdrop with malicious intent. It does mean you listen for the way people communicate rather than specific content. Your goals are to (1) determine the kind of conversation (from the list above) people are having, (2) determine the level of trust present in the observable relationship, and (3) observe any actions that facilitate or hinder this conversation.

> *I am afraid to tell you who I am, because, if I tell you who I am, you may not like who I am, and that's all I have.*
>
> —John Powell (Woods, 1997, p.128)

Relationships are complicated but are often the most rewarding experiences in our lives. We spend our lives communicating and sometimes find communication with others difficult or even frustrating. In this chapter we will examine how we communicate with ourselves and how relating to ourselves is connected to how we relate to others. Within the context of relationships, we'll explore the range of wants and needs we hope to meet, look at expectations, and discuss some common stages we go through in relationships. Finally, we will examine ways to improve relationships, linking what we have seen in previous chapters to what we learn in this one.

In the first exercise, did you find it relatively easy to find examples of relationships in your own life? Who did you list for your impersonal relationship? Conversations with a sales clerk, telephone operator, or telemarketer? How about for a close relationship? Family and friends? For each of us, the answers may be different, but the answers have common threads we will observe throughout this chapter.

In the second exercise, what did you observe? People having a conversation at a table opposite yours in a restaurant? Other students talking in the student lounge? Were you able to determine, as an outside observer, their level of trust? How did you make your determination? What led you to your observation about the conversations? Were any particular actions common in more than one observed conversation?

You will notice throughout this chapter, as you may have noticed in the second exercise, that you already know quite a bit about interpersonal communication. Take what you've learned from a lifetime of observation and experience and see how it relates to the material in this chapter. Some of the discussion may sound familiar. Some of the discussion may sound like a page out of your own life. Some of the discussion may not sound like something you've experienced. Throughout this chapter keep your own experiences in mind and see how looking at interpersonal communication through a formal, theory-based approach can give insight into everyday conversations. Also keep in mind that conversations and relationships do not fit well into categories, and, unlike words in boxes, they are dynamic and everchanging.

In Figure 6.1, both intrapersonal communication and interpersonal communication are occurring. Each person is talking to himself or herself, and one asks the other if they should have coffee. In a conversation in which the other person is talking, have you ever let your mind drift, only to get caught when he or she asks you a question? Your discussion with yourself is interrupting your active listening. Let's look at intrapersonal communication and how it relates to self-concept and listening.

What Is Intrapersonal Communication?

You may recall that we briefly addressed intrapersonal communication in the first chapter. The word *intrapersonal* means within one person. **Intrapersonal communication** is communication with one's self, including self-talk, imaging, and visualization. Shedletsky (1989) discusses intrapersonal communication within the context of the basic transactional model of communication, but all components of the model, from source to

FIGURE 6.1 *Intrapersonal/Interpersonal Communication*

receiver and so forth, happen within the individual. Pearson and Nelson (1985) discuss this interpretation, adding that intrapersonal communication is not limited to just internal monologue. They point to aspects of intrapersonal communication that include planning, problem solving, internal conflict resolution, and the evaluation of ourselves and others.

You view yourself in many ways within the context of your individual experiences. Once you learned how to use language, you began to implement on various levels the principles of communication, such as classifying and labeling. Did you perceive that an experience was a problem, that caused you harm, or did you perceive it as a challenge, to be learned from, or both? The way you interpret situations and circumstances, conversations and information, and the actions of others and yourself contributes to your knowledge and understanding of the world and your place in it. How you talk to yourself has a big impact.

Let's say you are taking a test and there are four answers to choose from. You choose how to respond to the question. You may eliminate options that don't make sense and choose the best option from the two remaining answers. Each step in that complicated process involves intrapersonal communication, where you talk to yourself and talk yourself through a problem, applying your previous knowledge to this new challenge.

Speaking of challenges, have you ever been in a competitive event like a sport, debate, or band or perhaps in an extracurricular activity like theater? You may have had moments where the spotlight, even if no one was watching, was on you. You are on the line in a race. You just recovered the ball and are pushing for a drive down the court. You take a breath and hit a high C on your trumpet as you begin a solo. Regardless of the challenge, the situations are in many ways the same. You are in a tense moment, and what you say to yourself makes a big impact. If you say "I can do it," you probably will hit close to your goal. If you say to yourself "there is no way I can do this," what effect do you think this has on your performance? You would be right if you said it certainly doesn't help, and probably hinders, your ability to focus on the task rather than pay attention to the nagging doubts.

Your intrapersonal communication, your conversation with yourself, is a significant part of your conversations with others. You seek affirmation that people see you like you want to be seen, perhaps how you see yourself. You look for actions, gestures, words, and attitudes in others that you relate back to how you see yourself and feel about yourself. This emphasis on feedback from others relates to your self-concept, which comprises two main aspects: your self-image and your self-esteem. As we discussed previously, **self-image** is how you perceive yourself and your **self-esteem** is how you feel about yourself. Your self-concept is generated primarily through interactions with others, and it is with this in mind that we place so much emphasis on intrapersonal communication.

Some researchers call it internal monologue, others self-talk. Both terms point to the same general idea, that you talk with yourself like a running monologue, which may be coherent and logical but can also be disorganized and illogical. Alfred Korzybski (1933), a scholar and philosopher of language best known for his system of linguistic philosophy and expression (general semantics), considered that the first step for one to become conscious of how we think (and, by extension, how we talk to ourselves) was to achieve a degree of inner quietness.

Exercise _____

To understand your own idea of self-image and self-esteem, take out a piece of paper and write ten things you like about yourself down the left side. As you are writing down things, use the right side to write down your self-talk.

> Example: I am strong.   (I am, but not as strong as some people. I
> need to spend more time at the gym.)

Once you are done with the ten items, think about the right side of the page as if someone else wrote it. Can you draw a picture of that person?

By recognizing that through communication with others we see ourselves, and how we view our strengths and weaknesses, we come to recognize the importance of intrapersonal communication. By understanding that our conversations with ourselves can interrupt conversations with others, we can learn to control who we are listening to and can learn to downplay our internal monologue. By accepting that we can choose what messages to say to ourselves, we can encourage ourselves to achieve our goals. See Intercultural Communication 6.1.

What Is Interpersonal Communication?

Have you ever had a conversation with someone in which you needed to listen or offer support? Then you already have a working knowledge of interpersonal communication. For our purposes, we'll say **interpersonal communication** is communication interaction typically between two people. This is a broad definition and is primarily defined in comparison to other forms of communication, such as group communication or mass communication. This emphasis on the number of people, usually referred to as a contextual definition, helps us understand interpersonal communication but lacks a discussion of the types of relationships between people. The developmental view of interpersonal communication places emphasis on the relationships and draws a distinction between a conversation with a

INTERCULTURAL COMMUNICATION 6.1 • *Face Negotiation Theory*

Have you ever heard of someone "losing face." How about "getting egg on their face?" Both phrases raise the issue of the loss of respect in a communication interaction. Stella Ting-Toomey (1993, 1994, 1998), a communication researcher originally from China, is well known for research concerning face and "face work," of the management of image you want others to perceive. To bring the concept to light, let's look at the following example:

Teacher: "Your assignments are due at the beginning of class."

Student: "But I got a ticket on the way to class, the police officer made me late."

Teacher: "You are an excellent student. I'm sure you will do your best next time."

Student: "You just don't understand."

The student is asking for an exception, questioning the teacher. The teacher asserts the position of an established rule and offers a kind remark as a face restoration strategy for the student. Ting-Toomey notes that there are two types of actions that make up the face-threatening process: face saving and race restoration. Face saving prevents the loss of face, whereas face restoration saves face once the loss has occurred.

This is a fascinating area of study, involving intercultural communication in many ways. Investigate further with information in "For More Information" at the end of the chapter.

government clerk and someone you care deeply about. In the developmental view, interpersonal communication involves people who have known each other previously.

Relationships with others are formed through communication, particularly interpersonal communication, and come in all sorts of shapes and sizes. A relationship with a parent or caregiver, a husband or wife, a boyfriend or girlfriend can be impersonal or close, professional or personal. Relationships can be enhanced (or not) through interpersonal communication. Can you recall a time when you noticed someone you did not already know and wanted to get to know them? How about a time when you knew someone but wanted to get to know them better? Why do you suppose you wanted to know more? Curiosity? Attraction? Possibly, but underlying your interest was the need to feel more confident, and less uncertain, about the person and the relationship. **Uncertainty theory** states that we seek to know more about others with whom we have relationships in order to reduce the anxiety created by the unknown (Berger & Calabrese, 1975; Berger, 1986; Gudykunst, 1995). Another motivation theory points to what we *want* from others. **Predicted outcome value theory** asserts that not only do we want to reduce uncertainty but we are also interested in the rewards that will result from the association (Kellermann & Reynolds, 1990; Sunnafrank, 1986, 1990).

Why do you do what you do? Is it to reduce uncertainty? To get something? Certainly this has something to do with your need to communicate with others, but is there more? Although each of us has different needs and wants, there is some common ground for all of us. We need to eat and stay warm. We need to feel safe and that we belong to a group and have a place in the world. We may even want to make a difference in our world. If we look at the issue of uncertainty within the context of security, we can see how we may want to learn more about others to feel safe and secure. Researchers Abraham Maslow and William Schutz offer two frameworks for us to consider when examining the following question: What makes us want to communicate?

Why Should We Engage in Interpersonal Communication?

Interpersonal communication is one form of communication we use to meet our needs and the needs of others. We engage in interpersonal communication to gain information, to get to know one another, to better understand our situation or context, to come to know ourselves and our role or identity, and to meet our fundamental interpersonal needs. In this section we will examine the functions of interpersonal communication, examining the many ways we choose to communicate with each other and why.

Maslow's Hierarchy

If you have taken courses in anthropology, philosophy, psychology, or perhaps sociology in the past, you may have seen Maslow's Hierarchy (Figure 6.2). Maslow (1970) provides seven basic categories for human needs and arranges them in order of priority, from the most basic to the most advanced. In this figure we can see that we need energy, water, and air to survive. Without any of these three basic elements, which meet our **physiological needs** (1), we cannot live. Once we have what we need to survive right now, we seek **safety** (2). Perhaps this once came in the form of a cave, or shelter, and in modern day it may mean a job or a safe place where your basic needs are met. Victims of domestic violence and abuse are sometimes given shelter (safety) at a facility designed to protect them from

FIGURE 6.2 *Maslow's Hierarchy*

their abuser. Once we have the basics to live, and feel safe from immediate danger, we seek affection from others, looking for a sense of **love and belonging** (3). This need builds on the foundation of the previous needs and underlines our need to be part of a group.

Once we have been integrated into a group, we begin to assert our sense of self and self-respect, addressing our need for **self-esteem** (4). By extension, once we are part of a group and have begun to assert ourselves, we start to feel as if we have reached our potential and are actively making a difference in our own world. Maslow calls this level the need for **self-actualization** (5). Beyond these levels, Maslow points to our basic human curiosity about the world around us. When we have our basic needs met, and do not need to fear losing our place in a group or access to resources, we are free to explore and play, discovering the world around us. Our **need to know** (6) drives us to grow and learn. Finally, beyond curiosity and the desire to know what makes things happen or why things work, we have an **aesthetic need to experience beauty** (7) for its own sake. Beauty takes many forms for many people, and the experience of skydiving or bungee jumping may for some rival the experience of seeing a famous painting or listening to music.

We can see in Maslow's Hierachy how our basic needs are quite concrete, but as we progress through the levels, we increase our degree of interconnectedness with others, relying on our relationships with others to support our level and, in turn, helping others achieve their goals.

It should be said at this point that Maslow's Hierarchy, although in many aspects universal, nonetheless focuses on individual needs. Western cultures typically promote the individual, and, by extension, their needs and wants, from concrete to abstract, are regarded as important. Other cultures see things differently. The Confucian concept of *Jen*, for example, holds that "benevolence" or "humaneness," or our treatment of others, is the highest form of virtue or excellence to which one can aspire (Kessler, 1998). This emphasis on the group, as opposed to the individual, promotes the meeting of the needs of all, and through meeting everyone's needs, your own needs are met. Rather than getting "my fair share" first, some cultures value the giving of your "share" to the group, through your effort and creativity, and by this giving your needs will be met by the group.

Exercise _____

Looking at Maslow's Hierarchy, how might this understanding help you if you are a supervisor responsible for a shift? A parent? A counselor? Write down one use of the information for each example.

Schutz's Interpersonal Needs

William Schutz, like Abraham Maslow, provides a useful framework for the discussion of interpersonal needs. In his theory (1966), Schutz points to three key interpersonal needs that are largely universal: affection, inclusion, and control.

The need for **affection**, according to Schutz, is the need we have to feel that people like us or that we can be loved and wanted. Can you see where this need may connect to one of Maslow's needs? Schutz takes this need one step further with his discussion of what happens when this need is not met and indicates two opposite categories. If a person does not feel liked, he or she may withdraw and not let others get close. Schutz describes people who exhibit these behavioral characteristics as **underpersonals**. The opposite of this withdrawn approach to interpersonal relationships is the **overpersonal** individual, who has such a strong need to be liked that he or she constantly seeks approval from others. The middle ground is where a person, called a **personal individual,** is mature and balanced in their approach to interpersonal relationships, both meeting their need for affection, but understanding that not being liked by everyone is normal.

After our need for affection, Schutz discusses the need for **inclusion,** the need for us to belong to a group. Our need for inclusion drives us to communicate with others, much as belonging is a basic human need according to Maslow. In new situations, where the majority of people already know each other, people can feel out of place. Take, for example, a chat room or bulletin board group on the Internet. The new person, or newbie, can read the rules of the group and even "lurk" or read messages without ever posting a reply to gain information and to understand how to communicate in this context. This alone, however, will not prepare the person adequately to leap into the group and post his or her opinion. As in group communication, the members will come to know one another through interaction, and until that step occurs, the newbie won't truly understand the chat group or bbs community. Nonetheless, our need to be included is fundamental across all cultures and languages, and meeting that need through interpersonal communication is important.

In terms of this need to be included or to belong, Schutz outlines three major categories: **undersocial, oversocial,** and **social.** As in the case of an underpersonal individual, an undersocial one does not seek out communication interaction with others, and when presented with a situation where communication occurs, he or she tends to be shy and withdrawn. The opposite of an undersocial person is an oversocial person, and they can be characterized by their need to constantly communicate, often dominating the conversation by taking the speech turns from others. A social person is balanced and both says what needs to be said and listens to others.

Related to this is the idea that interpersonal communication can involve messages on more than one level in varying social settings. **Content messages** focus on the superficial-level meaning of the message. Let's say you ask your friend for help and he or she replies in an upbeat way "sure" and maintains eye contact, waiting for you to relay how they can help. The literal meaning of the response is affirmative or yes, but the way they say it conveys meaning about your relationship. **Relationship messages,** which happen at the same time as content messages, focus on how the message was said. In this case, the upbeat tone of "sure" combined with clear eye contact communicates that the participants have a relationship. By paying attention to both types of messages, we can come to understand the degree to which someone is social and can discern relationships within conversations.

Finally, Schutz discussed our need for **control,** which also relates to one of Maslow's levels. Can you find which one? In our drive to control our surroundings, we at times may control others, the situation, or the type of interpersonal relationship. This need for control can be for some, called **abdicrats,** a burden of responsibility they would rather shift to others. For others, called **autocrats,** there is a need to control without input from others. **Democrats** share the need for control between the individual and the group.

Can you think of people you know who fit these categories? At the same time, can you remember an obstacle to communication that applies to these categories? People are not categories or labels, and although they exhibit similar behavioral characteristics, they do so in different ways to varying degrees. They are also involved in the dynamic process of communication, where self-concept is constantly redefined through interaction. This means that people can get caught in cycles where, for example, they withdraw from interpersonal relationships. It also underlines that people change over time, allowing for the possibility that people improve their relationships and strike a healthy balance.

Johari Window

At the end of the 1960s, when the relationship between a person and the world was a frequent topic of discussion, some individuals advocated

FIGURE 6.3 *Johari Window*

building bridges (lines of communication) between people and countries rather than walls. Joseph Luft (1970) and Harry Ingram investigated the realm of individual growth and the development of relationships with others. They presented their now famous Johari Window (the name was created by combining their two first names, Joe and Harry). In this window, or table, they present four types of information that are relevant to the self. In the first area (1), as you can see in Figure 6.3, is the open area, where information is known to both you and others, like how tall you are and your name. The next area (2) the window presents is that information that others know about us that we don't even know. Perhaps someone notices something in your hair that you didn't know was there or your supervisor recognizes in you potential that you didn't know you had. The third area (3) focuses on information you hide from others, considering the information private. Finally, the unknown area (4) covers information about you that no one, including you, knows. How would you handle an emergency? How would you do in a certain job? You haven't done it yet, so no one knows.

Self-disclosure

With this framework in mind, let's examine the process of self-disclosure. **Self-disclosure** is information, thoughts, or feelings we tell others about ourselves that they would not otherwise know. For example, if you tell someone that you liked or disliked a particular web site, your discussion of your attitudes is self-disclosure. However, if you tell someone you are tall or short, large or small, or wear eyeglasses (and you have them on), then your discussion of information is already apparent to the listener and therefore not self-disclosure.

As we discussed previously, for us to meet our needs we need people, and for them to know what our needs and wants are, we have to communicate them. In addition, we have basic human needs such as affection, inclusion, and control that are met through interpersonal relationships. One way we try to get our needs met and build relationships is through self-disclosure.

Can you recall a time when you met someone new that you wanted to get to know better? What did you talk about? Could some of what you discussed with the person been considered small talk? You may have told them your name or what you do. Where do you think this type of conversation falls within the framework of the Johari Window?

Let's say the person also wanted to get to know you better. How did they respond? Probably with similar information, like their name or area of study. Where did your conversation go from there? If it stayed on small talk for long, you may have felt you were not getting anywhere. That's because you are playing a game and it takes two to play. You disclose something about yourself, and they reciprocate, or also disclose something about themselves. Your conversation is off and running, and you both play the game.

Sometimes, however, conversations go awry and don't seem to work out. One key denominator across conversations is that the degree to which we adapt to one another impacts our communication. Roderick Hart (1972; Carlson et al., 1979), in his rhetorical sensitivity theory, discusses three different conversational styles and how they interact to cultivate or discourage communication. Conversational participants that Hart calls **noble selves** stand by their personal beliefs without adapting to others' attitudes, beliefs, or values. **Rhetorical reflectors**, however, change their messages to meet others' expectations. Between the firm stance on principals and the ability to change in conversation like a chameleon, the **rhetorically sensitive** find common ground with others. People often exhibit behaviors associated with all three categories, depending on the context and environment. Rhetorical sensitivity theory underlines the principle that effective communication is facilitated with sensitivity in adjusting what you say to the listener and how you say it. It also underlines the importance of the ability to understand and develop appropriate responses to situations based on your concern for yourself, your concern for others, and your knowledge of the context and environment.

Exercise

What do you think happens in a relationship when you disclose information about yourself and the response is negative?

Example: A teenager comes home and tells his mother that he has been drinking alcohol. His mother replies, "I should have expected that coming from you—you are just like your dad!"

Looking back at our previous example, you may recall that, through self-disclosure, people get to know one another. Taking into account the need to be rhetorically sensitive, you may discuss likes and dislikes, but you may also talk more about thoughts, ideas, or feelings you don't share with everyone. As you do this, the other person may disclose information about himself or herself, and you both get to know each other better, forming bonds of trust. As the trust grows, the level of intimacy can deepen.

Satisfactory communication involves a mutual understanding and agreement on whether or how much to self-disclose. If one person self-discloses a thought or feeling that is too personal, the other person may not be ready to handle it. For example, let's pretend you have known a new co-worker for only a day, and the next day you see them and ask, "How are you?" They then respond with a long response, going into great detail about their personal problems while you begin to look away. Your greeting was a social ritual, and the communication was meant to establish a connection, but not gain information, with a person with whom you have not developed a significant relationship. The other person, being rhetorically insensitive, missed the nature of your inquiry and instead self-disclosed information you did not request. By focusing on the types of self-disclosure that occur in a relationship, you can better reach that understanding or mutual agreement and avoid pitfalls. Which area in the Johari Window are we now talking about? Also see Case Study 6.1 and Computer-Mediated Communication 6.1.

Social Penetration Theory

The field of communication draws from many disciplines, and in this case, from two prominent social psychologists. Irwin Altman and Dalmas Taylor (1973) articulated the social penetration theory, which describes how we move from superficial talk to intimate and revealing talk. Altman and Taylor (1973) discuss how we attempt to learn about others so that we can better understand how to interact. With a better understanding of them with more information, we are in a better position to predict how they may behave, what they may value, or what they might feel in specific situations. We usually gain this understanding of others without thinking about it through observation or self-disclosure. In this model, often called the onion model, we see how we start out on superficial level, but as we peel away layers, we gain knowledge about the other person that encompasses both breadth and depth (Figure 6.4).

We come to know more about the way a person perceives a situation (breadth), but also gain perspective into how they see the situation through an understanding of their previous experiences (depth). Imagine these two spheres, which represent people, coming together. What touches first? The

CASE STUDY 6.1 • *Gender and Self-disclosure*

Who talks more about themselves, men or women? The answer depends on whom you ask and what underlying factor(s) might be considered. According to some researchers, women disclose more private, emotional information than men, stating that men risk getting hurt (Pearson et al., 1998; Rosenfeld, 1979). Others state that it depends on whom they are talking to. For example, Stokes et al. (1980) indicated that their study showed that men are more willing to talk about personal information with strangers, whereas women are more likely to talk to someone they know well. Do women prefer to disclose to other women more than men (Pearson et al., 1998)? Are women more accepting, more likely to view people as connected (Gilligan, 1982)? Do males view self-disclosure from females as seduction (Abbey, 1982)? What do you think?

The gender (role or behavioral aspects) as opposed to the sex (biological) of the person is a hotly debated issue. Which carries more weight, nature (biology) or nurture (environment, observation of others)? Add to this the dynamic of communication and the important process of self-disclosure, and the area of study gets quickly complicated. Isolating variables (that are themselves quite complicated), like culture, language, or background, from your gender within the context of communication is difficult. Some researchers have spent considerable effort in this area, but many have contradictory conclusions. Although we cannot take general statements as fact, we can observe how they have elements of truth in them. Some men may disclose feelings more than women. Some women may reveal more to strangers. We must be careful to avoid stereotyping, by reducing a complex process to simple labeling, on the basis of biological traits.

Try this: Write five questions concerning gender and self-disclosure. Ask an equal number of men and women, within a defined age range, the questions separately. Compare your results.

superficial level. As the two start to overlap, the personal levels may touch, then the intimate level, and finally the core levels may even touch. Have you ever known a couple that has been together for a very long time. They know each other's stories and finish each other's sentences. They might represent the near overlap, where their core values, attitudes, and beliefs are similar through a lifetime of shared experiences.

We move from public to private information as we progress from small talk to intimate conversations. Imagine an onion. The outer surface can be peeled away, and each new layer reveals another until you arrive at the heart of the onion. People interact on the surface, and only remove layers as trust and confidence grows.

Another way to look at it is to imagine an iceberg. What can you see from the surface? Not much. But once you start to go under the water, you

COMPUTER-MEDIATED COMMUNICATION 6.1 • *Mass Personalization: An Internet Marketing Trend*

Have you ever thought of how the Internet can serve you better? Rather than reading the same newspaper everyone else does, would you like just the information you want? Would you like to get the latest basketball scores, stock market reports, or news about your state delivered to your e-mail box? How about your very own web page, where you pick exactly what news you want to receive, for free? All of this is now possible, but the process called **mass personalization** has a price.

In exchange for you providing information such as your name, address, ZIP code, and age, and a little time spent on selecting what you want to read, you get your own "virtual newspaper," complete with short video and sound files. What does the Internet company, like Yahoo! or AltaVista, two personal content page providers, get in exchange? Information about you, and that's worth money.

Building relationships with customers has been a dominant phrase in many business circles for years. John Hagel and Arthur Armstrong, in their text (1997) *Net Gain: Expanding Markets Through Virtual Communities*, detail how businesses must move beyond individual relationships (shop keeper and customer) to building communities, where people come to interact and feel like they belong. The long-term goal is increased customer loyalty and increased sales.

By combining elements of mass communication with customization based on expressed interest areas, businesses can better target people who might buy their product. Do you think the consumer is receiving a service or that they are involved with a whole new level of marketing? Discuss your comments with a classmate.

gain an understanding of the large size of the iceberg and the extent of its depth. We have to go beyond superficial understanding to know each other and progress through the process of self-disclosure to come to know and understand one another.

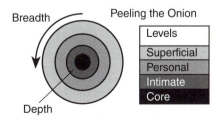

FIGURE 6.4 *Social Penetration Model*
Source: Adapted from Altman and Taylor's (1973) model of social penetration.

Review	Why do we engage in interpersonal communication?
Gain information	We engage in interpersonal communication to gain information. This information can involve directions to an unknown location or a better understanding about another person through observation or self-disclosure.
Understand communication contexts	We also want to understand the context in which we communicate, discerning the range between impersonal and intimate, to better anticipate how to communicate effectively in each setting.
Understand our identity	Through engaging in interpersonal communication, we come to perceive ourselves, our roles, and our relationships with others.
Meet our needs	As Maslow and Shutz discuss, we meet our needs through interpersonal communication.

How Do Relationships Develop?

Building on Altman and Taylor's (1973) social penetration theory, Mark Knapp, a professor at The University of Texas, outlined ten distinct steps that relationships go through as they form and dissolve. Keep in mind as we discuss Knapp's stages that no two relationships are the same and that many repeat or jump stages. The stages in Knapp's **model of relational development** (1978) serve to guide us through the discussion of common stages in relationships and offer insight into common characteristics that relationships share over time.

Coming Together

Stage 1: Initiating	People have short conversations and "size each other up," making initial judgments.
Stage 2: Experimenting	The conversational partners want to know more about each other. They share personal information, likes and dislikes, and continue to get to know each other better.
Stage 3: Intensifying	The participants recognize a desire to see each other more frequently, where the length of tie together increases, and the time apart decreases. There is mutual concern.

| Stage 4: Integrating | The participants recognize a relationship, and start planning their activities around those of their partner. Their friends see them as a couple, and if one is missing, people will ask about the other. |
| Stage 5: Bonding | The participants seek to formalize the relationship, through a public ritual like marriage or through a joint venture like buying a house. |

Growing Apart

Just as people grow together, they also grow apart. Sometimes people choose not to see each other after the initiation stage, or after the experimentation phase, or the couple fails to make the transition from integrating to bonding, and the relationship comes apart. Here are Knapp's five stages of **relational deterioration** (Knapp and Vangelisti, 1996), which outline the process by which relationships disintegrate.

Stage 1: Differentiating	The participants start emphasizing their individual differences instead of their similarities and common ground.
Stage 2: Circumscribing (blaming)	The participants spend less time together, and the times they spend together are farther and farther apart. Communication interaction decreases and takes on a negative tone.
Stage 3: Stagnating	The participants are actively engaged in other activities, and joint activities are not dynamic and require little interaction.
Stage 4: Avoiding	The participants actively avoid each other, viewing the other as in the way. While conversations may increase, so does the level of frustration and disagreement.
Stage 5: Terminating	The participants part ways and are no longer seen by others or themselves as a couple.

Exercise

Think of different relationships you have with other people, both male and female. Can you identify elements of each stage in a real relationship?

No two relationships are the same, but many go through these stages. If a relationship goes from stage one to stage five of relational development overnight, do you think there is any possibility it may go through stages one through five of relational deterioration as quickly? Counselors often point to the importance of bonding and the need to form strong connections at each level. In addition, knowledge of these stages can help couples recognize troubles early, and take a step back, possibly saving the relationship. It is important to note that a relationship can end at any stage and that sometimes relationships never end but instead become "polluted" as irrational conflict breaks out between relational partners as they try to hurt one another.

How Do We Manage Interpersonal Conflict?

Every interpersonal relationship experiences conflict at one time or another. **Conflict** can be defined as an expressed struggle between at least two interdependent individuals who perceive (1) incompatible goals, (2) scarce resources, and (3) interference from the other party in achieving their goals (Hocker & Wilmot,1991). People may avoid each other, blame each other, or even perceive that they have something to lose. None of these activities leads to effectively managing conflict. To create healthy, long-lived relationships, we need to learn how to manage conflict in a positive way. One way to do this is to consider the kind of climate, defensive or supportive, that we create when we communicate. A **defensive climate** is characterized by threatening one another's interpersonal needs.

COMPUTER-MEDIATED COMMUNICATION 6.2 • *Chat Rooms: Bringing People Together*

One way people connect is by setting up an "I-Seek-You" messaging program, similar to Mirabilis LTD's ICQ or America Online's popular Buddy List and Instant Messenger programs. It can be used as a conferencing tool by individuals (friends, family, or business associated, for example) on the Internet to chat,e-mail, perform file transfers, play computer games, and exchange information.

Another way people connect is through an Internet Relay Chat (IRC), a chat system developed by Jarkko Oikarinen in Finland in the late 1980s. According to www.interenet.com, a source for web-related information about history and current trends, IRC has become very popular as more people get connected to the Internet. The key features that contribute to the popularity are that (1) people can connect from anywhere and (2) the IRC can handle more than two conversation participants. This allows for discussions involving large groups, with each individual member receiving everyone else's comments as they contribute them to the discussion.

Source: http://isp.webopedia.com.

When one person shows indifference to another, they sacrifice inclusion and affection. When someone attempts to impose their will on another, the issue of control will divide rather than bring them together. A **supportive** climate, however, focuses on the task or problems to be solved instead of the judgments of others. It is also characterized by spontaneous, honest, and open communication, in which people ask each other's opinions and actively listen to responses.

Although competition may be present in some conversations, conversation is not by definition a competition. In the game of chess, the goal is to dominate your opponent and win. In interpersonal communication, one of the goals may be persuasion, but it also involves content messages and relational messages and is far more dynamic. Biologists once thought that the notion of "only the strong survive" was an indisputable idea. Modern biologists are now coming to consider the importance of cooperation as a strategy for survival in nature and note that many species practice cooperation to succeed. For example, dolphins will come to the aid of one who has been injured, defend one another, switch roles in terms of feeding if needed, and develop lifelong relationships with one another (Mann & Smuts, 1999). In conversations, we need to cultivate a supportive climate, focusing on assessing our own observations and interpretations, emotional responses, and intentional and/or unintentional requests for information or interaction rather than activities and behaviors that contribute to a defensive climate. See Case Study 6.2.

Improving Interpersonal Communication

Although there is no recipe for a perfect relationship, and we know that relationships are not static but rather dynamic systems that change over

CASE STUDY 6.2 • *Fighting Fair*

Think of a relationship you care about, and respond to the questions below. One (1) is the lowest level of agreement and five (5) is the highest.

Personal Assessment

It takes a long time to get over a fight.	1	2	3	4	5
Fights get personal.	1	2	3	4	5
I've forgotten what we fight about.	1	2	3	4	5
One or both of us uses foul or abusive words.	1	2	3	4	5
I want to prove my point.	1	2	3	4	5
My partner never listens to me.	1	2	3	4	5
My partner brings up past issues.	1	2	3	4	5
I sometimes blame my partner.	1	2	3	4	5

CASE STUDY 6.2 • *Continued*

If your score is:	1–10	The relationship may be static, but overall you fight fair.
	11–20	One or both of you make mistakes, but together you can improve your ability to discuss points of conflict.
	21–30	One or both of you make mistakes and may well hurt each other and the relationship. Seek ways to fight fair and not harm.
	31–40	You both should take time out to cool off, and then seek guidance from a professional.

Although this self-assessment is not meant to diagnose your relationship, it is intended to raise issues about how to conflict with your partner in ways that will not harm your relationship or each other. George Back and Peter Wyden (1973) state that verbal conflict can actually benefit a relationship, providing the couple follows positive guidelines. Here are a few suggestions (Stewart, 1998):

- Listen to each other. Take turns talking. Wait a few more seconds before speaking to make sure your partner has finished his or her turn.
- Do not mind read or second-guess each other.
- Stick to the subject. Don't bring up old issues.
- Show respect and empathy. Crossed arms show you are defensive, not open.
- Avoid arguing over details. Stick to the main points.
- Work it out; don't quit. Cancel other plans and complete your conversation.
- Chose a time when you will not be distracted (by family or work, for example).
- Show the other person that you really heard what he or she said.
- Remain calm. Don't engage in blaming, name calling, threatening, foul language, or sarcasm. They decrease intimacy and increase hostility.

Forgive and accept each other. Once you are finished, make up and move on together.

time, we still recognize how important relationships are to each other. The need for healthy relationships is universal, and here are a few strategies to help you improve yours. Canary and Stafford (1992) provide a useful framework for our discussion on improving relationships, and they identify five maintenance strategies that have proved successful in long-term relationships (Tubbs & Moss, 1999, p. 189).

1. Positivity

Be positive. The degree to which you can keep positive, about things in general and specifically the relationship, has a connection to the way your relationship will proceed. If you start thinking in negative terms, differentiating between your likes and your partners likes, you start to build a wall between you, one brick at a time. You may not even notice the wall as each of you build it, but one day you may not be able to see eye to eye, and it will take considerable effort to dismantle that wall, brick by brick.

2. Openness

Be open. Try new things together. See a movie, read the same book, or go camping together. Find some way to build common memories, a sense of shared history and common purpose, together. Part of openness is honesty. Be honest with the other person about your needs, and listen with empathy when they disclose personal information. Try to see things from your partner's perspective. Remember what you learned in Chapter 2, how our perspective makes a difference on how we act and react. Understand their actions from what they perceived to be the situation, not just from your own point of view.

3. Assurances

Value each other. Remind your partner what they mean to you. Give them a hug, tell them why you think they are great, or write them a letter. Do little somethings that convey clearly the message that you value the person as a friend or partner. Have you ever noticed the joy older couples have as they tell a joint story of something that once happened to them, even if they correct each other's version? Tell a story, and include your partner. People like to be reminded and assured that the relationship is on solid ground.

4. Networks

Keep connected. Call each other during the day. Write letters. E-mail. Bring them to the office and let them meet the people you talk about all the time. Form relationships with other people together. Make an effort to build common networks and clear channels of communication.

5. Sharing Tasks

One way to improve the communication is through action. If your partner typically cooks, and you know that today was a hard day for them and that cooking tonight is perceived as one more thing to do, pick up the spatula and get to work. Your partner will appreciate you taking the initiative, and

COMPUTER-MEDIATED COMMUNICATION 6.3 • *Rose*

> To be sweet to somebody via e-mail, you might add -/--@ to your message. The figure "-/--@" is another way of sending someone a rose.

he or she may take the time while you are cooking to relax, allowing for better communication later on.

This idea can extend to helping your partner find more time for what they like to do. Let's say your partner likes to garden, but the laundry pile is near the ceiling and the sink is full of dishes. Before they get home, get the laundry sorted and do the dishes. When they get home, hand them their gloves and trowel, and get back to the laundry. By using the principle of giving through your actions, in the same way Confucius presents the concept of *Jen,* you may meet your own needs through an improved relationship. See Computer-Mediated Communication 6.3.

Summary

In this chapter we discussed the difference between intrapersonal and interpersonal communication. Within these contexts, we examined self-concept and how we come to know and understand ourselves. We also addressed what motivates us to form relationships, different theories on our interpersonal needs, the process of self-disclosure, and the importance of rhetorical sensitivity. Finally, we discussed the stages of relational development and relational deterioration and looked at five ways to manage conflict and improve interpersonal communication.

For More Information _____

Korzybski, A:	http://userwww.sfsu.edu/~rsauzier/Korzybski.html
Ting-Toomey, S:	"Cross-Cultural Face-Negotiation: An Analytical Overview." Presented on April 15, 1992, David See-Chai Lam Centre for International Communication. http://www.cic.sfu.ca/forum/ting-too.html
Gender and communication:	The anthology *Women and Men Communicating: Challenges and Changes* (1993) offers a wide range of studies and perspectives on the issue of gender communication. A copy can be obtained through Harcourt Brace Publishers. ISBN: 0-03-074656-6.

Review Questions

1. Factual Questions
   a. What are the levels of Maslow's Hierarchy?
   b. What three areas compose Schutz's theory of interpersonal needs?
   c. What are Knapp's stages for relational development? For relational deterioration?

2. Interpretative Questions
   a. Is it self-contradictory to say relationships are dynamic so be careful of generalizations in one part of the chapter and then provide generalizations as guidelines in another?
   b. What does the term *self* mean? The term *relationship*?
   c. Can you think of an example for each of Knapp's stages?

3. Evaluative Questions
   a. Do you think interpersonal communication impacts intrapersonal communication. Vice versa? Which has the greater effect?
   b. Do you think self-disclosure is natural? Is it the only way to come to know someone?
   c. Do you think Maslow's Hierarchy (1970) or Schutz's Needs (1966) still apply today?

4. Application Questions
   a. Create a list of examples of the stages of relational development and relational deterioration. Survey an equal number of men and women, asking whether any of the stages sound familiar, and document their responses. Compare your results.
   b. Create a list of Schutz's needs and ask people if there are any other needs that motivate people to form relationships. Do their responses fit within Schutz's three concepts, or did you create a new category?
   c. Record your self-talk in note form throughout the day. Do you notice any patterns?

Works Cited

Abbey, A. (1982). Sex differences in attributions of friendly behavior: Do males misperceive females' friendliness? *Journal of Personality and Social Psychology, 42*, 830–838.

Altman, I. & Taylor, D. (1973). *Social penetration: The development of interpersonal relationships.* New York: St. Martin's Press.

Back, G. & Wyden, P. (1973). *The intimate enemy: How to fight fair in love and marriage.* New York: Avon.

Berger, C. (1986). Response-uncertain outcome values in predicted relationships: Uncertainty reduction theory then and now. *Human Communication Research, 13*, 34–38.

Berger, C. & Calabrese, R. (1975). Some explorations in initial interactions and beyond: Toward a developmental theory of interpersonal communication. *Human Communication Research, 1*, 98–112.

Canary, D. & Stafford, L. (Eds.). (1992). *Communication and relational maintenance.* New York: Academic Press.

Carlson, R., Hart, R. & Eadie, W. (1979). Attitudes toward communication and the assessment of rhetorical sensitivity. *Communication Monographs, 47*, 1–22.

Gilligan, C. (1982). *In a different voice.* Cambridge, MA: Harvard University Press.

Gudykunst, W. B. (1995). Anxiety/uncertainty management theory. In R.W. Wiseman (Ed.), *Intercultural communication theory* (pp. 8–58). Thousands Oaks, CA: Sage.

Hagel, J. & Armstrong, A. (1997). *Net gain: Expanding markets through virtual communities.* Princeton, NJ: Harvard Business School Press.

Hart, R. (1972). The rhetoric of the true believer. *Speech Monographs, 38*, 249–261.

Hocker, J. L. & Wilmot, W. W. (1991). *Interpersonal conflict.* Dubuque, IA: William C. Brown.

Kellermann, K. & Reynolds, R. (1990). When ignorance is bliss: The role of motivation to reduce uncertainty in uncertainty reduction theory. *Human Research, 17*, 5–75.

Kessler, G. (1998). *Voices of wisdom: A multicultural philosophy reader* (3rd ed.). Belmont, CA: Wadsworth.

Knapp, M. (1978). *Social intercourse: From greeting to goodbye* (pp. 3–28). Boston: Allyn & Bacon.

Knapp, M. & Vangelisti, A. (1996). *Interpersonal communication and human relationships* (3rd ed., pp. 34–40). Boston: Allyn & Bacon.

Korzybski, A. (1933). *Science and sanity.* Lancaster, PA: International Non-Aristotelian Library Publishing.

Luft, J. (1970). *Group processes: An introduction to group dynamics* (pp. 11–14). Palo Alto, CA: National Press.

Mann, J. & Smuts, B. B. (1999). Behavioral development in wild bottlenose dolphin newborns. *Behaviour, 136*, 529–566.

Maslow, A. (1970). *Motivation and personality* (2nd ed., pp. 35–150). New York: Harper & Row.

Pearson, J. C. & Nelson, P. E. (1985). *Understanding and sharing: An introduction to speech communication* (3rd ed.). Dubuque, IA: William C. Brown.

Pearson, J., West, R. & Turner, L. (1998). *Gender & communication* (4th ed.). New York: McGraw-Hill.

Rosenfeld, L. (1979). Self-disclosure avoidance: Why I am afraid to tell you who I am. *Communication Monographs, 46*, 63–74.

Shedletsky, L. J. (1989). *Meaning and mind: An intrapersonal approach to human communication.* Bloomington, IN: ERIC Clearinghouse on Reading and Communication Skills. ED 308 566.

Schutz, W. (1966). *The interpersonal underworld* (pp. 13–20). Palo Alto, CA: Science and Behavior Books.

Stewart J. (Ed.) (1998). *Bridges, not walls : A book about interpersonal communication* (7th ed.). Dubuque, IL: McGraw-Hill.

Stokes, J., Fuehrer, A. & Childs, L. (1980). Gender differences in self-disclosure to various target persons. *Journal of Counseling Psychology, 27*, 192–198.

Sunnafrank, M. (1986). Predicted outcome value during initial interactions: A reformulation of uncertainty reduction theory. *Human Communication Research, 13*, 3–33.

Sunnafrank, M. (1990). Predicted outcome value and uncertainty reduction theory: A test of competing perspectives. *Human Communication Theory, 17*, 76–150.

Ting-Toomey, S. (1993). Communicative resourcefulness: An identity negotiation perspective: In R. Wiseman & J. Koester (Eds.), *Intercultural communication competence.* Newbury Park, CA: Sage.

Ting-Toomey, S. (1994). *The challenge of facework: Crosscultural and interpersonal issues.* Albany, NY: SUNY Press.

Ting-Toomey, S. (1998). Intercultural conflict styles: A face negotiation theory. In Y. Y. Kim & W. B. Gudykunst (Eds.), *Theories in intercultural communication.* Newbury Park, CA: Sage.

Tubbs, S. & Moss, S. (1999). *Human communication* (8th ed.). Dubuque, IL: McGraw-Hill.

Woods, J. (1997). *Communication in our lives.* Belmont, CA: Wadsworth.

Group Communication

Chapter Objectives

After completing this chapter, you should be able to:

1. Describe the types of groups.
2. Understand how groups meet our basic needs.
3. Define a group and identify how many members make a small group.
4. Understand how groups form rules and norms for interaction.
5. Identify and describe five steps for group problem-solving.
6. Identify and describe five types of group members.
7. Identify and describe positive and negative group member roles.
8. Understand how group members become leaders and the styles of leadership.

Introductory Exercise 7.1

Take a moment and write down the types of groups to which you belong or interact. Think of a week and which groups you interact with. Do you go to a chat room online? Post messages on a BBS or bulletin board? Do you go to club meetings? Or classes? List all the groups with which you interact.

Introductory Exercise 7.2

Now that you have considered groups to which you belong or interact, consider groups to which you are no longer a member. List the group(s) and try to write reasons associated with your decision to no longer participate in these groups.

Introductory Exercise 7.3 _____

Examining the list of groups to which you currently belong or interact, and the list of groups to which you no longer affiliate, consider what types of leaders you have come into contact with. This list may include previous or current supervisors, teachers, club presidents, or perhaps social groups and groups of friends. Try to write qualities that you associate with each leader.

> *Home is not where you live, but where they understand you.*
>
> —Christian Morgenstern

When you enter a new place with strangers all around, how does it make you feel? When you go home to a familiar environment and family members, do you feel differently? Do you ever feel like others have different expectations of you in distinct groups or settings? Do you ever feel at home or comfortable, where you can just be yourself? As humans, we form groups naturally, and as people, we are still learning all the different ways groups and individuals within groups interact, become members, and grow apart.

In this chapter you will learn about groups, like families and work groups; what makes group communication distinct from interpersonal communication; and how your participation in a group can be a rewarding experience.

Types of Groups

First let's examine the various types of groups. Look back at the list you created in the first exercise. How many different types of groups did you list? Did you write any of the following groups? Which groups did you list that are not in this table? Compare with a classmate, fellow student, or the entire class and see to what degree your lists are similar or different.

Family	Church	Social groups
Clubs	Work groups	Department
BBS or bulletin board	Committee	Online chat groups

Why do you belong to the groups you listed? Where do you feel you belong? Do you feel close to a group of friends? When you get together, what do you do? How does what you do as a group influence how the group becomes and stays "a group." Has anyone left a group that is important to you? Chances are that you have experienced a lot of what this chapter is all about. By learning about the various types of groups, what patterns are common to groups and leaders, and the various roles group member's play, you will increase your understanding of a fascinating area of communication.

How Groups Meet Our Basic Needs

Through conversations and a shared sense that you and your friends belong together, you meet many of your basic human needs, including the need to feel included and the need for love and affection (Shutz, 1966). **Primary groups** meet these kinds of needs for you. They are normally the most important groups to you and may include family, friends, clubs and social groups, or church.

Groups that meet some of your needs, but not to the extent of primary groups, are called secondary groups. **Secondary groups** generally include work groups, where the main goal is to complete a task or solve a problem. These groups have a clear purpose in mind—to build a faster car or a better web site interface, for example. In terms of problem-solving, work groups often help people accomplish far more as a group than they can as individuals. This occurs as people, each of whom have specialized skills or talents, come together in new combinations with new challenges. They approach these challenges, and through interaction, come to combine skills and new perspectives to formulate unique approaches that they themselves would not have formulated alone. Look back at the list you created and see if you can identify and categorize your groups into primary and secondary groups. See Case Study 7.1.

CASE STUDY 7.1 • *Television Violence and Group Interaction among Children*

Have you ever thought about how television influences children's behavior with peers or how they perceive the world? Communication researchers have been investigating this issue for more than 40 years, and a leading researcher testified before Congress that "(t)here can no longer be any doubt that heavy exposure to televised violence is one of the causes of aggressive behavior, crime, and violence in society. The evidence comes from both the laboratory and real-life studies" (Eron,1992, p. 1). Through these social science research studies, it has become possible "to predict some effects of violent viewing in conjunction with specific plot elements (Aidman, 1997):

- "**Aggressive Behavior.** Learning to use aggressive behavior is predicted to increase when the perpetrator is attractive, the violence is justified, weapons are present, the violence is graphic or extensive, the violence

CASE STUDY 7.1 • *Continued*

is realistic, the violence is rewarded, or the violence is presented in a humorous fashion. Conversely, the learning of aggression is inhibited by portrayals that show that violence is unjustified, show perpetrators of violence punished, or show the painful results of violence."

- **"Fearful Attitudes.** The effects of fearful attitudes about the real world may be increased by a number of features, including attractive victims of violence; unjustified violence; graphic, extensive, or realistic violence; and rewards to the perpetrator of violence. According to the work of George Gerbner and Larry Gross (1980), heavy viewers of violent content believe their world is meaner, scarier, and more dangerous than their lighter-viewing counterparts. When violence is punished on television, the expected effect is a decrease in fearful attitudes about the real world."

- **"Desensitization.** Desensitization to violence refers to the idea of increased toleration of violence. It is predicted from exposure to extensive or graphic portrayals and humorous portrayals of violence and is of particular concern as a long-term effect for heavy viewers of violent content. Some of the most violent programs are children's animated series in which violence is routinely intended to be funny, and realistic consequences of violence are not shown."

The debate over to whether or to what extent television violence influences children's behavior is a fascinating topic to investigate. Research the topic online and share your results in class.

How Many Members Does It Take to Make a Group?

Each group is made of members, but how many? As we discussed previously, when one person talks to himself or herself it's called **intrapersonal** communication. When two people communicate, it's often called **interpersonal** communication, and can range from not very personal to quite intimate. When a third person enters the group, the same level of closeness is no longer possible. With each additional group member, the number of possible interactions increases (Harris & Sherblom, 1999).

Number of group members	2	3	4	5	6	7	8
Number of possible interactions	2	9	28	75	186	441	1,056

Small groups contain three to eight people. With more than eight people the ability to have equal participation, where everyone has a chance to speak, be heard, listen, and respond, becomes difficult. Small groups need to have enough people to make sure there will be no lack of ideas and information but not so many people that the ideas and information that each brings cannot be shared (Galanes et al., 2000). Groups that grow to nine, ten, or more members often tend to break into smaller groups, subdividing the larger group.

Intrapersonal communication	One person
Interpersonal communication	Two people
Group communication	Three to eight people

Groups Play by Their Own Rules

Small-group communication is different than one-on-one communication. Have you ever participated in a group and tried to express an idea and found that you weren't able to get a word in the conversation? Taking turns is part of everyday life, from standing in line at the ATM machine to saying what you think around the dinner table. In small groups, the formal rules people follow in a meeting or class are not normally observed. In class, the instructor calls on each student in turn, and each person hopefully has a chance to speak. In a meeting, there is someone in charge who acts like the instructor, recognizing who gets to speak and when. Sometimes a leader will be designated in charge of a group, or someone will emerge to become leader, and they will help group members take turns. For the most part, however, group members' comments are spontaneous.

Here are a few helpful hints to get heard:
- Make sure you relate what you are trying to say to something someone else was saying
- Use common words
- Speak clearly

Problem Solving in Groups

One of the most common reasons groups form is to solve a problem. Once you are a member of a problem-solving group, one of the first challenges to address is how to go about solving the problem. One way that has shown results over time is John Dewey's reflective thinking sequence seven-step process (Adler, 1996).

1. Define the Problem

If the group doesn't understand the problem, how will they know if it is solved? One way to begin to understand is by clearly defining the problem. If the definition is too broad, the problem can seem overwhelming. If the problem is more specific, the problem may not seem so complex. In the following example, we have a web-based division of a "brick and mortar" company that needs to increase its customer base and ultimately sales:

Too Broad:	"Our numbers are down. We need more customers. How can we increase our web traffic?"
More Precise:	"Sales have dipped slightly. We need to better retain customers and attract new customers. We need to increase and diversify our customer base. How can we maximize customer resource management, ensuring quality customer service while encouraging new customer referrals from our existing customer base?"

2. Analyze the Problem

In the second step of the process, the group tries to learn more about the problem. Group members may be assigned "homework" where each one learns about specific areas of the problem to be studied.

Stan is the head of customer resource management. He oversees the handling of the customer from the point of initial contact through purchase and delivery and handles returns and complaints. Stan is interested in ways to better serve the customer, and through superior service, retain customers while attracting new ones. He will first study the cycle of customer service and see if there are any points, from order taking to returns, at which customers do not receive prompt and courteous service or where they report problems.

Andres is in charge of data management and handles the gathering, analysis, and presentation of information gathered in the supply chain, sales, and marketing. He will investigate two specific issues: (1) the age and gender distribution of our current customer population and (2) any points in the process at which the customer typically abandons his or her "basket."

Mary is responsible for products—both products currently offered and exploring new products to add to the line—and the discontinuation of products that are not performing well. She will analyze current sales and produce a report that specifically identifies how each product is presented to the customer, how each product is selling, and to what degree there may be issues in the supply chain where specific products may not always be in stock.

3. Establish Criteria

Next, the group needs to establish the criteria for a solution. After carefully analyzing the problem from diverse perspectives, group members have provided preliminary conclusions, from general to specific, that approach the problem from their knowledge base.

Stan: We need to clearly communicate to the customer at the time of purchase a reasonable estimate of the time of delivery.

    Customers report that the specific product they want is "never in stock." The interface is not capable of cross-checking inventory to provide instantaneous information concerning back-orders. It takes repeated communications to receive their product. Customers indicate that they want to save time but end up spending more time than "if I just went downtown, found parking, and went and bought the product myself."

Andres: Our customers are aged 30–50, with above-average incomes, and are not abandoning "baskets" at any specific, localized point in the process.

    Our customers are typically in the 30- to 50-year-old age range, with a near equal gender distribution between males and females, with above-average incomes. The average time for a sale, from product selection to processing payment option, is under one minute. No point in the process was found to more likely experience "basket abandonment."

Mary: We routinely sell out of specific products.

    There are nine products that we routinely sell out of, and we have failed to find a reliable source. In addition, the store downtown receives shipments first and then the product is received at our warehouse.

4. Consider Possible Solutions to the Problem

Now the group becomes creative, imagining all the possibilities to improve the product while trying to stay within the limitations. Someone should record the ideas because each idea may not work but may start a whole new process or solution later.

Stan: Create a cross-index feature, linking the product desired with a report of how many are in stock, which can identify stock in real time and communicate to the customer expected delays.

	Have customer service representatives respond quicker to orders that have products that are back-ordered, communicating the delay promptly to the customer.
	Create a referral premium, where existing customers can refer their friends and receive a discount for each referral.
Andres:	Expand our current customer base to include younger customers. Reexamine our product line, better track age to purchase information, and explore new product lines to broaden our base.
	Improve the data management features to deliver the best up-to-date information to the customer at the point of purchase, saving them time.
Mary:	Explore the supply side of the business and examine new sources for the product, routing of the product to the traditional store second, and alternatives to the product that may be more readily available.
	Explore new and related product lines that may appeal to customers in the 18- to 29-year-old age category.

5. Decide on a Solution

Through discussion, the group weighs the positive and negative aspects of each option against limitations and possible success. This may include a cost-benefit analysis of the time and resources necessary to accomplish each proposed solution.

Stan:	Integrate the cross-index feature as soon as possible.	High Cost
	Customer service representatives contact customers.	Medium Cost
	Premiums for referrals.	Medium Cost
Andres:	Develop cross-index feature.	High Cost
	Develop a better tracking system to correlate customers, age, and desired products.	Medium Cost
Mary:	Discuss with the corporate office the issue of supply and routing.	Low Cost
	Search for similar or alternative products.	Low Cost
	Search for related products that may appeal to younger customers.	Low Cost

6. Implement the Solution

On paper an idea may look good, but making it a reality is challenging. The group now puts their well-developed plan into action but chooses to delay certain solutions until they are prepared to handle possible outcomes. Stan recognizes that there is a problem getting the desired product to customers, so he can implement a customer service contact concerning the delay as soon as possible. Rather than attract new customers and not be able to fill their orders, he may elect to wait on the premium for referrals plan until the supply issue is resolved. Andres will work on the cross-index feature from the data management side and also examine better ways to track customers and sales. Mary will go to the corporate office first to discuss supply and also will initiate a search for similar, related, and possibly new products that they can add to their current line.

7. Follow up on the Solution

Not every idea works out as planned. Careful follow-up allows group members to know, according to their criteria, how well they solved the problem.

Stan:	Customers report satisfaction with the prompt replies, although they express concern over getting the desired products. The majority of orders are not cancelled.
Andres:	The problem of cross-indexing the information is a challenging one and will take time and resources, possibly even new software.
Mary:	The corporate office altered delivery routes, placing the online orders first in priority. She will actively explore alternatives.

We discussed a strategy to solve problems from beginning to end. In real life, problems do not always follow this process in a clear, distinct order, but knowledge of the process has enabled Stan, Andres, and Mary to work together effectively. Now let's examine the process of becoming a member of a group, staying a member, and finally leaving a group.

How Do Groups Develop?

Groups are dynamic systems that are in constant change. Group development, which involves growth and change across the group's lifecycle, occurs in all groups. Just like we examined with interpersonal relationships, groups grow together and eventually come apart. People join groups and others leave, producing a turnover that changes and transforms the very nature of the group. Group socialization, or how the group members interact with one another and form relationships, is an important part of group development.

To better understand group development and its lifecycle, many researchers have described the stages and phases groups go through, but most agree with Tuckman's model (1965), which specifies the usual order of the phases of group development.

Tuckman (1965) describes how groups form and come together in the **forming stage.** This stage is also called the orientation stage because individual group members, who are new to each other and can't predict each other's behavior, come to know each other. Individuals initially are tentative as they learn the purpose or goal of the groups as well as a little more about each other.

Individual group members become independent as they work together, and in the **storming stage,** there may be subtle or obvious conflict. There may be more than one way to approach the group's goal, and without a clear leader or a set agenda, group members may experience a sorting out period. Group members may side with one plan or another, or look to one member as leader and criticize rivals, and everyone may express on some level a sense of dissatisfaction with the group. While this may sound uncomfortable, it is generally considered a normal stage of development for the group.

As the group moves beyond division and forms a sense of consensus, the group becomes more cohesive and members begin to bond to one another. The **norming stage** is where the group forms norms for behavior and communication. Group members know one another better and can predict each other's behaviors more accurately, lowering tensions and reducing uncertainty. This stage is marked by less division and a heightened sense of unity, and members generally express more satisfaction with the group at this point.

After working together, the group reaches a point at which it can perform the designated task or achieve the goal. In the **performing stage,** productivity is key. Sometimes groups can get over conflicts and work well together but still not accomplish the group goals. The group may or may not reach this stage, but the next stage is one all groups eventually reach.

In the **adjourning stage,** the group dissolves and members go their separate ways. Group members, who were once independent and apart from the group, have gone through stages to become interdependent. This group interdependence may be hard to leave. Group members have changed and become accustomed to the norms, habits, and unique aspects of the group. The end of the group can come suddenly, or on schedule, but may be marked by the anxiety of separation.

Tuckman's Linear Model of Group Development

Stages	Activities
Forming	Group members come together and learn about each other and the purpose of the group.
Storming	Group members become more comfortable with each other. Conflicts between group members will arise, establishing status, rank, and roles in the group, as they feel more comfortable with one another.
Norming	Group members establish spoken or unspoken rules about how they communicate and how they are working toward a common goal.
Performing	The group reaches their goal and performs the goal.
Adjourning	With the job completed, the group members go their separate ways.

While Tuckman offers a useful model to understand group development, it is important to remember the socialization aspects within the group. **Group socialization** is the development of interpersonal relationships within a group context. You may have noticed how each stage is marked by communication interactions, both verbal and nonverbal, that contribute to conflict, conflict resolution, bonding, and separation. Group success is built on the foundation of the relationships that form as a part of group development. You can emphasize activities and environments that create a supportive group climate, paying attention to relationship messages as well as content messages. In the next section we will examine group socialization in relation to the group lifecycle.

Lifecycles of Groups

Think about a group you belong to—why did you choose it? Your choice to become a member of a group is one part of a predictable process called the **group lifecycle** (Moreland and Levine, 1982). Keep the group you thought about in mind as we go through the steps.

The first step is to investigate what the group is all about and why you should choose to participate. Collecting information through your five senses, and paying attention to what group members say and the way they say it, you'll start to make some general observations about the group. You may study information about the topic the group is formed around or learn more about the problem they are to solve. You're a **potential member.** Once your curiosity is satisfied and you decide to join the group, you move to the next step.

As a **new group member,** your level of acceptance by other group members will increase as you begin learning the group's rules—both spoken and unspoken (Fisher, 1970). When you have learned the rules, the other group members will view you as a full participating member, no longer an outsider or new. You have become a full member of the group.

Full members of the group enjoy the privilege of knowing the rules and customs and can even create new rules. New group members just entering the group look to full members for leadership and guidance. Full group members can control the agenda and have considerable influence on the group. There are many ways to know if you are a full group member.

One is ritual, where there is a ceremony marking your passage from new member to full member. A good example is a quinceñera, or a coming out party. In many Latin American cultures, the child, who is a new member of society and is learning society's rules, becomes a full member at age 15 through a ceremony held by her parents. After the ceremony, she is considered a full member of society, with both rights and responsibilities of membership. Another way is to watch and see who people listen to, who they look at, and where the attention is directed. Group members listen to full group members to learn information about the rules, to gain a better understanding of the central issue, and to express their participation.

Full members of a group, however, do not always agree on everything. Differences of opinion between group members often lead to people focusing on their differences instead of their similarities—how we are not like them. This leads to less communication and less interdependence. Group members then diverge, or come apart. They come apart in a variety of ways. When the group comes apart, the space between divergent group members often increases. As group members diverge they meet less frequently, so they do not share the same space they once did. Even if they still come together at the same time in the same room, **divergent group members** will sit apart and move to the margins of the room.

Communication also decreases as a group comes apart. Divergent group members have less eye contact and seek out each other's opinion less frequently. Finally, divergent group members begin to notice their differences. In the beginning of the process, group members investigated the group and found the members interesting and felt they could belong. This stage is the reverse, where once a person belongs, they start to see the differences and choose to become a more marginal member. **Marginal group members** start to look outside the group for their needs. Can you think of an example of a group that you once belonged to but have since left?

The last step of participating in a group is when the group member removes themselves from the group, becoming an **ex-member.** This means that they no longer participate and think of the group as something they once were involved with but they instead now belong to new groups and activities.

1. Potential member   Interested in becoming involved
2. New member   Wants to participate
3. Full member   Knows the "rules"
4. Divergent member   Not as interested in being involved
5. Ex-member   No longer involved

This process has no set timetable and may be different for everyone. One person might stay a full member for years, whereas another becomes marginal and leaves quickly. Some people may move back a step, reexamining why they should belong, or forward a step, and suddenly quit the group. Groups also come together and grow apart. Recognizing this process is an important part of being a group member.

Why Do People Stay in a Group?

Group members stay in a particular group for a variety of reasons. They may have been assigned to the group and come to feel a part of the group as they strive for a common purpose. People generally feel a commitment to a group if the group is well regarded and respected. They belong because they have an opportunity to share their skills and knowledge. They meet their **interpersonal needs** but also see their role within the larger group as productive. Group members celebrate reaching important stages, and their acknowledgement of success becomes self-reinforcing for group membership. **Group synergy** (Trenholm, 1995), the idea that two heads are better than one, works to reinforce the concept that everyone benefits from being part of the group and produces better outcomes as a group than individual members could by themselves. **Interdependence** is an important group function, and the feeling a group member has that he or she is contributing and making a difference encourages continued membership. Finally, group members that stay with groups perceive **support** from the group that reinforces their own commitment to continue membership.

Group Members Have Roles to Play

Not everyone can be the boss or there wouldn't be any workers. If we all do the same job in a group nothing gets done. These two observations underline the same idea—for a group to work effectively everyone has to do their job, and everyone must know what that job is. Groups have people who motivate others to be at the meeting, people who take notes on important decisions, people who gather information and bring it to the group, and people who coordinate activities and bring the coffee. Here is a table listing both positive and negative roles people sometimes play in a group setting

(Benne & Sheats, 1948). Do you find any group members that come to mind, past or present? Where do you fit?

Types of Roles

Positive Roles	Tasks
Initiator - coordinator	Suggests new ideas or new ways of looking at the problem
Elaborator	Builds on ideas and provides examples
Coordinator	Brings ideas, information, and suggestions together
Evaluator-critic	Evaluates ideas and provides constructive criticism
Recorder	Records ideas, examples, suggestions, and critiques

Negative Roles	Tasks
Dominator	Dominates discussion, not allowing others to take their turn
Recognition seeker	Relates discussion to their accomplishments, seeks attention
Special-interest pleader	Relates discussion to special interest or personal agenda
Blocker	Blocks attempts at consensus consistently
Joker or clown	Seeks attention through humor and distracts group members

Everyone is important and contributes to the group "feel" of being a group, but how do people know their roles? Most people either self-select a role or are assigned one. Perhaps you have a full-time job, children, and this group project. Your time is limited and you don't want to lead. You may self-select to follow rather than lead and to gather information on just one topic to contribute. If, on the other had, you do have the time, energy, and commitment to play a leadership role, you may want to show other group members your willingness, expertise on the topic, and superb organizational skills.

Factors that Influence Roles

Groups will vary by the number of people, their backgrounds, and the range of experiences they bring to the group. Perhaps you or other group members speak a second language, or English is not your first language, or you have traveled and seen how other people live. All of these experiences combine to contribute to your perception of how the world works, but in a different part of the world, people see the world operating by different sets of rules. One example is the value of conformity versus individuality. In cultures that value conformity, or the group over the individual, people seek to get along. In cultures that value individuality over conformity, competition and dissent are much more prevalent. Here are a few examples (Pearson & Nelson, 2000):

Collectivist cultures	Value conformity	Venezuela, Peru, Taiwan
Individualistic cultures	Value individual differences	United States, England

Another example of cultural differences that influence group dynamics is the ability to tolerate the unknown and uncertainty. In some cultures, equality among group members is the norm, and an individual's title is not necessarily needed. People often use first names in conversation rather than titles, and uncertainty about where someone comes from is normal. In other cultures, where a person comes from and their place in society is important and needs to be established to participate in group communication. Examples include (Pearson & Nelson, 2000):

Uncertainty-accepting cultures	Flexible rules are the norm; high tolerance for ambiguity	Australia, New Zealand
Uncertainty-rejecting cultures	Clear rules are expected; a rigid hierarchy is expected	Japan, Greece

One example of how two cultures can perceive a situation differently came when Michael Fay was arrested and pleaded guilty to vandalism charges in Singapore in 1994. His sentence was to be struck with a cane by a government official as punishment for his offense. Many people in the United States, Michael Fay's home country, perceived that his personal rights were violated when the sentence was carried out. Many Singaporeans regard group standards as more important that individual rights and saw it essential that Fay was treated the same as any citizen of Singapore. See Intercultural Communication 7.1.

When Groups Come Together Via Computers

The Internet, a system of connected computers, has brought people together in new and challenging ways. If you go to a search engine web site, such as Excite!, you will see "People and Chat" in bold letters, followed by a number, often more than ten thousand. This is the number of people in the "chat room" gathered to talk via e-mail. By clicking with your mouse on these words, this hyperlink takes you to the conversation.

INTERCULTURAL COMMUNICATION 7.1 • *Travel Information*

> If you would like to learn about other cultures, including helpful hints on intercultural communication, and if you plan to travel, the State Department has a web site that features a wealth of information on many countries: http://www.state.gov/index.html. Also available in text-only and K–12 editions.

Businesses as well are creating spaces for their employees to communicate online. The most common is e-mail, or electronic mail. Just like in face-to-face group communication settings, there are social customs and norms for communicating via computers.

A good example of an active BBS group can be found at Pelican Parts, a web-based company that supports an interactive bulletin board. Owners of Porsche® and BMW® automobiles and motorcycles can post messages and respond to one another. Both groups have a common connection through their choice of automobiles and have common concerns such as repair, maintenance, and modifications. As a BBS member, each person has an online name and develops an extended conversation with other owners, creating community, while allowing the sponsor company to build a strong customer base. You can examine this example at http://www.pelicanparts.com.

Groups form around common interests and vary from cars to fashion. Regardless of the forum, there are a number of guidelines members should be aware of when interacting in a chat room or posting on a BBS. *Netiquette* by Virginia Shea, can be found in electronic form at http://etiquette.net. Shea summarizes customs in the business setting, discusses how to argue, and even addresses issues of love and romance. She proposes that anyone participating in electronic-mediated communication remember that you are communicating with a human, someone who has feelings like you, and always communicate with respect for others. See Computer-Mediated Communication 7.1.

Some people use **emoticons** to add meaning to a message. An emoticon, sometimes called a **smiley,** is a symbol composed of a few text characters that represents an emotion (tilt your head left). As you can see, people can be pretty creative.

:-) or :)	Smiling, happy faces. For comments not intended to be taken seriously.
:-(or :(	Sad faces, showing disappointment
;-) or ;)	Winking faces, just joking
%-^	A Pablo Picasso fan

COMPUTER-MEDIATED COMMUNICATION 7.1 •
Participating in Groups on the Internet

There are many ways to connect to people on the Internet. Learning the rules before you jump into a chat room or post a message can be a positive way to become more comfortable with the technology while enhancing your own experience.

You may have questions that include:

- What is correct form for business mail?
- Guidelines for children participating in discussion groups?
- What is "Spamming?"
- Business e-mail practices and personal e-mail?
- How to maintain e-mail privacy?
- What are appropriate salutations and closing statements?
- How to get receipts and handle rudeness?
- What is offensive language on the Internet?
- How do you cite Internet resources?

One source for answers to these and many questions can be found at *The Net: User Guidelines and Netiquette,* by Arlene Rinaldi at:
http://www.fau.edu/netiquette/net/questions.html

In addition, you can also find guidelines for participating in groups at the Michigan Electronic Library at:
http://mel.lib.mi.us/internet/INET-netiquette.html

Group Members as Leaders

> *A person does not become a leader by virtue of the possession of some combination of traits, but the pattern of personal characteristics, activities, and goals of the followers. . . . The evidence suggests that leadership is a relation that exists between persons in a social situation, and that persons who are leaders in one situation may not necessarily be leaders in other situations.*
>
> —R. M. Stogdill (1948)

What does it take to make a leader? Think about the groups you belong to and their leaders. Does everyone always participate in the same way, regardless of the group, or are there some groups in which someone may be a leader, and in other settings they may be a follower? Take a moment and write some of the traits of leaders that come to mind.

Did you write intelligent and decisive? How about a good talker and sociable? How about a quick thinker with a good dose of common sense? If you wrote down any of these, you're right. If you wrote down traits that were not mentioned, you may also be right. No doubt if you participate in a class discussion about what traits leaders possess, you will have a diverse and rich list of traits, though not everyone would agree. That diversity of opinion wasn't always taken into consideration, and historically philosophers like Plato thought there was one ideal list of traits.

The universal traits approach is the theory that states there are some specific traits, such as intelligence and strength, that leaders have in common (Stogdill, 1974). This concept does not apply well in modern society, where people can be smart in many ways or physically limited and still lead groups to success. Simply, there are no traits that leaders possess that followers do not, and different traits serve different situations. The traits required to guide a classroom discussion are not the same as the traits required to lead a platoon under enemy fire or to coordinate the capture of a suspect. Finally, this idea assumes that just leaders are born that way, which means others are not. Have you ever seen a newspaper or online article saying that someone was a hero, saving a child from a fire, or finding resources for a community just hit by a tornado? Situations like this one happen every day at every level. Everyone has different strengths and weaknesses, and there are times when your strengths are the ones needed to solve the problem. Most are not as dramatic, but they do show us there is no exact ideal leadership style and that the situation matters.

> *The art of communication is the language of leadership.*
>
> —James Humes

How Does One Become a Leader?

Now that we've seen there are no specific leadership traits, let's examine how one becomes a leader. Perhaps you are not tall and handsome, and don't have a quick comeback to every comment someone makes. Does that make you less of a leader? Not at all. Your ability to think quickly, or to put ideas together and communicate them, or your ability to use a computer or to solve a math problem are all traits leaders need. Our specific blend of traits, given the situation, makes leaders out of all of us at one time or other.

Leadership varies from person to person, but researchers generally agree that these can be divided into three categories: the appointed leader, the elected leader, and the emergent leader (Harris & Sherblom, 1999).

Appointed Leader

An appointed leader is exactly that—someone of authority pointed at them and said you're it—you're the leader. There is no discussion among the group members as to who they would like to lead or whether the leader wants the new role. Can you think of an appointed leader?

Elected Leader

An elected leader means that there was an election and they won with a majority of votes. Examples include positions of leadership you are probably familiar with—mayor, senator, and president. These elections may be held in many contexts, including a stockholder's meeting or a general public election.

Emergent Leader

The emergent leader emerges from the group. There are two types of emergent leaders. The first is when a group has no leader and an individual comes forward to fill the role.

The second way a leader emerges is when a group has a leader but another member rises to a leadership role alongside the existing one. Someone may have a lot of knowledge about one subject that the group needs, and the person rises from expert to the position of leader. Have you ever been in a group when this has occurred? Can you think of other reasons why this might happen?

We have addressed the issue of how one becomes a leader. Now let's look at three classic types of leaders and see if you recognize any traits.

Autocratic Leader

The instructor finishes explaining a group problem-solving exercise to you and your group. You start to look toward each other and to discuss the exercise when one member says, "Here's what we'll do." He or she then proceeds to take over the discussion, assigning roles and duties, and you are left wondering who made him or her the boss. The answer is he or she did and you did. He or she chose to make the plan, and others followed along. There was no consideration of the thoughts or ideas of the group members.

A group with an autocratic leader has little group member input or discussion. Autocratic leaders tend to decide the best plan of action on their own. They are often "task oriented," making decisions about the who, what, how, where, when, and why aspects of the task. Can it ever be an advantage to have this kind of leader? Can you think of an example?

In a hospital setting, you wouldn't want the surgeon asking for discussion and a vote about what to do next when someone had a heart attack. In a military setting, you might need to trust in your platoon leader's orders while under enemy fire. Autocratic leaders serve a purpose in certain settings, but there are other styles of leadership that may be more effective depending on the group's needs.

Democratic Leader

The instructor finishes explaining a group problem-solving exercise to you and your group. You start to look toward each other and to discuss the exercise when one member says, "What will we do?" He or she then proceeds to lead the discussion and actively solicits others' opinions. The discussion is open, and each person has the opportunity to share.

This style of leadership can be very effective when individual group members possess a wide range of talents and ideas, when the group has not formed yet, or when the goal is not exactly clear. Through discussion and gathering of everyone's input, the group can examine more than one way to solve a problem. On the other hand, if the task is to perform surgery, a democratic style of leadership may not be effective.

No Initiative or Laissez-Faire Leader

The instructor finishes explaining a group problem-solving exercise to you and your group and assigns the role of leader to the student on your right. The instructor leaves and the leader is silent. The discussion starts slowly, and then someone starts talking and won't let anyone else speak. Group members look to the leader to facilitate the discussion, letting others take their turn, but the leader just listens. A good laizze-faire leader has the skill and expertise to know when to ask a good question to stimulate discussion or elicit comment from a quiet group member. A less skilled laizze-faire leader may not know when to facilitate discussion and when to direct attention to the task at hand.

Take just a minute to think about the three types of leaders you've read about and the traits we've discussed. How do the leadership styles fit in the groups to which you belong? Did the type of leadership ever affect the group's success?

The three previous styles have been studied extensively but reflect a traditional way of looking at a leader. To keep up with the times, let's take a look at three styles that may combine traits we've seen previously (Harris & Sherblom, 1999).

Leader as Technician

As our society becomes more dependent on technology, many of the problems we are confronted with, from city water issues to networking computers, require technical expertise and specialized education. When a group is formed to solve a problem involving technology, an expert in the area is often called on to lead. This can lead to the traditional autocratic style of leadership, which may present us with challenges. Electricians look at a system differently than water resource engineers, and if they do not listen to the pumps specialist, the water may never get where it is supposed to go. Specialization, or expertise in one area of knowledge, may influence the way an expert perceives the problem or possible solutions. The electrician may look at it from his or her area of specialty but might miss information that the other two group members have seen. An effective leader as technician combines the democratic style with technical knowledge to lead the decision-making process and facilitate information from the group to solve the problem. Knowing what you do not know can be as important as knowing what you do know.

Leader as Conductor

To understand this leadership style, imagine a symphony and the role of the conductor. The musicians that play the drums must coordinate with the violins, and they must coordinate with the trumpets, and they must coordinate with the flutes. It gets pretty complicated. One person helps bring each group of musicians together, blending their strengths into beautiful music. To be successful, the conductor or leader must know a lot about each group, or team of musicians, and particularly their instruments. Many conductors play a number of instruments and understand the difference between a trumpet and a French horn and when and how one should be heard. It's easy to see how this style of leadership runs the risk of micromanagement. Have you ever had a supervisor who asked you to do something and then stood over you, making sure you did it correctly? They are making sure you play your part, just like a conductor. Although the conductor may coordinate a group in creating a beautiful piece of music, there is no room for individual interpretation. If the lead violinist suddenly plays a solo or changes a couple of notes in a symphony, everyone will hear the chaos and the music that once sounded pleasurable will now sound irritating. Can you see where this leadership style might be effective in the same situations as the autocratic style?

Leader as Coach

Most people have worked with coaches sometime in their lives. You may even remember your favorite coach. What did they do that made them your favorite? Write the traits that come to mind in the margin.

You may have written that they helped you improve your skills, maybe they helped you improve your morale and got you motivated, or maybe they told you about their experience of how they overcame an obstacle that you had to deal with. Maybe they also pushed you to improve yourself. These are all positive traits of coaches, and it is easy to see how this kind of leader is many people's favorite.

Now that you've learned about the three current leadership styles, how can you relate these to a group to which you belong?

What traits could have a positive influence on the group? Peters and Austin (1985), two researchers in the study of group communication, answered that question, and they identified five important coaching roles.

1. Coaches orient and educate—they explain clearly the goals, positions, and skills needed to succeed.
2. Coaches nuture and encourage talents—they notice the individual talents of each member of the team and work with each person, strengthening the player and the team.
3. Coaches make corrections—they provide critical feedback on where individual players and the team needs to improve.
4. Coaches listen—they listen to players and offer helpful suggestions when problems interfere with peak performance.
5. Coaches confront problems that are not getting better—they can address important issues that, if not addressed, threaten the stability or even survival of the team.

What have we learned from this discussion of leadership? That people all possess traits that make them leaders. There is no one set of traits that make some people leaders and other not leaders. We've also learned that the situation matters. If you are a conductor in a symphony or a platoon Sargent, certain styles of leadership may be necessary. If you are in a business, or even a class, and you do not facilitate the sharing of experiences and knowledge, you may miss the key that solves the problem.

Summary

In this chapter we examined what is a group, the seven steps to problem solving, and why people become members of groups. We also examined group development, group socialization and the lifecycles of groups, how people come to be members, the various roles they play within the group, and how they eventually leave the group. We discussed leadership styles, examining different models of leadership, and recognized that each model has a distinct purpose.

For More Information

To learn more about small-group communication, Allyn & Bacon offers a comprehensive site at:
http://www.abacon.com/commstudies/groups/group.html

To learn more effective workplace communication, the COABE Incentive Grant Project by Nancy Hampson, Bobbi Paul, and Maxine Patrick-Williams offers practical lessons at:
http://www.workplace-eti.com/coabe/coabe.htm

Review Questions

1. Factual Questions
   a. How many people does it take for intrapersonal communication? For interpersonal communication? For small-group communication?
   b. What are the seven steps to problem solving?
   c. What are three reasons people stay in groups?

2. Interpretative Questions
   a. How do our basic needs influence our participation in groups?
   b. Do groups help us, harm us, or both?
   c. How does the lifecycle of group participation mirror the stages of interpersonal relationships? How is it different?

3. Evaluative Questions
   a. Is it possible to completely learn enough about how to problem solve in groups to be able to improve the outcome?
   b. Is it necessary to understand group communication to participate effectively?
   c. Can knowledge about group processes improve group communication?

4. Application Questions
   a. What do people consider their primary groups? Create a survey, identify a target sample size, conduct your survey, and compare the results.
   b. What groups or clubs are available on your campus? What percentage of the student population is involved? Investigate the issue and share your findings.
   c. Research one group that you would like to know more about. Compare the results.

Works Cited

Adler, R. (1996). *Communicating at work: Principles and practices for business and the professions.* Boston: McGraw-Hill.

Aidman, A. (1997). *Television violence: Content, context, and consequences.* Washington, DC: Education Resources Information Center (ERIC). Also available at: http://www.ed.gov/databases/ERIC_Digests/ed414078.html.

Benne, K. & Sheats, P. (1948). Functional roles of group members. *Journal of Social Issues, 4,* 41–49.

Eron, L. D. (1992, June 18). The impact of televised violence: Testimony on behalf of the American Psychological Association before the Senate Committee on Governmental Affairs, *Congressional Record,* 1.

Fisher, B. A. (1970). Decision emergence: Phases in group decision making. *Speech Monographs, 37,* 56–66.

Gerbner, G. & Gross, L. (1980). The violent face of television and its lessons. In E. L. Palmer & A. Dorr (Eds.), *Children and the faces of television: Teaching, violence, selling* (pp. 149–162). New York: Academic Press.

Galanes, G., Adams, K., & Brilhart, J. (2000). *Communication in groups: Applications and skills* (4th ed.). Boston: McGraw-Hill.

Harris, T. & Sherblom, J. (1999). *Small group and team communication* (pp. 8, 226–228, 232–234). Boston: Allyn & Bacon.

Moreland, R. & Levine, J. (1982). Socialization in small groups: Temporal changes in individual-group relations. *Advances in Experimental Social Psychology, 15,* 153.

Pearson, J. C. & Nelson, P. E. (2000). *An introduction to human communication: Understanding and sharing* (pp. 216–218). Boston: McGraw-Hill.

Peters, T., & Austin, N. (1985). *A passion for excellence: The leadership difference.* New York: Random House.

Shutz, W. (1966). *The interpersonal underworld* (pp. 13–20). Palo Alto, CA: Science and Behavior Books.

Stogdill, R. M. (1948). Personal factors associated with leadership: A survey of the literature. *Journal of Psychology, 25,* 35–71.

Stogdill, R. M. (1974). *Handbook of leadership: A survey of theory and research* (pp. 63–82). New York: The Free Press.

Trenholm, S. (1995). *Thinking through communication: An introduction to the study of human communication.* Boston: Allyn & Bacon.

Tuckman, B. (1965). Developmental sequence in small groups. *Psychological Bulletin, 63,* 384–399.

8

Communication at Work

Chapter Objectives

After completing this chapter, you should be able to:

1. Understand the importance of communication in the work environment.
2. Identify strategies to search for employment.
3. Identify and describe the interview process and the types of interviews.
4. Describe key qualities employers seek in applicants.
5. Identify and describe communication in meetings.

Introductory Exercise 8.1

Think for a moment about what you want to do for a living. What kind of profession would you like to work in, what kind of service would you like to provide, or what skills do you want to use as you work?

Look back at the first exercise at the beginning of Chapter 1. You examined the employment section of a newspaper for jobs you might be interested in and found the many different ways that communication skills are referenced in the job advertisements.

Now take the information you collected, or if you set it aside find another employment section of a newspaper, and create a list of all the types of communication from the areas we have studied in the areas you are interested in.

Compare your results with those of a friend or classmate.

Introductory Exercise 8.2

Interview a friend who has a job or a fellow co-worker, asking them specific questions about the types of communication skills they use on the job. Compare their responses to the information you gathered for Introductory Exercise 8.1. What did you find?

> *We certainly believe in communication at The Coca-Cola Company. It has helped to make ours the world's most widely known trademarked product. In addition to our corporate communicating, what our people say and the way they conduct themselves in the communities around us have played an important role in the high regard Coca-Cola enjoys around the world. Those contacts may be as small and informal as the conversation at the PTA meeting, or they may involve one of our executives addressing a large group, but whatever the occasion, that person speaking represents Coca-Cola to his or her audience.*
>
> *We encourage our people to communicate effectively by speaking directly, by knowing their subjects and audiences, and by speaking directly and listening attentively. The ability to do these things well is definitely a factor in how we judge the readiness of our managers to move up the corporate ladder.*
>
> —Roberto C. Goizueta, Former Chairman and
> CEO, The Coca-Cola Company

Consider this: If you work at a job for forty hours a week, take a two-week vacation each year, and have a twenty-five–year career, you've worked fifty thousand hours. This example fails to account for the many anticipated job changes you will make in your lifetime, all the retraining you will do to increase your knowledge and improve your skills, all the overtime you may work, and the delay in the anticipated retirement age. Work, like communication, is a dynamic process that changes as the need for skills and services change, shifts as markets move, and evolves as knowledge and technology develop.

In this chapter, we will discuss communication in the work environment, including researching potential employers, making connections with people who may know about positions as they become available or needed, interviewing, interpersonal interaction and listening skills, and the diverse ways you will communicate as part of employment. Apply what you've learned from experience and your understanding of material from previous chapters to these areas and you will see how important communication is in your work environment.

To illustrate the importance of communication, a 1997 survey of Fortune 500 company executives indicated that employers want employees who know how to communicate, get along well with others, are sensitive to differences in cultural perspectives, and make good decisions as individuals and in groups (American Council on Education, 1997; Seiler & Beall, 2000).

Effective communicators in the workplace, according to a number of surveys, can explain ideas clearly, can give good directions, can be good listeners, can work well with others, can deal sensitively with people of diverse backgrounds and cultures, and can represent their companies well in small group and large group settings. Personnel directors have described their needs in prospective employers as follows:

"Send me people who know how to speak, listen, and think, and I'll do the rest. I can train people in their specific job responsibilities, as long as they listen well, know how to think, and can express themselves well."

—Seiler and Beall, 2000, p. 7.

Given the importance of the job interview, do you think good communication skills are key? In fact, in related research, oral communication skills were identified as the number one factor, ahead of self-motivation, problem solving, decision making, leadership, work experience, and appearance (Maes et al., 1997).

In a survey of 480 companies and public organizations, communication abilities were ranked first among personal qualities of college graduates sought by employers.

—*The Wall Street Journal*, 12/29/98, p. A1

For many people, the job interview is an experience they do not look forward to, fearing that they will make a mistake. As we saw in the discussion of speech anxiety, one of the best ways to get the butterflies to fly in formation is to train them with practice and preparation. We'll examine constructive steps you can take before, during, and after your interview to help you be more aware of the process and your role. Have you ever taken a test you were not prepared for? How about a test over material you didn't have in class? How well did you perform? Now let's reverse the situation. Have you ever taken a test you were very prepared for, one where you knew the content and the material, and were ready to take? Now how did you perform? Most people do reasonably well when they have clear objectives, know what is expected of them, and have time and the opportunity to prepare and perform.

A job interview is both a test and a performance. It is a test of your knowledge and skills, and performance much like a speech. You hear questions and try to respond to each question while making sure you reference your skills, work experience, and appropriateness for the job. Wouldn't it be advantageous if you had the questions before the interview? In many cases, you actually do have the same or similar questions.

164   Chapter 8

www.ablongman.com/mclean

What Do You Know Already?

Chances are you already know a lot more than you think you do about the job you would like to have, people who work in that field, and possible interview questions. First let's look at who you know, and then we'll examine what you know. You may have heard the saying "It is not what you know, but who you know," and there is some truth in it. One researcher contacted 280 people in Boston who had taken a new job in the past year. He discovered that the majority found their jobs through people they knew but were not close to, like former college friends, colleagues, and friends of the family (Granovetter, 1973). Another researcher also found similar results and noted that associates and people we are less familiar with, but nonetheless in some way connected to, often know valuable information that can assist us in finding new jobs (Rogers, 1983). Give some thought to people you have known and stayed in contact with. Perhaps there are parents of a friend you played with as a child that will remember you. You may never know where the connection may assist you in your research, but getting the word out concerning what you are looking for means you enlist the help of several other sets of eyes and ears, and the more people helping you the better.

Now let's examine what you know. No doubt you have given serious consideration to what you want to do for a job or profession. You liked something about the field or area, and hopefully your curiosity led you to explore it. Perhaps you have examined related fields, talked to people who currently work or have worked in the past in the area you are considering, examined the employment advertisements to get an idea of basic and desired qualifications, and perhaps you even had an internship in your desired work environment. The accumulation of knowledge from your research and experience is what you know about the job right now. If you have missed any of these steps, it may be in your best interest to spend more time on background research, getting to know more in general terms about what you want to do or where you would like to work. Many college campuses have student counseling about employment, with tests to help reveal your strengths and weaknesses, interests and goals. Your investment in thoroughly researching your chosen profession or job is an investment in yourself, and considering that you may work more than fifty thousand hours in the job or a series of jobs, it is worth the effort.

From the information you have gathered, through interviews with people in the field, from books about your field, from discussions with your professors or colleagues, and via your research on basic and desired job qualifications, you can create a list that briefly summarizes what you know so far. Take a moment to write down simple words to reflect what you've gathered to date. You may want to consider keeping a journal, both as you complete this exercise and as you research your chosen job or profession.

What Do You Need to Know?

Once you have completed the list, you should reexamine it to see if there are any patterns. You may have lots of friends who work in the industry, and you may have even had an internship, but your background research into the field may be lacking. What is the turnover rate in the industry? What are the future prospects for the business? Are you preparing to becoming a video-player repairperson when the rest of the world is going digital? Looking at the big picture from a variety of sources will help you know more about your subject so that you can better adapt the information for yourself and to your audience, your future interviewer or employer. Perhaps you have done your homework and know about the growth and future in the industry, but you don't know anyone who actually works in the field. Look to your list to see where you are lacking information, and then try to fill in that gap. Do you know anyone who knows someone who does the job you want to do? Perhaps as part of this course you could interview an employer in your area of interest, stating that you are not actively seeking employment but rather researching the field. Again, consider keeping a journal to keep your information organized and accessible and to show yourself what you have learned as your research progresses. See Computer-Mediated Communication 8.1.

Making Contact

Once you have thoroughly investigated your field of interest and are confident that you want to work in the area, you need to identify potential employers you want to work for. You'll want to consider factors like location, potential for growth within the company, and the degree to which your skill set matches what the company needs. If you want to work overseas, look for employers who send their employees abroad rather than hiring people within the country (Intercultural Communication 8.1). If you want to reach a certain position, but know you lack experience, look for a job that will use some of your skills while allowing for growth and promotion to your goal.

You've Got the Invitation to Interview!

First of all, congratulations are in order. The invitation to interview means you already passed a series of tests. You have been found to have the basic qualifications, and now they want to learn more about you. It is now time to consider who is going to interview you and what they want to learn from you.

COMPUTER-MEDIATED COMMUNICATION 8.1 •
Investigating Employment on the Internet

There are many job and employment web sites, both nonprofit and commercial, that offer advice, guidance, and actual job listings. Here are a few popular sites:

To search for employment, with listings available and updated frequently, go to: www.monster.com

America's Job Bank is a searchable database of national job listings. Go to: http://www.ajb.dni.us/

CareerMosaic features job postings and resumes with special sections for college students. Go to:
http://www.headhunter.net/jobseeker/index.htm?siteid=cmhome

CareerBuilder offers job listings and career advice at:
http://www.careerbuilder.com/

CareerPath.com features an online search of newspaper employment ads from major U.S. cities at: http://www.careerpath.com/

CareerSite offers comprehensive employment services for employers and job seekers in all industries at: http://www.careersite.com/

If you have the opportunity, see if you can learn who is going to interview you. Will it be one individual or a group? Will it be a human resources professional or the supervisor who has hiring authority? Will it be a panel of people who work with the position? Audience analysis, or a clear understanding of your audience and their characteristics, is key to being prepared. The degree to which you can analyze your audience will help you better prepare, adapt, and feel comfortable with the interview process.

If you do not have the opportunity to learn who will be interviewing you, make some educated guesses and consider various scenarios. What can you learn about the company in general? How about the specific departments that interact with the position? Who is the supervisor for the position? Pretend you have interviews with each person, from a human resources professional to the boss. What information would they like to know when considering you for the position from their frame of reference? What has led them to offer the job in the first place? What skills or services does the position involve, and what needs does the employer have to be met by this position? Answering these questions and others you come up with will help you focus your preinterview preparation.

As you can see in Case Study 8.1, there are many interview questions that you are already familiar with. It may seem difficult to answers all the

INTERCULTURAL COMMUNICATION 8.1 • *Working Overseas*

Have you ever dreamed of working in another country? You can make your dream a reality if you research, prepare, and explore the many ways people have successfully gone to work abroad before you.

Consider a study-abroad term as a possible first step toward your goal. Many colleges and universities have programs that allow you to earn credit toward your degree while taking classes at universities outside the United States. Six months in a country will give you valuable first-hand experience, a better understanding of the culture and your ability to adapt, and perhaps important contacts for employment later.

You may also want to consider a volunteer position with the Peace Corp or want to teach English as a Second Language (ESL) to support your travel habit. This can provide you needed experience, develop your language skills, and make you more attractive to the overseas employer.

If you've got the skills and experience, then perhaps you are ready to explore the possibilities for employment. There are many sites available online that can give you guidance and referrals to position announcements.

To start your search, with questions to guide your research, questions to ask potential employers, and links to international job banks, go to: http://www.hendrix.edu/career/workingoverseas.htm

To learn more about working abroad, go to:
The Expat Network at: http://www.expatnetwork.co.uk/index.asp
OverseasJobs.com at: http://www.overseasjobs.com/

There is an informative article available from USA Today entitled *"Tips for Women Working Overseas"* at:
http://www.usatoday.com/2000/global/globe001.htm

Dave's ESL Café offers a wealth of information about teaching ESL abroad as well as actual position announcements at: http://www.eslcafe.com/

questions in preparation for the interview, but consider how the questions are similar. The questions have common themes that you can categorize into groups. Through practice, you can learn how to hear the interview question and recall how it is similar to a question you have prepared for, allowing you to adapt your response to the new question with the benefit of preparation. You will also want to examine these questions and categories, preparing and practicing responses for twice as many questions as you are likely to be asked. The better prepared you are, the more equipped you are to adapt to new questions in the interview process.

Now let's examine a popular but difficult question: "Tell me about yourself." This is not an invitation to tell your life story but rather an

CASE STUDY 8.1 • *Common Interview Questions*

1. Tell me about yourself.
2. Have you ever done this type of work before?
3. Why should we hire you?
4. What are your greatest strengths? Your weaknesses?
5. Give me an example of a time when you worked under pressure.
6. Why did you leave your last job?
7. How has your education prepared you for this position?
8. Why do you want to work here?
9. What are your long-range goals?
10. Are there any questions that you have?

There are also many resources available online that discuss common interview questions.

CareerBuilder.com offers a comprehensive site, with questions, guidance, and tips, at: http://www.careerbuilder.com/gh_int_htg_questions.html

Victory University of Wellington, New Zealand, offers both questions and guidelines for responses at:
http://www.vuw.ac.nz/st_services/careers/common.htm

To learn more about the job interview process, as well as job opportunities in Canada, go to:
http://jobsearchcanada.about.com/aboutcanada/jobsearchcanada/library/weekly/aa123099c.htm

opportunity to state a little about your background and experience, and how you came to acquire skills and knowledge central to the job. Try to include references to the basic qualifications, and include information about how your experience also relates to the desired qualifications. Employers typically focus on five key areas: educational background, work experience, knowledge of the company or organization and the specific job tasks, and your own career goals (Adler & Elmhorst, 1999). Consider them when preparing for your interview.

Your first interview may be a **telephone interview,** and it is important to understand the purpose of this type of interview as well as the medium in which you will be communicating. Telephone interviews are often used as a low-cost way of screening candidates that have met the required qualifications and of getting a sense of the person through a series of questions. Since the purpose is to screen, some candidates will be eliminated from the list, while others will move forward in the process. You'll want to be by the phone before the actual interview and be prepared, with your research on the company readily available in an easy-to-read format. You don't want to be hunting for information during the interview. You may want to make friends and family aware of the interview to prevent them from calling during your scheduled interview time. The employer will have a set schedule and will have brought people together specifically for this time with you.

Once the phone rings, typically the human resources professional will confirm that you are ready and then will introduce each person in the interview. Respond with a short hello, and write down each person's name. If there is an opening after the round of introductions, thank them for the opportunity to speak with them today. They will then ask you a series of questions, with some time at the end should you have any questions. Keep in mind that there is a set time for this interview, so keep your answers short and to the point, usually less than two minutes. Use your words effectively, underlining your experience and how it applies to each question, with connection to the stated (or unstated) needs of the employer. Brief examples can help capture interest and make you memorable, but be careful not to get carried away. After you have completed their questions, and if there is time remaining, you may have the opportunity to ask a question of your own. Perhaps you are interested in management style, or want to know examples of projects the person selected may be involved with, and here is your opportunity to research the potential employer further. Leave questions of salary for later in the process.

Keep in mind that you are communicating over the telephone, and your voice is the channel for your messages. The employer lacks the nonverbal cues present in face-to-face interactions, and your attention to the pauses, and when they are ready for you to answer, is important. Try not to overlap or interrupt, as the interruption may be accentuated simply because of the medium. Be enthusiastic, and it will carry through to your voice, encouraging people to listen. Before you leave the telephone interview, thank the employer for their time, and once you have finished, promptly write a thank you note to go out in the mail the same day. This simple act can reinforce your interest and help reinforce a positive perception of you as a potential employee.

The next type of interview may be a **personal interview.** A personal interview will feature verbal and nonverbal components, and you will want to consider both aspects as you prepare. How you **dress** is important. Professional dress is usually expected, and you will generally want to dress one level above what you believe the employer expects during the normal course of business. If tan slacks and a button-down, collared shirt are the standard, a well-fitting suit or dress may work well. Prepare your clothes ahead of time and have an alternate outfit should you need to change, spill something on your clothes, or otherwise find yourself needing a quick change of clothes.

Walking in the door, you should already **know the company or organization** from prior research. You should familiarize yourself with the company, getting a feel for the pace and the employees. Introduce yourself to the receptionist, and make sure you have time to be at the right place at the right time. Be courteous to everyone you meet. Employers have been known to consult secretaries about potential candidates, and should you come to work for the company, they will be able to assist your settling into your new role. You should also **know the job,** having a good idea of specific tasks and functions prior to the interview. Interviewing someone in the company or a similar company who works in a related position during your research phase can help you understand the position and give you a more insightful perspective. Always **consider the employer's needs** and how you can, through a combination of your education, training, and experience, meet those needs. The position was created for a reason, and your understanding of the job will help you prepare and be confident when your interview takes place.

When the interview starts, much like in the telephone interview, be attentive to cues from the employer. A brief hello, and firm handshake, and take your assigned seat. Taking notes while maintaining positive eye contact with each person present for the interview can communicate your interest and listening skills.

Be honest in your responses, drawing from your actual experience. You may remember the story of Pinocchio, where each lie makes his nose grow longer. Your employer may not catch your exaggeration, but your nonverbal communication may give you away. Regardless, you want to present yourself honestly and sincerely. Your goal is to obtain a job where you want to work, not one where your false impression of yourself sets up unreasonable expectations or one you grow to dislike months later only to have to start the search all over.

Be positive in your responses, discussing challenges and ways you solved problems in a positive way, demonstrating respect for people you have worked with in the past. If you are negative about a previous employer, this is not the place to demonstrate your feelings. Your employer is considering how well you would represent them, and negative communication will not serve you well.

Be brief in your responses, usually under two minutes, allowing for discussion and follow-up questions as you get to know each other. Keep in mind that brief should not be too short, where the response fails to answer the question. Instead, consider the content and your key examples, but watch out for getting off track or wandering in your response.

In addition, **incorporate "because"** into your response with a concrete example. If the interview question is "How do you handle deadlines?" an effective response is "I believe I am very good a working under a deadline because when I wrote for my college newspaper, I learned how to start promptly on an assignment and how to budget enough lead time to so that I always had my submission in on time." The "because clause" gives the interviewer more vivid detail to remember, encouraging active listening, and builds credibility through the effective use of evidence.

Finally, consider what you want to learn from the interviewer(s). What do you want to know about the company, possible opportunities for growth, or work abroad? Leave questions for salary until the interviewers decide to interview you again or offer the job.

In addition to the job interview, there are two other types of interviews. The first is the **information-gathering interview.** The purpose of this interview format is to gain information and insight into an area or subject from the person you are interviewing. They can offer a unique perspective, information, or referrals to new sources of information for you to explore. You can't get answers to the question "what is it like to work for Company X" from a book or perhaps an Internet site the way you can from an employee. More than one interview can broaden your base of information and give you a wider perspective.

The second type of interview is the **performance appraisal interview.** Once you have accepted the position, and have time on the job, you should anticipate periodic evaluations of your performance and productivity. The purpose of this interview format is to establish and strengthen a relationship between the employer and the employee, to inform the employee of how they are doing, to discuss what has been accomplished, and to set goals for future performance. You will know from specific job duties what the position involves, and taking notes while you work about projects completed and goals reached can help you prepare for the performance appraisal interview. Be aware of the specific duties your job description calls for, and keep notes so that when it comes time for your interview, you are prepared and can take advantage of the opportunity to showcase your accomplishments.

Effective Communication in Interpersonal Interaction

We previously examined language and communication and common barriers to effective communication. Now let's apply this knowledge to the work context. We'll start with using language that reduces possible misunderstandings. Specific, concrete terms are much less open to possible interpretation, and misinterpretation, than abstract terms. Using terms that can be easily understood the first time will help decrease misunderstandings. For example, if you send an order out for one hundred units to be sent to Miami University, make sure you write "Miami University in Ohio" or the shipper

COMPUTER-MEDIATED COMMUNICATION 8.2 • *Sexual Harassment*

Sexual harassment is a serious issue and one that you will want to investigate. Here are a few online resources:

The U.S. Equal Employment Opportunity Commission offers a comprehensive summary of facts involving sexual harassment at: http://www.eeoc.gov/facts/fs-sex.html

The University of North Carolina–Greensboro offers a site that provides a wealth of links at: http://library.uncg.edu/depts/docs/us/harass.html

You can also test your knowledge and learn more through *BusinessWeek's* interactive test at: http://www.businessweek.com/1997/41/b3548040.htm

might send it to Florida. Simpler terms are also preferred over more complex ones. As we saw in the discussion of jargon and doublespeak, words that abstract a concept can result in misunderstandings.

Demographers predict that in the year 2050, one of every two Americans in the United States will be black, Hispanic, or Asian American (Kikoski & Kikoski, 1996). Between now and then, the workplace will continue to become more culturally diverse. Not everyone will have the same cultural background as you or be familiar with your favorite clichés. Clichés and trigger words can lead to problems and misunderstandings. Clichés, or often-used phrases, may not be known by everyone you work with. Saying "You're such an early bird," or making a reference to the "early bird gets the worm" cliché may be misinterpreted by someone who is not familiar with the saying. Trigger words can cause an emotional response in some listeners who have strong emotional associations with them. For example, referring to the ability to manage money with a reference to Jews is both racist and offensive. Find concrete terms to describe the idea you are trying to communicate or simply say, "You certainly handle the money well in this organization."

Avoid using terms that have an **inherent language-based bias.** Gender-specific language, which fails to include a large percentage of the workforce, may inhibit the listener's desire to accept your information. Choose words like "law enforcement officer" as opposed to "policeman" to avoid a gender bias. Can you think of an example when abstract language or language-biased terms led to confusion or misunderstanding in the workplace or school environments?

Sexual harassment refers to a hostile work environment where sex is an issue in the course of completing job functions. The Civil Rights Act of 1964 and the many court cases that have followed focus on two types of sexual harassment. The first is *quid pro quo,* or "this for that," in which sexual favors are directly or indirectly attached to employment, such as promotions. Hostile work environment refers to both the verbal and nonverbal behaviors in the work environment that intimidate, offend, or are hostile. Avoid terms that are not appropriate, and treat everyone with respect in your verbal and nonverbal communication. See Computer-Mediated Communication 8.2.

Listening skills are also related to work communication, and lack of attention to them can lead to problems. Here are five barriers to effective listening that may impact workplace communication:

1. Physical barriers	Hearing for some can be a challenge. It may involve the vocal range of your voice combined with the selective hearing loss in that range by a co-worker. Modern hearing aids are increasingly effective in tailoring the amplified range to match the specific hearing loss of the individual.
2. Psychological barriers	You may be preoccupied, which may impact your ability to concentrate on the speaker. You may not listen unless you think the information directly benefits you. You may not want to reveal your lack of knowledge in a certain area. By focusing on the speaker and actively listening, finding value in the information regardless of its direct benefit to you, and being open to asking clarifying questions, you can improve your listening skills.
3. Sociocultural barriers	If someone speaks with an accent, you may focus on the accent and not on the content, creating psychological noise. Psychological noise, differences in need for context, differences in values, and cultural values of silence all impact the listening process. Being aware of these differences can be the first step to improving your ability to actively listen.
4. Assumptions	Predicting is an important skill in the communication process, but assuming you know what someone is going to say may influence your ability to hear the whole message. Effective communication requires interaction, and the responsibility lies with both sender and receiver.
5. Environmental barriers	Noise, interference, and even too much information at once can all be present in your work environment. By taking the time to have a conversation in a quieter setting, you may be able to listen better, get more out of the message, and communicate more effectively.

Praise and criticism are inherent in the work environment. You may hear your boss congratulate a team on reaching its goal or your supervisor asking you to work harder in a specific area. How praise and criticism are presented has a significant impact on their effectiveness and the degree to which they positively or negatively contribute to the work environment. Praise should be sincere and should follow several guidelines that reinforce its effectiveness. Make sure you offer **praise for specific tasks, performance, or activities** rather than vague generalities. For example, you might say, "Your extra effort in working with that client made the difference!" rather than "You work well with clients." Your praise will acknowledge the job well done and reinforce what you consider a job well done. **Incremental praise** at the completion of steps in progress toward a goal instead of just at completion of the project will both acknowledge incremental accomplishments and motivate employees as they work toward the next step in the process. For example, you might hold a staff party during the lunch hour to honor the completion of an important goal and then, toward the end of the lunch, lead a meeting that covers the next goal. **Criticism** should come in the form of a constructive goal, with a clear definition on an area to be improved, with suggestions to address the issue. Be careful not to allow criticism to become negative, as this can arouse feelings of defensiveness, impact the ability to effectively listen, and fail to constructively address the issue. Finally, **relay praise** from third parties such as customers or clients. "I want you to know the clients on this project told me directly how happy they are with your handling of their project" carries more weight than you just stating your own satisfaction with the employee's progress.

Effective Communication in Teams and Groups

Group communication is a dynamic process that involves leadership, purpose, and interactions distinct from interpersonal communication. As we've discussed previously, your ability to understand group communication will contribute to a positive group climate that draws on everyone's talents and expertise.

Here are five ways to promote effective communication in groups and teams:

1. Recognize goals	The group should set clear goals and objectives, with ways to measure progress. Recognize that you and others have personal goals but that your group goals should come first.

2. Establish positive group norms	Each group will create norms, but focusing on this task and establishing positive norms from the beginning can help everyone feel more comfortable and can contribute to a creative environment.
3. Focus on cohesiveness	Group members need to feel committed to the group and want to stay a part of it. Shared values, common goals, recognition of progress, and interdependence all contribute to cohesiveness.
4. Avoid groupthink	Although conflict may be uncomfortable at times, it is more desirable than all group members agreeing to tasks and ideas for the sake of group harmony.
5. Create a creative environment	Brainstorming, mapping, and engaging group discussions where individual members are allowed to share freely creates a more creative environment and discourages groupthink (Janis, 1983)

Effective Communication in Meetings

Meetings are part of the work environment and, like working in teams, require an understanding of the purpose of the meeting, what the group hopes to accomplish, and your role in the meeting. Here is a brief summary of the four common types of meetings you may encounter:

1. Sharing information or knowledge	Everyone brings a different skill set and level of experience to the group, and the sharing of information or knowledge is an important task. Be prepared when you gather, have your information organized, and use your active listening skills.
2. Problem solving	Problems are part of the work environment. Coming together to brainstorm solutions, or to delegate further information gathering to use to solve the problem, is key to effective problem solving. Bring your insight to the problem, use your active listening skills to gather insight from others, and record specific steps to solve the problem.

3. Decision making

Like problem solving, decision making is an important activity on the job. Employees may use information gathered after a problem-solving meeting to decide where to buy a product or service, to develop a new product to meet a need in the marketplace, or to set new group goals.

4. Social meetings

Relationships in the workplace are important to an interactive, dynamic work environment. Getting to know your co-workers while discussing a problem or possible decisions may also be a goal of meetings.

As we discussed in verbal communication, turn-taking (Sacks et al., 1974) is an important part of discussions. Be open to listening to others, giving them the time and space to complete their idea or sentence, and take turns with the goal clearly in mind. Side discussions can be productive, but you are gathered to learn from and benefit from each other in your job functions and ultimately the company or organization. Keep side discussion to a minimum and focus on effective listening habits. Finally, consider the cultural environment in which you work. As we have seen, silence is an important part of conversation in many cultures, and your ability to actively listen and adapt to distinct turn-taking styles will influence your ability to effectively participate in meetings.

Effective Communication in Virtual Meetings

We increasingly meet or gather in virtual space, either via a teleconference, videoconference, or, increasingly, online conferences. New technology and adaptations of existing technology allow us to connect in new and innovative ways without having to travel extensively, holding down costs while often allowing us to exchange information more effectively.

Teleconferences allow more than two people to have a discussion over the telephone. Job interviews, particularly information-gathering interviews, allow the company or organization to get to know the job candidate briefly without the expense of travel. This allows the committee or supervisor the ability to screen a larger number of candidates before selecting a few for face-to-face interviews. Intraorganization teleconferences may involve all of the types of meetings we have examined but again require less travel. Preparation and organization are still key to effective teleconferences. In this format for gathering, remember there are no visual cues, and the channel of voice and sound carries the messages. This can allow you to focus on the words but also means that turn-taking skills are important and that interference, such as background noise or the speaker's proximity to the microphone, may influence the quality of the sound.

Videoconferences allow a group to gather in an interactive television environment. Now you have both visual and vocal channels, allowing for a more lifelike meeting. Job interviews may also incorporate this meeting strategy, and with the proliferation of sites in locations such as Kinko's, the possibility that you may participate in this type of meeting is increasing. Like teleconferences, turn-taking skills are key, but you also add the dimension of dress and presentation, much like a speech, to establish your credibility. Videoconferences can bring together people in remote locations and allow for interaction that until recently was only feasible in a teleconference format.

Online conferences use the Internet and a private chat room or bulletin board to exchange information. Messages can be typed and read in real time, allowing for dynamic interaction with a large number of people. Turn-taking skills again are important, and the ability to follow the thread of the discussion cannot be underestimated. As in a teleconference setting, this format allows for only one channel, the written word, to convey your thoughts and ideas. Placing emphasis on concrete, specific terms can assist you in getting your message across in an online discussion. In addition, with the integration of visual images over high-speed and large-bandwidth lines connecting people, a hybrid videoconference is possible, with the added capability of sharing files or attaching documents.

Summary

In this chapter we examined the various types of interviews, including the preinterview phase of information gathering and preparation, and focused on skills to use in interview settings. We discussed interpersonal communication in the workplace, with an emphasis on sensitivity to the increasingly diverse workplace. Working in teams effectively means recognizing common problems, and we examined five common barriers to effective meetings. In addition, we discussed the various types of meetings, including virtual meetings, and how they are changing the work environment.

For More Information _____

To learn more about effective job interview skills, the CIBC Company maintains a website entitled "How to Succeed in a Job Interview" at:
http://www.cibc.com/inside/careers/hrr01dir/hrr07.html

Two additional sites that offer effective job interview tips are:
http://www.jobsearch.about.com/careers/jobsearch/library/weekly/aa061398.htm
http://www2.jobtrak.com/help_manuals/jobmanual/

To learn more about simple body language rules in the work environment, go to
USA TODAY by Anita Bruzzese of the Gannett News Service at:
http://www.usatoday.com/careers/news/usa024.htm

To learn more about turn-taking, see Robert E. Nofsinger's book *Everyday
Conversation*, published by Sage. ISBN: 0-8039-3310-X.

To learn more about online conferences, the Department of Communication
Studies at the University of Kansas maintains a website entitled "The Virtual
Meeting Assistant" at:
http://www.ukans.edu/cwis/units/coms2/vma/vms.htm

To learn more about communication in the work environment, Ronald B. Adler
and Jeanne M. Elmhort have a comprehensive text with a wealth of information
entitled *Communicating at Work: Principles and Practices for Business and the Professions*,
published by McGraw-Hill. ISBN: 0-07-303433-9.

Review Questions _____

1. Factual Questions
   a. What are three common interview questions?
   b. What are the five main areas in which employers ask questions?
   c. What are five barriers to effective meetings?

2. Interpretative Questions
   a. How does the interview process serve both potential employees and
      potential employers?
   b. What are successful strategies to learn of available positions?
   c. How does the process of interviewing mirror the stages of interpersonal
      relationships? How is it different?

3. Evaluative Questions
   a. Is it possible to completely learn enough about a company to anticipate
      possible needs?
   b. Is it necessary to understand the company's needs to interview effectively?
   c. Can knowledge about the company improve interview communication?

4. Application Questions
   a. What do people consider their tasks in a given position or job? Create a
      survey, identify people who hold similar positions, conduct your survey,
      and compare the results.
   b. What job-related resources are available on your campus? Investigate the
      issue and share your findings.
   c. Research one company or industry that you would like to know more
      about. Look for trends and identify possible needs. Compare your results.

Works Cited _____

Adler, R. & Elmhorst, J. (1999). *Communicating at work: Principles and practices for business and the professions.* New York: McGraw-Hill.

American Council on Education (1997). *Spanning the chasm: Corporate and academic cooperation to improve work-force preparation.* Washington, DC: American Council on Education.

Granovetter, M. (1973). The strength of weak ties. *American Journal of Sociology, 78,* 20–21.

Janis, I. (1983). *Groupthink: Psychological studies of policy decisions and fiascoes* (2nd ed.). Boston: Houghton Mifflin.

Kikoski, J. & Kikoski, C. (1996). *Reflexive communication in the culturally diverse workplace* (pp. 2–3). Westport, CT: Quorum.

Maes, J., Weldy, T. and Icenogle, M. (1997). Oral communication competency in the workplace. *Journal of Business Communication, 34,* 67–80.

Rogers, E. (1983). *Diffusion of innovations* (3rd ed.). New York: Free Press.

Sacks, H., Schegloff, E. & Jefferson, G. (1974). A simplest semantics for the organization of turn-taking for conversation. *Language, 50,* 696–735.

Seiler, W. & Beall, M. (2000). *Communication: Making connections* (4th ed.). Boston: Allyn & Bacon.

9

Mass Communication

Chapter Objectives _____

After completing this chapter, you should be able to:

1. Understand the importance of mass communication and its role in the communication process.
2. Identify and describe nine types of mass communication.
3. Describe the effects of mass communication.
4. Understand how mass communication is created and shaped and how it in turn influences our perception, culture, attitudes, and behavior.
5. Identify and describe ways to be a critical media consumer.

Introductory Exercise 9.1 _____

When were the following media invented?

Gutenberg Press	_____	Telephone	_____
Television	_____	Camera	_____
Wireless Communication	_____	Internet	_____
Radio	_____	Video Games	_____
Movies/Film	_____	Billboard	_____
Typewriter	_____	Paper	_____

Let's say you are a local business owner just starting out and you want people to know about your products, services, and location. If you want to communicate to yourself, you may use a PDA (Personal Digital Assistant) to keep notes of things to do or people to contact. If you want to communicate with one other person, you may speak to them in person, call, or send an e-mail. If you want to communicate with a group of people, how would you send them the message? You could not possibly speak to everyone, and calling each person might take you forever. You could, however, set up a listserve with your e-mail program, creating a list of everyone who should receive the message, create the message once, and click on "send." Mission accomplished. Or is it? Did you reach everyone? Are there some people you want to communicate with who do not have access to e-mail? Perhaps you want commuters on a nearby highway to know about your business. How would you reach them? Billboard? An advertisement on the radio? Flyers on their windshields at the local park-and-ride parking lot? You would probably have to use more than one way to communicate with people, because no one way is sufficient to reach everyone.

Reaching everyone is exactly what mass communication is all about. According to Alexis Tan, author of *Mass Communication Research and Theories* (1985, p.1), "The field of mass communication (includes) the study of mass media, the messages they generate, the audiences they attempt to reach, and their effects on these audiences." From this comprehensive perspective, we will define mass communication, examine the various types and effects of mass communication, and look critically at mass media and its messages.

What Is Mass Communication?

According to Wilson and Wilson (1998), "Mass communication is a process in which professional communicators using technological devices share messages over great distances to influence large audiences." Another way of saying it is mass communication is a form of communication in which a source addresses a large audience with the same or similar message. Mass communication is not direct communication, but just because it is not one-on-one does not mean it is not powerful or important. Indeed, mass communication has become one of the most powerful forces in our daily lives. We increasingly learn language, societal values, and even behaviors through mass communication.

Traditionally, the model of mass communication featured three major components: a source, "the media," and a large, diverse audience. The **source** could be you the businessperson with the new store and a desire to promote it. The **media** might be the local radio station that will do a live broadcast from your store and tell everyone listening, including (hopefully) those commuters driving by, all about your products and services. The **audience** would be all the listeners of that particular station at that specific time, regardless of their physical location.

Mass communication is transforming with the increasing prevalence of technology in individual's lives. The source and the media are merging at a rate never seen before. No longer are professional communicators the exclusive source of mass media messages.

Once it was the Gutenberg press, the first mechanical printing press, that revolutionized books, placing copies in the hands of people like never before. With the advent of closed-circuit television, desktop publishing, local- and wide-access networks, e-mail, and wireless communication, the source can communicate directly with employees, departments, customers, or suppliers in new and creative ways. The net result is more direct communication. You as an employer can e-mail everyone in the accounts receivable department with a department-specific message. Then you can produce an advertisement, make multiple copies, and send it out via traditional mail, sometimes called "snail mail" because of how long it takes to reach the receiver, to each customer on your list.

Traditional media remains a powerful force and will not disappear anytime soon, but it is changing rapidly. Let's examine the types of mass communication and see how they have changed over time, their functions, and their effects on society.

Types of Mass Communication

The Development of Newspapers

From Ice Age (after 25,000 BC) pictographic communication to hieroglyphic inscriptions in ancient Egypt (3100–3000 BC), people have long used symbols and pictures to capture events, tell stories, and share information with one another. The first known alphabet (seventeenth–sixteenth centuries BC), found in Palestine; the invention of paper (second century BC) and block printing (prior to 800 AD) in China; the first movable type (fifteenth century AD); and the Gutenberg printing press (1436) in Europe all contribute to the mass-produced newspapers we read today (Robinson, 1999). According to Lewis Mumford (1999, p.85), "The invention of printing from movable types is second only to the clock in its critical effect on our civilization."

Prior to the newspaper, and its historical versions, people still had a desire to get the news. How did they find out what was going on? According to John Thompson (1999), people in Europe generally got their information in one of four ways. First, those in charge, such as kings and monarchs, established their own communication systems to learn what was happening at a distance and throughout their territories. Business and commerce facilitated the second type of communication system, allowing early business-to-business communication. Third, they got it through the extensive network of the Catholic Church. Finally, travelers carried news with them as they traveled all over early Europe. Merchants and particularly traveling entertainers such as storytellers, ballad singers, and actors shared information with people in local areas.

Which of these four communication networks do you think the common person had access to? Did early kings and monarchs share their information with the villagers? Probably not. Did merchants share their business information? They might lose their competitive advantage. That leaves the Catholic Church and travelers as the two main sources of information for most people.

The printing press and the mass production of the written word took the information from the hands of the scribe, where someone hand-wrote a copy of the text, to the printer's workshop. From there it quickly made its way into the hands of the people and gave rise to an increase in the reading public (Eisenstein, 1999). Information, once held by a small group of people, was now in the hands of a much larger, and increasing, group of people. If knowledge is power, then this shift of information transferred power more than any other single event in history.

Newspapers in North America had a significant impact. Just like several hundred years before in Europe, the increased availability of information allowed people to have more control of their lives. In that role, the U.S. press has long been regarded as the "watchdog" of the American people against abuse by its own government. The First Amendment of the U.S. Constitution reads:

> Congress shall make no law respecting an establishment of religion, or prohibiting the free exercise thereof; or abridging the freedom of speech, or of the press, or of the right of the people peaceably to assemble, and to petition the Government for a redress of grievances.

We can see the important role of the press, but given this special role and its constitutionally protected status, some critics have warned of abuse of power by the press (Fallows, 1997), with their ability to selectively influence public opinion. Can you think of an example where you perceived that the press set the agenda, controlled discussion of an issue, or limited access to information? Conversely, can you think of an example where the U.S. government has been accused of similar actions? See Case Study 9.1.

People have also questioned the extent to which the First Amendment covers speech that advocates violence, or exploits minors, or is "offensive." The Supreme Court has made decisions that have impacted the freedom of speech, excluding some hate speech, child pornography, or speech that incites violence. These restrictions underline the interpretation that some types of speech fall outside the original intent of the First Amendment.

Modern newspapers have changed a great deal in the past one hundred years. Each town and city used to have its own newspaper, and with it

CASE STUDY 9.1 • *Censorship and the Internet*

Have you ever seen a blue ribbon icon on the Internet? Did you wonder what it meant?

The Federal Communications Decency Act of 1996, a controversial piece of legislation signed into law by President Clinton on February 8, 1996, banned the communication of "obscene or indecent" material via the Internet to anyone under 18 years of age (Telecommunications Act of 1996, Section 502, 47 U.S.C. § 223[a]).

People who opposed this legislation opposed censorship on the Internet. Proponents for legislation claimed that the Internet, just like other forms of media, required certain restrictions. Opponents organized a grassroots effort and utilized a blue ribbon in their campaign of solidarity.

On June 26, 1997, the United States Supreme Court declared the Communications Decency Act's ban on "indecent" Internet speech unconstitutional. Although the Court indicated in the majority opinion that it appreciated the law's purpose of protecting children from indecent material, it ruled that "[t]he interest in encouraging freedom of expression in a democratic society outweighs any theoretical but unproved benefit of censorship."

The interpretation of the First Amendment has and will continue to be a source of considerable debate. What do you think is appropriate limitation of free speech? Is it ever justified? Are there appropriate forms of censorship? Research this case study and gain a more in-depth understanding of the issues. Compare them in class or with classmates.

Telecommunications Act of 1996 http://www.fcc.gov/telecom.html

Electronic Privacy Information Center http://www.epic.org/cda/

came a wide diversity of ideas. As competition increased among all media and people became more mobile, daily newspapers gradually gave up afternoon editions and newspapers merged to pool their strengths. Now, relatively few media companies own many newspapers, regardless of their service area. What do you think may be possible outcomes of a decrease in this diversity of ownership?

In addition, newspapers have adopted writing styles, graphic presentations, and delivery methods from other forms of media. See Intercultural Communication 9.1. *USA Today* newspaper presents a wide range of information in small paragraphs with sidebar graphics that can be quickly read, adopting a more visually engaging format from other media, like television and magazines. The *Wall Street Journal* features almost no color but focuses instead on in-depth content in its area. Finally, newspapers have moved to the Internet to keep pace with the growth in electronic media, and many people now read their "newspaper" online, without ever holding a page.

INTERCULTURAL COMMUNICATION 9.1 • *Minorities in Print Cartoons*

> All comic characters, from Dagwood to Ming of Mongo, are socially significant in the sense that they propagate images that play upon our prejudices.
>
> —Jules Feiffer

Have you ever read the Sunday comics? Do you have any comic strips that you read frequently? Have you ever thought about the characters, who creates them, or how they are portrayed?

The history of print cartoons is fascinating, and which characters are popular, which strips are carried by a large number of newspapers (or increasingly online news sources), and how those characters are portrayed tell us a lot about what we want to see.

Print cartoons were first developed to attract interest and increase readership. Richard F. Outcault created the first comic strip character when he drew *The Yellow Kid*, a small child in a yellow nightshirt (Kanfer, 1994). In one of his first strips, Outcault demonstrated racist overtones that continued throughout the print life of his character. In one strip, he beats up a black child, dislocating his jaw. The child lies on the ground and a billy goat comes over and munches on the 'wool' of his hair.

Arthur Asa Berger conducted a comprehensive study of comic strips, and specifically described an African American character portrayed in an early strip called *The Katzenjammer Kids*. He wrote, "The blacks in the strip fitted into the stereotype of the time—the African savage with a fancy loin dress and names like "Captain Oozy Woopis" or "King Doo-Dab." In one strip, "Sammy Snowball," an African American child, is caught by the teacher playing with ink but is not punished. As the white children are punished, Sammy states, "Ise glad ise black" (Berger, 1973, p. 39). Berger follows up his description with a discussion of how the characters portrayed the accepted stereotypes of the era in which they were produced, with characters of color often portrayed as savages, ignorant, dependent on white characters, or as comic relief.

Minority characters in print cartoons have historically been the "butt of the joke" and suffered denigration, exaggeration, and exemplified overt racism (McLean, 1998). There have been changes, however, and modern comic strips are becoming increasingly diverse while eliminating many stereotypes. Read the Sunday comics in your local paper. Count the number of characters and decide whether they are primary or main characters, secondary characters, or tertiary or minor characters that play relatively minor roles. Compare your analysis with your classmates.

Magazines

Magazines offer specialized and focused content to readers (or viewers) via a printed and bound format or increasingly through the Internet. Magazines first became available in 1704 and quickly became popular, including the launching of the *Saturday Evening Post* in 1821 and *Reader's Digest* in 1922 (Wilson & Wilson, 1998). From magazines that focus on current affairs, such as *Newsweek* and *Time*, to magazines that focus on narrow interests, such as *Backpacker* and *Hot Rod Magazine*, magazines have become popular in America. See Computer-Mediated Communication 9.1.

Books

As we discussed previously, the Gutenberg press revolutionized the art of printing and allowed printed information to flow, over time, from the hands of the few to almost everyone. Modern books are divided into fiction and nonfiction categories and are often further categorized by their subject, reading level, and focus. Books are produced, like this one, to compile information in one handy place but also serve to tell stories, create new worlds, and excite our imagination. Books have evolved over time, and like other media, the Internet has had a significant impact. Authors could once only publish via publishing houses, and there were generally more manuscripts than organizations that wanted to publish them. Now individuals can publish themselves on the Internet by posting a web page with their content. Stephen King, a well-known and prolific author, became the first author to actively sell his writing directly to consumers through the Internet with the release of *Riding the Bullet* in 1999. Subscribers paid a fee and were allowed to download into their computer a chapter of the book at a time.

COMPUTER-MEDIATED COMMUNICATION 9.1 • *Web Sites of Major Newspapers and Magazines*

Here are a few major newspapers and magazines that also have significant online delivery formats:

USA Today	www.usatoday.com
The New York Times	www.nytimes.com
The Wall Street Journal	www.wsj.com
The Washington Post	www.washingtonpost.com
Newsweek	www.newsweek.com
Time	http://www.time.com/time/

He later followed up in 2000 with a second e-book (electronic book) entitled *The Plant* (Dubner, 2000). Although this first step to web-only publishing did not rival print book sales, it nonetheless indicates a trend in publishing books in the future.

Radio

Like newspapers, radio helped bring information to people in a new way and helped accelerate the movement toward a "mass society." Whereas newspapers came out once a day, or once a week, radio came on the moment something happened. This immediacy meant that regardless of where you were in the country, you could know about the event right away. This immediacy contributed to the sense of a larger, connected society and meant stiff competition for newspapers.

Early radiotelegraphy was used to send Morse code messages across great distances to communicate military, maritime, or civilian information. It was first viewed as a novelty, but the *Titanic* changed all that. In 1912, when the *Titanic* ocean liner hit an iceberg, it was able to radio for help, and it kept in contact with five different ships. Although many were lost in that tragedy, many were saved in their lifeboats by ships that heard the calls for help via radio.

Radio went from a hobby or a business tool to a mass medium from 1920 to 1930. This rapid change brought significant changes in U.S. society. People could increasingly access entertainment from the comfort of their own homes, tuning into radio dramas much like the "soap" operas of television, so called because of their soap company sponsorship, into hit programs. This meant people stayed home more, preferring to catch their favorite broadcast rather than go out and see a play or listen to an orchestra.

Radio in the 1930s became mainstream, and broadcast sports, dramas, comedies, and music programs were available in attractive formats in a way that drew large audiences and national attention. It also became a tool to bring people together, and President Franklin Roosevelt's fireside chats have long been called a milestone in radio history. Many programs from radio successfully made the transition to early television, and the combination of sound and the visual image only made the well-known characters even more popular. In 1952, mass communication pioneer Edward R. Murrow changed the name of his successful program "Hear it Now," covering news and international issues, to "See it Now," reflecting the transition to television (Wilson & Wilson, 1998).

Modern radio can be accessed by your car radio while driving to work, your portable radio and headphones while working out, or increasingly via your computer, where live broadcasts can be picked up or streamed in RealAudio, MP3, or XM into your computer from all over the world.

Music

Music has long held an important role in many cultures and has a powerful effect on the audience. From Chuck Berry to the Rolling Stones to Kid Rock, music has defined generations and served to communicate to large audiences individual points of view, values, and beliefs.

Recent discussion over the lyrics of rap music, for example, and the appropriateness of some content for young audiences has brought up issues of censorship, warning labels, and debates that certain kinds of music influence people in negative ways. When Elvis Presley first took the stage, many of the same arguments were heard, and many of the same debates held. Music has long been a means of expression to a large audience and a way in which to communicate values, beliefs, and points of view to the public.

In recent years, music as a mass medium has been more often referred to as the Music Industry. It's called an industry because it is big business, and the control and presentation of talent (singers) and content (songs) has become an important part of the U.S. economy.

In addition to entertaining us, music plays an important role of communicating our customs, beliefs, and traditions to future generations. Children in the United States are raised learning the alphabet song. Generations are defined in part by the style of music they listened to when they came of age. For some cultures, the preservation of music is an important way to record the language and its inherent values and beliefs. Sam Morris and other Nez Perce tribal members recorded traditional Native American songs and speeches on bees wax cylinder rolls in 1897, 1900, 1907, and 1909. These recordings, now converted to digital recordings, serve as an important historical record for not only the tribe but also historians, linguists, ethnomusicologists, and anthropologists (Nez Perce Tribe and Washington State University, 1995).

Music plays an important part in our daily lives, affecting our moods and helping us recall special moments. It influences our perception and how we see the world, much like newspapers and radio.

Photography

It has been said many times that a picture is worth a thousand words, and there is a reason that this cliché lives on—there is truth in it. Photographs do carry information in ways that no other medium can, capturing moments that can be studied endlessly. One clear example is the work of Edward S. Curtis.

In 1887 Curtis left his childhood home in Wisconsin for Seattle and the Puget Sound of Washington State. Although only nineteen years old, he was skilled with a camera and fascinated by the coastal Native American tribes. Many of these tribes had only signed treaties with the United States in the past twenty-five years, and their cultures were in many ways intact, but integration was bringing change to Native Americans. Curtis set out to produce a large inventory of images, preserving the culture and its traits through photographic record (Curtis, 1992).

> Alone with my campfire, I gaze about on the completely circling hilltop, crested with countless campfires around which are gathered people of a dying race. The gloom of the approaching night wraps itself around me. I feel that the life of these children of nature is like the dying day drawing to its end; only off in the West is the glorious light of the setting sun, telling us, perhaps, of light after darkness.
>
> —Edward S. Curtis, 1905

How does one capture this image? Curtis accomplished this through his photographs and attention to detail. His images today are studied for their record of customs and traditions that, through the process of cultural assimilation, have become lost. Native Americans endure, and reservations are reflecting a rebirth in interest in tradition, culture, and language. These images contribute to the wealth of information available for study and use.

Through photographs, we have captured moments in time and, in our captured expression, the emotions of that time. Newspapers incorporate photographs to convey information in an engaging way, both providing more information than a written transcript of the event and making information more readily accessible to everyone. Photographs and pictures, however, are changing too with the advent of electronic media.

We now see digital photographs where the "red eye" can be eliminated. We attend movies where each frame is a picture painted within a computer program, and the computer animation rivals real pictures or footage. The blur between objective photographs of reality, while never free of bias, and the complete fantasy of digitally enhanced or created images is increasing in modern media.

Billboards

With the expansion of highways across America came a new form of advertising, billboards. These large signs on the sides of highways communicate simple messages of where to get gas, a hotel room, or other information and services to countless travelers each day. Some people, like the Outdoor Advertising Association, consider them essential tools for the traveler and key to economic success for businesses along the roads. Other people, like the group Scenic America, consider them scenic pollution, blocking the view of beautiful scenery with intrusive advertising. Currently, twenty states limit the number and placement of billboards, and Vermont, Maine, Alaska, and Hawaii prohibit them (Shelton, 2000). National Public Radio

(NPR) reporter Missy Shelton broadcast a report on the proliferation of billboards on Missouri's roads. In response to the possible threat of legislation to halt billboard construction, construction prior to the election skyrocketed to more than fourteen thousand billboards, making many highways overrun with roadside advertisements (Shelton, 2000). Voters in the state narrowly defeated legislation to stop billboard construction. Billboards take a simple message and broadcast it via images and words, and their role and place in society is the source of continuing debate.

Movies

What is the last movie you saw? What about it do you remember? The special effects? The development of the story? The characters? Movies, motion pictures, or films are enjoyed by countless people worldwide every day.

In 1895, the Lumière brother's began projecting motion pictures in a Paris café, and Edwin S. Porter's *The Great Train Robbery* became the first U.S. film to tell a complete story in 1903 (Wilson & Wilson, 1998). Charlie Chaplin entertained us with silent comedies, and *Gone with the Wind* broke all box office records in 1939. George Lucas released *Star Wars* in 1977, and its latest edition continues to draw attention. From *Toy Story* to *Jumanji* to *Titanic*, movies have come to amaze audiences and play a central role in mass media (Wilson & Wilson, 1998).

Television

How many television sets do you have in your home? How often are they on? How much time do you spend watching television? Are you aware that television sets outnumber bathtubs in the United States? It is estimated that Americans own on average two television sets per home and watch on average seven hours a day (Wilson & Wilson, 1998). More time is spent watching television than any other single activity, besides sleeping. According to Wilson and Wilson (1998), it is believed that the average child will watch eighteen thousand hours of television by the time they reach age fifteen. In contrast, that same child will be in school only eleven thousand hours.

Television, invented in 1923, was not widely developed until 1941 because of World War II. Television borrowed a great deal from radio, and its popularity and access spread rapidly. Soon a main fixture in living rooms across the United States, television impacted interpersonal communication in family relationships. According to Lynn Spiegel (1999, p. 268), "the television set became a central figure in family relationships," transforming modes of communication.

Television has been both celebrated and condemned for its ability to educate and entertain. Some critics have seen the television as an important tool in education and socialization, with programs such as "Sesame Street" promoting early reading and predicting and reasoning skills to young children. Others have pointed to the violence in the media and the portrayal of violence in comical or playful contexts as having negative effects on society (Larsen, 1968). While this debate continues, the power and impact of television on the viewing individual and society has been significant.

Videogames

Videogames are relatively new within the field of mass communication, and the messages they portray have a powerful impact. Whether you are playing a first-person driving game, with your hands on a force-feedback wheel that makes the driving experience almost real, or a spy with a gun maneuvering back streets, the videogame is increasingly casting you, the player, as the central figure in a movielike experience.

Perhaps you remember Pong or Asteroids from the late 1970s, where quarters in the arcade versions generated astronomical sales overnight. From relatively simple games to increasingly complex 32-bit systems in 1993, Sega 's 1998 128-bit system, to Dreamcast, Xbox, GameCube, and PlayStation 2 systems, videogames have become more vivid and realistic each year.

The realism of the graphics and scenarios is often touted by the gaming industry, but at the same time videogames are described as fantasy, with players able to clearly perceive the difference. To make the games as real as possible, game producers use live motion sensors on real people to capture authentic motions within three-dimensional modeling. This means basketball players look and act just like basketball players. At the same time, scenarios that do not normally exist in the real world, such as first-person games involving killing others, are portrayed with the same realism. This merger of realism and fantasy, combined with the popularity of videogames, makes them an interesting new area of study.

How do videogames portray men, women, and minorities? If you have seen Duke Nukem, a hypermasculine character, or Lara Croft, a female with exaggerated proportions, you may have noticed how videogame characters reduce, simplify, and exaggerate features like traditional comic strip characters. Men are often portrayed in powerful roles, where action and might are prized, and females are often cast as "damsels in distress," in need of being rescued. Lara Croft as a character does not need to be saved, but her physical exaggeration nonetheless perpetuates a stereotypical image. Minority characters are often relegated to secondary or tertiary roles in videogames, as we often see in traditional comic strips. A game called *Kingpin*, for example, takes place in an inner city ghetto and reinforces both violent ghetto images and stereotypical images of African American characters. This too is changing in both comics and videogames, but difference is often enhanced, making it exotic or abnormal.

With videogame popularity rivaling television, and with crossover characters such as Lara Croft, who star in their own movies and videogames and are represented by live models at promotional events, videogames have become a powerful force within the mass media.

Internet

From the 1960s U.S. Defense Advanced Research Projects Agency (DARPA) and their development of linked computers via ARAPNET and the 1973 development of Transmission Control Protocol (TCP) and Internet Protocol (IP), allowing systematic computer-to-computer communication, the Internet has a fascinating history. The Internet is a relatively recent arrival in the world of mass communication. The U.S. National Science Foundation (NSF) began the development of the NSFNET in 1986 and now provides a major communication service for the Internet. Use of the Internet, essentially an unstructured web of computers worldwide linked via telephone lines, satellite, and microwave transmissions, has exploded in recent years. Just ten years after NSFNET came to serve as a major Internet conduit, Pacific Bell Telephone Company in California reported it had more minutes on its networks used by computers than people (Shore, 1996). More computers were talking to each other than people.

The Internet allows individual users to search for information on other computers, communicate with each other via e-mail and chat rooms, and gather and broadcast information in ways never previously possible. Once the gatekeepers of major newspapers, radio, or television stations selected what the number one story was for the morning edition or evening news. Now the concept of time and the notion that you have to wait until the newspaper arrives or the five o'clock news comes has been replaced by information immediacy. As soon as information is available, it can be uploaded to a web page and is immediately accessible by countless "viewers." Visits to web pages are measured as "hits" and reflect the now common idea that you can actively get the news that interests you when you want it rather than passively awaiting delivery or broadcast.

This news consumer activity has extended to increased individualization or customization of content based on the customer's specific interests. For example, rather than read a newspaper that has information designed to attract a wide audience, you can now register at no cost on web sites like Yahoo! and Altavista for your own "newspaper," or web page of content. This content is gathered from many of the news information services as it is posted and is presented on your specific page in the order and way you have previously selected.

This selectivity, and your visits to web pages of interest, can be tracked via small computer programs called cookies, stored in the cache file of your web browser on your computer hard drive. With these small programs that report back to the source or third-party computers, you can be recognized each time you visit a site, and everything, from the banner advertisements to the lead article or picture can be tailored to your demographic profile cross-indexed to your previous Internet activity. This level of mass customization, where general information can be presented in a myriad of specific ways based on individual characteristics, breaks out of the classic mass communication paradigm, where one message reaches a large audience. This new dimension of mass communication raises the possibility of increased efficiency but comes with risks, including loss of privacy and possible isolation, where you only see, hear, or read what interests you and miss common concerns in the community or country.

Functions of Mass Communication

According to Charles Wright (1975), mass media has four important functions, surveillance, correlation, cultural transmission, and entertainment. **Surveillance** is the "watchdog" function previously described in newspapers, where the media watches those in authority for signs of abuse or misconduct. It involves the active gathering and disseminating of information to the audience through the specific medium, print, radio, or television, for example. **Correlation** takes surveillance and adds a new dimension, the analysis and evaluation of information. This interpretation places a value on some information over other information and impacts the information you receive. **Cultural transmission** involves the display of social codes and behaviors, including those involving values and priorities, ways of social interaction, and customs that are "normal" in mainstream society. People view the interaction of characters within the context of a television program or film and internalize these patterns of behavior in their own lives, with the characters serving as role models. Finally, **entertainment** is a distraction from everyday life, allowing the audience to see a different perspective, world, or even galaxy that in real life does not exist. Entertainment appeals to our sense of curiosity and provides a way to "escape" from our daily lives.

Effects of Mass Communication

Mass communication is a powerful force, with a long history in the United States. As we have seen, this force has an effect on the audience, shaping attitudes, opinions, values, and sense of priorities.

Gatekeeping, according to Pearson and Nelson (2000, p. 133), is "a process of determining what news, information, or entertainment will reach a mass audience." The term "gatekeeping" was originally used by Kurt Lewin as a metaphor, featuring a series of gates that information must pass through before ever reaching the audience (Wilson & Wilson, 1998). Gates and gate-keepers may include media owners, editors, or even the individual reporter. Another function of gatekeeping is **agenda setting.** Setting the agenda, just like the agenda of a meeting, means selecting what the audience will see and hear and in what order. Who decides what is the number one story on the evening news? According to Wilson and Wilson (1998), professional communicators who work in the media industry set the agenda for us.

In addition to gatekeeping and agenda setting, the media **shapes attitudes and behavior.** This is done through framing and content. **Framing** involves placing an imaginary frame, much like a frame around a picture or a window, around a story. What lies within the frame that we can see? What lies outside of the frame that we cannot see? Which way does the window face? All of these variables impact our perspective, and by the acts of gatekeeping and agenda setting, the media frames the stories we see and information we learn. **Content** means, like framing, what is in the program that we can see and/or hear. People sometimes imitate what they see and hear, and in the case of media and its effects on individuals, this effect can be dangerous. Take for example the case of Touchstone Films and a movie about football players. In one scene, to demonstrate their "courage," the football players would lie on the highway at night as cars rushed past. After viewing the film, there were several young men nationwide that imitated the scene and died as a result (Wilson & Wilson, 1998). Links of violent behavior and television displays of violence, while long suspected, have yet to be conclusively proven. Nonetheless, there is increasing evidence that indicates a link and is a topic of increased communication research.

According to Pearson and Nelson (2000, p. 132), **culture within the context of mass communication** is "a set of beliefs and understandings a society has about the world, its place in it, and the various activities used to celebrate and reinforce those beliefs." Themes of independence, overcoming challenging circumstances, and hard-fought victory are seen repeatedly in U.S. programming and reflect an aspect of U.S. culture. In the case of football, it is sometimes viewed as a male sport, and its importance on Thanksgiving Day is nothing short of a ritual for many Americans. In you went to a country in Latin America, you would probably find the television set tuned to a soccer game, where soccer is the revered sport. What do these sports say about culture? One might interpret that U.S. football is aggressive and that although the team is important, the individual's effort and record are celebrated in all the time between plays. Significant attention is given to how much each individual player makes for a salary. In South American football or soccer, the announcer emphasis is on the team, and at breaks, some discussion of key players is present, but not to the same degree, though this is changing.

What do these differences tell us? Our interpretation of these differences may point toward ways in which the media reinforces national culture and its values, but take care not to overgeneralize. To state that U.S. football is a male-viewer–dominated sport may be an accurate observation, but to exclude women when discussing the sport would lead to a generalization that is not accurate and may even perpetuate a stereotype.

The media is an active participant in the perpetuation of stereotypes in many ways. Julia Wood (1994) makes an interesting observation of the world according to television:

> It is a world in which males make up two-thirds of the population. The women are fewer in number perhaps because less than 10 percent live beyond 35. Those who do, like their male counterparts and the younger females, are nearly all white and heterosexual. In addition to being young, the majority of women are beautiful, very thin, passive, and primarily concerned with relationships and getting rings out of collars and commodes.
>
> —Pearson and Nelson, 2000, p. 136

This limited view, itself a product of gatekeeping, agenda setting, and the profit motive, has little connection to the "real world." Most people are not rich. Most people are not the projected "ideal" body type. Many people, particularly in a diverse country that is undergoing dramatic demographic changes, are not members of just one racial, ethnic, or cultural group but rather are members of many groups.

Critical Analysis of Mass Communication

By now we have examined the definition of mass communication, explored various types and their functions, and come to recognize the powerful force of the mass media. Who would you rather have control your view of the world—the media or you? Be a critical consumer of mass communication. Ask yourself the following eight questions when you read a newspaper, watch a movie, or go to a web page. The questions will help you focus on getting information you need while recognizing its limitations, exaggerations, and distortions.

1. What Is the Goal?

Professional communicators want to inform you, but they also want to make a living. Who decided what was important and how I should see and/or hear it? The function of correlation, the analysis of an issue, in addition to surveillance, the gathering of information, leads to gatekeeping and agenda setting—choosing what the gatekeeper wants you to see is often based on the assumption of what they think you want to see.

This allows the media to sell advertising space based on past performance and projections of how large and what the demographic traits of an audience will be. This selection of content, including news, is tied to how large and what type of audience a program attracts. While the media plays an important role as a "watchdog," never forget that the dog needs to eat (or make a living).

2. Is the Problem as Important as It Is Portrayed?

This question expands on the previous question, allowing you to look more closely at it, within the agenda the media has established. Is the number one or two story really as important as it appears to be? What evidence is offered to support this claim and from whom is the evidence offered?

3. Is There Enough Evidence Presented to Justify the Claim or Main Point?

This question builds on the experience of the two previous questions, asking you to examine the credibility of the sources and the evidence supplied as justification for the main point of the story. If the main claim or point is that the sky is falling, and the only evidence is a Professor Chicken Little and his single observational study, you may want to question the claim and look for more evidence. As in the scientific process, one needs to gather as much information to prove or disprove the hypothesis, claim, or main point based on that information.

4. What Has Not Been Said?

As we have seen previously, the importance of silence as a component of communication cannot be understated. Silence can speak volumes. If a story is aired that features extensive interviews with the sources that were willing to talk to the media but offers nothing "from the other side," be careful not to believe only in the side of the issue presented. What information has been left out? What information did not make it past the gatekeeper(s)? What did not make it on the agenda? Lack or omission of information can give you important clues about the validity of the story and the credibility of the evidence.

5. Have Sources Been Provided?

"Anonymous sources close to the President" is not as credible as "According to the President's Official Spokesperson." Anonymous information has no direct source, and although some people may not want to talk "on the record," it is harder to substantiate. Some editors used to refuse to publish or broadcast any information that came from an anonymous source to prevent gossip and innuendo from becoming de facto truth simply because it appears on the news agenda. Failure to reference sources and give credit where credit is due is a clear sign that the information being provided needs further evaluation.

6. How Credible Are the Sources?

Credibility, or *ethos* according to Aristotle, is one of the key features in an effective presenter. Lack of credibility means the audience will not believe what the speaker is saying, and may even decline to listen to him or her. Is the source of the information someone who should know about the subject in question? What is their experience in the field? Their education and background? Why were they chosen to speak on the topic? All of these questions lead to an assessment of a source's credibility and the degree to which you should consider their information valuable and accurate.

7. Are the Arguments Logical?

"If all humans are mortal, and I am human, I therefore must be mortal." This example of classic logic illustrates logical model rarely found in media today. More often than not, the logic goes like this: "Attractive young people like this brand. You want to be young and attractive so buy this brand." This second example is not logical. The assertion that attractive young people like this brand should be questioned. Do they really like this brand? If so why? Who studied young people's buying preferences and made the claim? The same people selling the brand? How would its purchase alter your life, and is the ideal represented a worthy goal for you? We use logical short cuts like "If it costs more it must be better," or "This new product is made by a company I know so it must be good" all the time. Thinking for yourself and questioning the information presented and the logic (or lack thereof) is an important skill. Logical short cuts are used to persuade us as well, and our knowledge of them can help us be better consumers of mass communication.

8. Has the Message Tried to Manipulate Me by Appealing to Emotions or Needs I May Have?

This question builds on the previous question concerning logic. If a program or advertisement attempts to influence you and its main appeal is to your emotions or sense of goodwill, it is a fair question to ask, "Where is the evidence?" While appeals to emotions can be effective, they should be suspect for the implication we should only use our "hearts" and not our minds.

Summary

In this chapter we discussed the role, types, functions, and effects of mass communication. Within each type of mass communication, we examined the changes over time and how each medium is continuing to change. Finally, we discussed ways to critically analyze mass communication and looked at several questions to ask to help us be more informed consumers of mass media.

For More Information _____

To learn more about Edward S. Curtis's photographic collection, go to: http://www.curtis-collection.com

To learn more about the Sam Morris Collection, contact the Northwest Interpretative Association at: http://www.nps.gov/whmi/nwia.htm

To listen to KSMU reporter Missy Shelton's report on billboards, broadcast during the show Morning Edition on December 7, 2000, go to: http://search.npr.org/cf/cmn/cmnpd01fm.cfm?PrgDate=12%2F07%2F2000&PrgID=3

To learn more about Stephen King and his role in e-publishing, go to: http://www.nytimes.com/books/97/03/09/lifetimes/king.html

To learn more about media analysis and critique, read Arthur Asa Berger's (1991) *Media Analysis Techniques,* Newbury Park: Sage. ISBN: 0803943628.

To learn more about videogames and their history, go to: http://www.videogamespot.com/features/universal/hov/index.html

Review Questions _____

1. Factual Questions
   a. What are the types of mass communication?
   b. According to Charles Wright (1975), what are the four functions of the mass media?
   c. What are eight questions to help critically analyze the media?

2. Interpretative Questions
   a. Will all print media become electronic in the future?
   b. Is there fair and equal access to computers in the United States to allow for equal distribution of information via the Internet?
   c. To what degree is there diversity of content in traditional media (newspapers, books, magazines, music, radio, television, and movies)? Is there more or less diversity of content on the Internet?

3. Evaluative Questions
   a. Do you think mass communication is a powerful force in America today? Which type of mass communication has the greatest effect or impact?
   b. Do you think billboards are useful or scenic pollution?
   c. Do you think gatekeepers make decisions about content and order or priority based on your needs as a media consumer, their needs as a media producer, or both?

4. Application Questions
   a. Create a list of your favorite newspaper, movies, television programs, or similar types of mass communication. Ask your friend to do the same. Compare your results and see where you prefer to get your information and entertainment.
   b. Create a list of Schutz's interpersonal needs and ask people why they watch, read, view, or listen to mass media. Do their responses fit within Schutz's three concepts?
   c. Consider to what degree mass communication has influenced and shaped your view of the world. Discuss Julia Wood's view of "television-land" and how it relates to "reality."

Works Cited

Berger, A. (1973). *The comic-stripped American: What Dick Tracy, Blondie, Daddy Warbucks, and Charlie Brown tell us about ourselves.* Baltimore: Penguin Books.

Curtis, E. S. (1992). *Portraits from North American Indian life* (p. viii). New York: Promontory Press. Reprint of a 1907 limited edition text.

Dubner, S. (2000, August 13). What is Stephen King trying to prove? *The New York Times* web site. Available at: http://www.nytimes.com/library/magazine/home/20000813mag king.html.

Eisenstein, E. (1999). The rise of the reading public.. In D. Crowley & P. Heyer (Eds.), *Communication in history,* (3rd ed.). New York: Addison, Wesley, Longman.

Fallows, J. (1997). *Breaking the news: How the media undermine American democracy.* New York: Random House.

Kanfer, S. (1994, May/June). From the *Yellow Kid* to yellow journalism. *Civilization: The magazine of the Library of Congress, 2 (3),* 32–37.

Larsen, O. (1968). *Violence and the mass media.* New York: Harper & Row.

McLean, S. (1998). Minority representation and portrayal in cartoons. In Y. Kamalipour & T. Carilli (Eds.), *Cultural diversity and the U.S. media.* New York: State University of New York Press (SUNY).

Mumford, L. (1999). The invention of printing. In D. Crowley & P. Heyer (Eds.), *Communication in history* (3rd ed.). New York: Addison, Wesley, Longman.

Nez Perce Tribe and Washington State University. (1995). *Nez Perce music archive: The Sam Morris collection.* Seattle, WA: Northwest Interpretive Association. Two volumes on compact disc.

Pearson, J. & Nelson, P. (2000). *An introduction to human communication* (8th ed.). Boston: McGraw-Hill.

Robinson, A. (1999). The origins of writing. In D. Crowley & P. Heyer (Eds.), *Communication in history* (3rd ed.). New York: Addison, Wesley, Longman.

Shelton, M. (2000, December 7). Billboards in Missouri. In *Morning Edition* (3:37). Washington, DC: National Public Radio.

Shore, N. (1996, July 8). Phone users face splitting headache. *Long Beach Press-Telegram,*
    p. A1.
Spiegel, L. (1999). Making room for TV. In D. Crowley & P. Heyer (Eds.), *Communication in
    history* (3rd ed.). New York: Addison, Wesley, Longman.
Tan, A. (1985). *Mass communication theories and research* (2nd ed.). New York: Macmillan.
Thompson, J. (1999). The trade in news. In D. Crowley & P. Heyer, *Communication in history*
    (3rd ed.). New York: Addison, Wesley, Longman.
Wilson, J. & Wilson, S. (1998). *Mass media/mass culture* (4th ed., pp. 261–275). New York:
    McGraw-Hill.
Wood, J. T. (1994). Gendered lives: Communication, gender, and culture (pp. 231–244).
    Newbury Park, CA: Wadsworth.
Wright, C. (1975). *Mass communication: A sociological perspective* (2nd ed., pp. 8–22). New York:
    Random House.

Speech Preparation

Chapter Objectives

After completing this chapter, you should be able to:

1. Describe how to choose a topic for a speech or oral presentation.
2. Conduct an audience analysis, determining whether a topic is appropriate for a speaker, audience, or situation.
3. Formulate statements concerning the general and specific purpose of the speech or oral presentation.
4. Describe the relationship between the speaker, the speech, and the audience.
5. Create an outline of your speech.

Introductory Exercise 10.1

Complete the following self-inventory by brainstorming as many items as you can for each category. Think about anything you know, find interesting, or are involved in that relates to the topics below. Have you traveled to a different city? State? Country? Do you have any projects in other classes you find interesting? List them below.

BOOKS & NEWSPAPERS	SPORTS
TELEVISION	STATE ISSUES

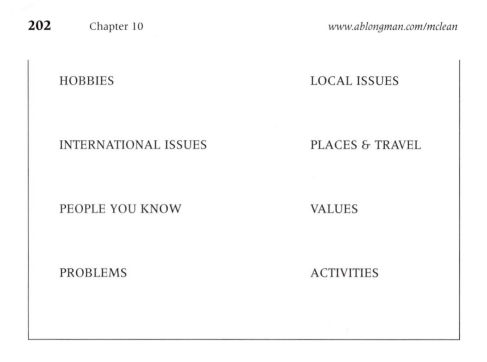

HOBBIES	LOCAL ISSUES
INTERNATIONAL ISSUES	PLACES & TRAVEL
PEOPLE YOU KNOW	VALUES
PROBLEMS	ACTIVITIES

Introductory Exercise 10.2 _____

Choose your three favorite categories on the list above and circle them. Then ask a friend what he or she would be most interested in hearing about. Ask more than one friend, and keep score of which item attracts the most attention. Make sure you keep track of who likes which category.

Do you have to give a speech or an oral presentation? If you have been assigned a topic by the teacher, you may be able to go straight to the section on narrowing your topic. If not, then the first part of this chapter will help you. This chapter will take you step by step and help you prepare for your speech or oral presentation. By the time you have finished this chapter, you will have chosen a topic for your speech, narrowed the topic, and analyzed the appropriateness of the topic for yourself as well as for the audience. From this basis, you will have formulated a general-purpose statement and specific thesis statement to further define the topic of your speech. Building on the general and specific purpose statements you formulate, you will create an outline for your oral presentation.

Through this chapter, you will become more knowledgeable about the process of creating a speech and gain confidence in your organizational abilities. Preparation and organization are two main areas that, when well developed prior to an oral presentation, significantly contribute to a reduction in levels of speech anxiety. If you are well prepared, you will be more relaxed when it comes time to give your speech.

How to Choose a Topic

First, if you have not already completed the first introductory exercise, please work with it, identifying as many activities, areas of interest, places you've travel to, and things you find interesting as possible. Once you have completed the exercise, identify three broad subject areas where you have some knowledge or experience. As stated in the directions for Introductory Exercise 10.2, please circle them and then survey people you know to find out which of the three they prefer to hear about. Make sure you keep score by writing down factors such as age, gender, and any other elements you think your audience may have in common.

Getting Started
1. Do you already have a project you are working on, perhaps in another course? Save yourself time and adapt the project material and information into a speech.

2. What are you currently studying in your other classes? What interests you? What topics do you want to know more about? Since you are going to be gathering information, make sure it is about a topic that truly interests you. If you find the topic interesting, your enthusiasm will show through and your audience will become interested too.

3. Which subjects or aspects initially drew you to this topic or area? Chances are that whatever peaked your interest the first time will also get your audience interested.

4. Conduct a search (use a search engine on the Internet, explore the library, or interview people you know) in your subject area to get an overview of the subject. Choose a topic that is interesting to you.

5. Explore topics, issues, places, or people that fascinate you. You will need to motivate yourself to stay on track as you develop your speech, and the more intriguing your topic is to you, the more likely you are to "stick with it!"

Factors in Choosing a Topic

A few key factors you should consider before you choose your topic include the purpose of the speech, projected time length of the speech, your ability to access information, and the appropriateness of the topic. Is the purpose of the speech to inform or persuade, to demonstrate or to entertain? Depending on the purpose, you may decide to take your subject area or issue and make sure it can meet the stated goals of the speech.

Speech to inform	To inform the audience, to teach about a topic or issue, to share your knowledge.
Speech to persuade	To persuade or influence the audience, changing attitudes, beliefs, or values.
Speech to demonstrate	To demonstrate to the audience how to use, operate, or do something.
Speech to entertain	To entertain the audience, engaging them in a relatively light-hearted speech that may have a serious point or goal.
Ceremonial speech	To perform for the audience a ceremonial function, such as a toast at a wedding or a eulogy at a funeral.

Give some consideration to the issue of how well your topic will lend itself to the purpose. How long is your speech going to be? A speech might be five to seven minutes, which is not a lot time to cover a topic in great detail or depth unless you plan carefully. Make sure you have a topic that is specific enough that you can adequately cover it in the time given. Try to choose a topic that can be researched in your college or university libraries. You may need to do some initial checking of sources to be sure material is available.

Appropriateness is especially important because some topics do not work as well in a classroom setting. Regardless of where you give a speech, you should always choose topics that will not offend members of the audience or promote harmful or illegal actions. Also, avoid topics that the audience already knows a lot about or about which they have strong feelings.

Consider topics that are:

- new
- possibly controversial
- clear
- supported by information you can find in outside sources
- interesting to you

Individual classrooms vary, so make sure that your instructor approves your topic and that your topic is appropriate for the audience. At some colleges and universities, broad topics are designated as part of the curriculum, including, for example, environment, diversity, and technology. Some colleges and university instructors may also encourage you to not choose topics that have been done repeatedly over the years, such as abortion or the death penalty, unless you can connect the issue to a current event or new perspective. Don't avoid all controversial topics, as they often intrigue your audience and help maintain interest. Just make sure you consider the preexisting attitudes of your audience when attempting to create an effective, engaging speech.

Choosing a topic can be difficult, but your self-inventory of things you already know should get you started. By doing a little exploring, you can often help yourself come up with several possible topics. The topic itself will not exclusively make a "good" or "bad" speech. How you develop that topic and discuss its points and issues, however, will make a significant impact. Before moving on to the next step in this chapter, make sure you have a topic in which you are relatively confident. If you have trouble selecting a topic, take your self-inventory to your instructor or librarian. They may be able to help guide you to a topic that works for you.

Write General-Purpose and Thesis Statements

If this is an assigned speech, you will already know the purpose but you will still need to write your own specific purpose. To help you come up with this purpose, consider these three questions:

1. What specifically are you going to inform, persuade, demonstrate, or entertain your audience with? A clear goal makes it much easier to develop an effective speech. Try to write in just one sentence exactly what you are going to do.
2. How much of this topic can I fit into the time period allowed? Typically your speech will be five to seven minutes or possibly ten minutes. In those ten minutes, it would be impossible to tell your audience about the complete history of the Ford Mustang automobile. You could, however, tell them about four key body style changes since 1965. If your topic is still too broad, narrow it down into something you can reasonably cover in the time allotted. Focus on just the classic Mustangs, for example, and the individual differences by year and how to tell them apart.
3. What about my topic will be the most interesting for the audience? What information will they actually use once my speech is over? Informing your audience about the body features of the Mustang may not be as useful as informing your audience on how to buy a classic car and what to look for. General issues of rust or how to determine if the engine is worn out may be more relevant.

When you have answered these three questions, then you should have a pretty good idea of what your specific purpose will be for the speech. You should be able to state this purpose in one sentence. For example, the specific purpose of our "classic cars" speech could be stated as, "By the end of my speech, I want my audience to be more informed about three ways they can determine if a classic car is a rust bucket or a diamond in the rough." Complete the following sentence for your speech: By the end of my speech, I want the audience to be more informed (persuaded, have a better understanding of, entertained by) about _____.

If you can't finish the sentence, you need to go back and work though the three questions again. Make sure you have given them sufficient time and attention. An effective speech requires planning and preparation, and that takes time. Know your goal, and make sure you can write it in one sentence. If you don't know your goal, the audience won't either.

A thesis statement, or central idea, should be short, specific, and to the point. Beebe and Beebe (1997, pp. 121–122) recommend five guiding principles when considering your thesis statement. The thesis statement should:

1. be a declarative statement.
2. be a complete sentence.
3. use specific language, not vague generalities.
4. be a single idea.
5. reflect consideration of the audience.

These principles should help you write your thesis statement. Take a moment and write a couple of draft versions. Once you have a thesis statement you like, its specific nature should help you focus on what information you need to find.

Finding Resources

Now that you have a topic, know your general purpose, and have written your thesis statement, it's time to gather information. If you have taken the topic from your own list, you probably already know a lot about it. You will still need information from sources other than yourself to establish credibility, create a more comprehensive speech, and make sure no important aspect of your topic is left out. See Computer-Mediated Communication 10.1.

Planning Your Investigation for Information

When giving a speech it is important to gather information from books, magazines and newspapers, electronic sources, and interviews with people who know a lot about your topic. With more information from a variety of sources, you will have more possibilities when it comes to the development of your speech. Remember that this investigation will be more fun if your topic is one in which you are actually interested.

COMPUTER-MEDIATED COMMUNICATION 10.1 • *Copyright*

You know when you create something it is your creation. You known when someone else creates something it is their creation. What happens when you want to create a speech and use other people's ideas, statistics, or formulas? You need to give credit where credit is due. Give the author(s) full credit and do not pretend, to yourself or to the audience, that the information is your own. Your unique creation will be the speech itself, which integrates diverse sources in new and innovative ways, with a fresh perspective.

For an insightful article on the topic, read *An Ethical Edge in Education: Cognizance of Copyrights and Copy Wrongs* by Duane Goehner, presented at the International Conference: The Social and Moral Fabric of School Life, on October, 4 1997, in Seattle, Washington. Go to: http://www.goehner.com/copyright.htm

Staying Organized

1. Before you go to the library or computer, make sure you have a space where you can keep all your materials in one place. A cardboard box, clearly labeled, can be a great space to put all the information you gather into.

2. If you are gathering information online, open a new document in whatever writing program you use and save it as "Sources." Every time you find information, copy the web address or reference/ citation information and paste it into your document. If you are gathering information from books or periodicals, use one sheet of paper as your "Sources" document. This will save you a lot of time later.

3. Plan to use your time effectively. What information do you hope to find in the library? Make a list. Try to combine tasks and get your investigation completed efficiently. Go to the library once with a list rather than three times without one.

4. Ask the research librarian for assistance in grouping information and where to find it.

Searching for Information Via Electronic Sources

The World Wide Web is an amazing source of information, but for that very reason it is difficult to get information you actually need. Let's look at two issues that make searching online easier: where and how to search for information.

Knowing where to go for information is as important as knowing key words and concepts related to your topic. Do you need general information? Do you need to survey what's available quickly? Do you prefer searching only reviewed sites? Is your topic education related? Depending on your answers, you may want to consider where to start your search.

Here's a summary of main search engines and how they might work for you:

Browse a general topic?	www.yahoo.com
	www.dogpile.com
	www.lycos.com
	www.northernlight.com
	www.stpt.com
Search for a specific topic?	www.altavista.com
	www.excite.com
	www.infoseek.com
Search a large amount of the Internet at once?	www.metacrawler.com
	www.allonesearch.com
	www.mamma.com
	www.profusion.com
	www.askjeeves.com
	www.search.com
	www.gosearch.com
	www.isleuth.com
	www.thebighub.com
	www.altaseek.com
Search only reviewed sites?	http://magellan.excite.com/
	www.clearinghouse.net
	www.miningco.com
Search specific databases	www.switchboard.com
	www.mapquest.com
	www.itools.com/research-it/

When you first start using a web search engine, getting a response like "487,230 web pages found" may sound amazing. It does not, however, mean you found a lot of valuable information. It means that you need to consider ways to narrow your search to find that valuable fact, reference, or piece of information that will make an impact on your audience.

As we discussed previously, let's say you want to focus on classic cars and specifically on the Mustang's four major style changes. A search on Yahoo! with the keyword "Mustang" yields nine categories and 367 sites. Taking a closer look, we can see that the P-51 Mustang airplane from World

War II; sports teams such as the Milwaukee Mustangs (football), Phoenix Mustangs (hockey), and Billings Mustangs (baseball); wild horses; and a number of Ford Motor Company references are included in this broad list. By adding the year and manufacturer ("1965 Ford Mustang") we narrow the search to eleven sites. As we continue to narrow our information, and compare our results across various search engines, we can quickly find the information we need. Here are a few tips to help you narrow your search:

Use this to help you narrow your search:	AltaVista Simple Search www.altavista.com	Altavista Advanced Search www.altavista.com
For both words, AND, +, or &	+1965 +Mustang	1965 AND Mustang 1965 & Mustang
For either word, OR	Ford Mustang	Ford OR Mustang
For one word but not the other, NOT	+Mustang -horse	Mustang AND NOT horse
Exact phrase, quotation marks " "	"1965 Ford Mustang"	"1965 Ford Mustang"

In addition, many search engines offer advanced search engines and specific tips on how to focus in on just documents, just audio files, just pictures (black and white or color), and just video. Exploring these tools will both improve your web search skills and yield better information for your speech.

Getting to Work

Before you go to the library, look over your own information sources. Do you read a magazine that relates to the topic? Was there an article in the newspaper you read that might work? Is there a book, CD-ROM, or music CD that has information you can use? Think of what you want the audience to know and how you could show it to them. Perhaps cover art from a CD or a line from a poem may make an important contribution to your speech. You might even know someone who has experience in the area you want to research. Consider how you are going to tell and show your audience what your speech is all about.

As you begin to investigate your topic, make sure you consider several sides of an issue. Let's say you are going to do a speech to inform on the history of the transcontinental railroad. At first you may have looked at two sides, railroaders versus local merchants. Railroad tycoons want to bring the country together, moving people, goods, and services in a more efficient way, and make money. Local merchants want to keep out competition and retain control of their individual markets. Take another look at this issue and you see that several other perspectives have bearing on this issue. Shipping was done primarily by boat prior to the railroad, so shippers would not want the competition. Recent Chinese immigrants were in need of work. Native Americans did not want to lose their culture or way of life, and a railroad that crossed the country would cut right through the buffalo's migration patterns. We now have five perspectives to the central issue, which makes the topic all the more interesting.

Make sure as you start your investigation for information that you always question the credibility of the information. Sources may have no review by peers or editors, and the information may be misleading, biased, or even false. Be a wise information consumer. The questions at the end of the chapter on mass communication can help you assess the credibility of the information.

Getting to Know Your Audience

Knowing your audience well before you speak is essential. Here are a few questions to help guide you in learning more about your audience:

1. How big is the audience?
2. What are their backgrounds, gender, age, jobs, education, and/or interests?
3. Do they already know about your topic? If so, how much?
4. Will there be other speakers? If so, who do you follow and what is their topic?
5. How much time have you been given for your speech, including time for questions and answers?

Demographic Traits

Demographic traits are the traits people have that make them an individual but that they have in common with others. For example, if you were born male, then your view of the world, based on your heredity and environment, may be different than that of a female. Being male, however, means you have this trait in common with roughly half the world's population. In addition, if you were born in 1940 and someone else was born in 1980, your views of the world may be different. By showing common demographic trends in our audience, we gain insight into our audience and their possible experiences, interests, and goals.

Gender   Although gender differences may be less clearly defined than in generations past, knowing the gender of your audience can still offer you insight.

Employment	What is the work experience level of your audience? Are they just starting out or do they have years of experience in their fields?
Education	Has the majority of your audience graduated from high school? From college? Do they have a technical skill? Education and educational background may contribute to different interests.
Age	An audience where the majority of the members are traditional college age (eighteen to twenty-four years) will have different interests and goals than one made up of returning students older than forty years who all hold full time jobs.
Marital status	Is your audience composed of mainly married or single people? These two groups will have different experiences and interests. The importance of child safety seats may be more appealing to an audience with a higher proportion of married people.
Membership	Do people in the audience belong to any groups, professions, or similar interest groups? This may be a common link that could support your speech.

Situational Traits

Although demographic traits may give you a better idea of the people in the audience, there are still a couple of factors specific to your individual speech and the speech event itself that you need to consider.

Physical setting	Will you be speaking on a stage? In a classroom? The type of room you are in will have a significant impact on the ability of the audience to hear you, the rate at which you can present information, and the ability to involve the audience in your topic.
Seating and visibility	Are the chairs hard or soft? How far away are they from you? Will you be on stage, "above the audience"? Are there facilities for your visual aides (slide screen, for example)? Will the podium block a portion of the audience's view of the visual aid?
Temperature	Never underestimate the power and influence of temperature. If the audience is cold, they will have a hard time concentrating on your message. If they are warm, they may be sleepy and

	unattentative. The temperature should be taken into consideration when planning the aspects of your topic and how to cover them.
Audience size	Generally, the bigger the audience, the more "formal" the speech. This often means that it is harder to involve individual members of the audience. Is also means that your visual aids, already big, should be even bigger!
Proximity to last/next meal	If people just ate a big lunch, they may be inclined to be sleepy. Turning down the lights to show slides may mean your audience goes to sleep. If people are hungry, and dinner is right after you finish speaking, it is a safe bet that at least a portion of the audience is more focused on their stomachs than your message.
Distractions	Is there a window in the room where people in the audience may be distracted? Beyond the window, will there be any distracting activity? Try to assess distractions before they get you off track in your speech.
Degree of formality	Will this be a formal lecture hall with levels and a podium? Will people be eating while you are speaking? Are they required to be in the audience? These factors will help you with your topic, investigation, and the development of your speech.

Audiences tend to be interested in ideas, issues, and things that relate to their needs and wants, goals, and motivations. By taking an "audience-centered" approach to your topic, and making sure you have information about your audience, you will better tailor your message, establish more common ground, and make more effective connections to their needs and interests (Beebe and Beebe, 1997). See Intercultural Communication 10.1.

Organization

Now that you have a better idea of who your audience is and what you want to focus on, you will need to consider how to organize your information. The first step is to write three key points that relate to your main topic. Once you have completed this step, with your key main points identified, you will need to consider how to bring them together to create a cohesive speech.

INTERCULTURAL COMMUNICATION 10.1 • *Adapting Your Speech to Different Learning Styles*

Howard Gardner (1993) is known for his theory of multiple intelligences, and he discusses the ideas that people learn better if the message is presented in a strategy that compliments their learning styles. Consider each style when preparing your speech. What styles might work best? Perhaps asking your audience to reflect on a point, and then to write a few sentences at the conclusion of your speech might reinforce your central message.

Here is a quick summary of the seven styles and strategies:

Styles	Examples	Strategies
Linguistic	Language, reading, verbal expression, speaking, writing, memorizing words (names, places, and dates).	Reading, oral presentations such as debates, reports, or storytelling.
Logical/mathematical	Use of numbers, perceiving relationships, reasoning (sequential, deductive, inductive), computation.	Problem solving, graphic organizers, categorizing, classifying, working with patterns and relationships.
Spatial	Think in three dimensions, mental imagery, design, color, form, and line within space.	Maps, charts, graphic organizers, painting or drawing, visual aids, working with pictures or colors.
Musical	Discern rhythm, pitch, and tone; interpret music; identify tonal patterns; compose music.	Rhythmic patterns and exercises, singing, music performance
Bodily/kinesthetic	Sense of timing and balance, athletics, dance, work that takes physical skill.	Drama, role playing, touching and manipulating objects, demonstrating.
Interpersonal	Organizing, leading others, communicating, collaboration, negotiating, mediating.	Group projects, interaction, debates, discussions, cooperative learning, sharing ideas.
Intrapersonal	Reflection, thinking strategies, focusing/concentration.	Individual projects, self-paced instruction, note taking, reflection.

On a separate piece of paper:

1. Write your general-purpose statement.
2. Write your thesis statement.
3. Define your main points.

You should be able to take your general-purpose statement and thesis statements from earlier in this chapter. As you took notes and gathered materials, some information must have appeared more important or relevant. Choose two or three key points from your list of information issues of facts that relate to you're your main topic. See Case Study 10.1.

Let's return to the topic selection of the transcontinental railroad. The general purpose is to inform the audience on its impact on a young but developing United States. The thesis statement focuses:

Topic	Transcontinental railroad
General-purpose statement	I want the audience to be more informed about the impact of the transcontinental railroad
Thesis statement	The transcontinental railroad changed shipping, communication, and cultures across America.

With the information we have so far, we can now list three main points.

CASE STUDY 10.1 • *Organize Your Information in Three Parts*

People generally like information in groups of three. Common examples include introduction, body, and conclusion; beginning, middle, and end; and breakfast, lunch, and dinner.

Information in groups of three helps us retain the information.

Sigmund Freud defined personality in three parts: id, ego, and superego.

Jürgen Habermas divided language into three categories: private, colloquial, and formal.

Even Agatha Christie, in her play *Rule of Threes*, uses three characters to weave a suspenseful tale.

Regardless why we remember things well when they come in small groups of two or three, it is in your best interest, when considering your speech, to limit yourself to just a couple of main points.

1. Change in shipping.
2. Change in communication.
3. Change in cultures.

Think of each one of these main points as a separate but shorter speech. The point is to develop each of these main points like you have developed your overall speech. What do you want to focus on? The major types of shipping in the time of the transcontinental railroad? One aspect you may want consider is to what degree is your audience familiar with this time in history. If they are not very familiar, a little background and context can help make your speech more meaningful and enhance its relevance to your thesis statement. By taking time to consider what you want to accomplish with each point, you will help yourself begin to address how you need to approach each point. Once you have thought about what you want to focus on for each point, list each subheading next to the main points. For example:

1. Change in shipping
   A. Navigating the waterways via barges and boats
   B. Overland stagecoaches
   C. Timetables for modes of travel
2. Change in communication
   A. Letters in the days of the Pony Express
   B. How the Morse code telegraph system followed railroad lines.
   C. Bringing people together across distances
3. Change in cultures
   A. Pre-railroad immigration
   B. Impact on Native Americans
   C. Territories become states

The Eleven Types of Speech Structures

Here are eleven distinct organizational structures to consider for your speech. The second column illustrates the process and the third column provides you with an example within the context of our sample speech outline. As you read each organizational structure, consider how the main points and subheadings might change or be adapted to meet each pattern.

Structure	Strategy	Example
1. Time (chronological)	Structuring your speech by time shows a series of events or steps in a process, typically	Before the transcontinental railroad, the events that led to its construction, and its

	beginning, middle, and end. "Once upon a time" stories follow a time-ordered pattern.	impact on early America.
2. Comparison	Structuring your speech by comparison focuses on the similarities and/or differences between points or concepts.	A comparison of pre– and post–transcontinental railroad America, showing how health and life expectancy remained the same.
3. Contrast	Structuring your speech by contrast focuses on the differences between items/concepts.	A contrast of pre– and post–transcontinental railroad America by shipping times, time it took to communicate via letter, or how long it took to move out West.
4. Cause-effect	Structuring your speech by cause and effect establishes a relationship between two events or situations, making the connection clear.	The movement of people and goods out West grew considerably from 1750 to 1850. With the availability of a new and faster way to go West, people generally supported its construction.
5. Problem-solution	Structuring your speech by problem-solution means you state the problem and detail how it was solved. This approach is effective for persuasive speeches.	Manufacturers were producing better goods for less money at the start of the Industrial Revolution, but they lacked a fast, effective method of getting their goods to growing markets. The transcontinental railroad gave them speed, economy, and access to new markets.
6. Classification (categorical)	Structuring your speech by classification establishes categories.	At the time the nation considered the transcontinental railroad, there were three main types of transportation: by water, by horse, and by foot.

7. Biographical	Structuring your speech by biography means examining specific people as they relate to the central topic.	(1804) Lewis and Clark travel four thousand miles in more than two years and cross. America. (1862) President Lincoln signs the Pacific Railroad Act, which leads to, in 1876, the Transcontinental Express from New York arriving in San Francisco with a record-breaking time of 83 hours and 39 minutes. In 2002, President Bush can cross America by plane in less than five hours.
8. Space (spatial)	Structuring your speech by space involves the parts of something and how they fit to form the whole.	A train uses a heat source to heat water, create stream, and turn a turbine, which moves a lever, which causes a wheel to move on a track.
9. Ascending/descending	Structuring your speech by ascending or descending order involves focusing on quantity and quality. One good story (quality) leads to the larger picture, or the reverse.	A day in life of a traveler in 1800. Incremental developments in transportation to the present, expressed through statistics, graphs, maps, and charts.
10. Psychological—also called "Monroe's Motivated Sequence" (Ayres & Miller, 1994, p. 274)	Structuring your speech on the psychological aspects of the audience involves focusing on their inherent needs and wants. See Maslow (1970) and Schutz (1966). The speaker calls *attention* to a *need*, then focuses on the satisfaction of the need and *visualization* of the solution, and ends with	When families in the year 1800 went out West, they rarely returned to see family and friends. The country as a whole was an extension of this distended family, separated by time and distance. The railroad brought families and the country together.

	a proposed or historical *action*. Useful for a persuasive speech.	
11. Elimination	Structuring your speech using the process of elimination involves outlining all the possibilities.	The transcontinental railroad helped pave the way for the destruction of the Native American way of life in 1870. After examining treaties, relocation and reservations, loss of the buffalo, disease and war, the railroad can be accurately considered the catalyst for the end of an era.

Now that you've reviewed the eleven organizational structures, choose one and create an outline of your speech. Look back at the outline in the transcontinental railroad example. There are three main points and three subheadings per point. You can use this format as a model or modify it to meet your own needs in order to create your own outline.

The Five Parts of Any Speech

Although your organizational structure will vary from speech to speech, there are nonetheless five main parts of any speech: attention statement, introduction, body, conclusion, and residual message.

1. Attention Statement

The **attention statement** is the way you focus the audience's attention on you and your speech. An attention statement can be used at any time during your speech, but let's first discuss your opening attention statement that comes with your very first word. The audience will be curious about you and may even be more interested in you than in the speech itself. Your attention statement should address the need for the audience to learn a little about you but should also focus on common ground between you and the audience, establishing a relationship, in order to transfer attention from you to the speech.

For example, you may open with a question, "How many people here today have ever felt their life was at risk?" You may then take the attention and continue with, "Hundreds of people die every day in automobile accidents in the United States, and the majority failed to use their safety belts.

Today I am going to discuss what safety belts are, how they are designed and used, and why you should choose to use your safety belt every time you get into a car."

This is just one example, and what you choose to do to gain attention and engage the audience may depend on your topic, speaking style, and comfort level. You may be nervous and have anxious energy when you start your speech, and the attention statement or activity can help you channel this nervous energy into a positive start to your speech. Here are several devices that can be used to engage the audience and gain attention.

Device	Strategy	Example
Appeal to interpersonal needs	If you recall, Schutz (1966) discussed affection, inclusion, and control and Maslow (1970) outlined a hierarchy of needs. Appealing to our basic needs can gain attention.	"How many people here today have ever felt their life was at risk?"
Be specific	Concrete terms, dates, places, or actual events are more vivid and engaging than abstract concepts.	"On July14, 2002, four-year-old Stephanie Sanchez lost her life in a car accident. Authorities on the scene indicated a safety belt may have saved her life."
Use local references	Specific, local events or examples engage the audience with a reference they can readily identify.	"Last week two students from our student body were involved in a car accident at the entrance to the college. Even though both vehicles were going less than twenty miles an hour, both drivers were taken to the hospital. Why? Neither was wearing a safety belt."
Use familiar references or experiences	The audience may share common experiences and familiar references, and you can draw on this to create common ground and gain attention.	"Have you ever been in a hurry to get somewhere and forgotten to fasten your safety belt?"
Use unusual images or facts	The unfamiliar can also be used to gain attention, using surprise to relate to your topic.	(Holding up a safety belt) "Have you ever been on a plane and had the flight attendant give you instructions on how to use

your safety belt?" (clicking the buckle). "Just because we don't have a flight attendant in the parking lot doesn't mean the safety belt in your car is any less important."

Create a sense of suspense	Suspense, like surprise, can draw the audience's attention to your topic.	(Holding out a bag with a safety belt inside) "Who would like to guess what is inside?" (an audience member or members reach inside and guess)
Create a sense of humor	Humor, like surprise or suspense, can be effective in drawing attention.	"Has anyone ever been on a roller coaster? Were you aware or even thankful for your safety belts as you (including body motions) rolled and pitched along the track?"
Use body motions	Body motions that compliment or even replace the message can be used effectively to gain attention.	(Sit in a chair, pretend to buckle up, look to the audience, pretend to drive, and then have a mock accident, turning your chair on its side.)

You may notice that many of these attention-gaining devices combine elements of each other. You will need to know our audience and topic well in order to plan your attention statement or activity. You may consider planning several attention statements as you progress through your speech, keeping the audience engaged. If you have three main points, you may consider how to draw attention to each point and how to make successful transitions, highlighting for the audience what you've covered and where you are headed to facilitate active listening. An effective introductory attention statement draws attention from you, or whatever else the audience might be focused on, to your topic and leads right into your introduction.

2. Introduction

Your **introduction** introduces you and your topic and should establish a relationship with your audience and state your topic clearly. To establish a relationship with the audience, you have to establish trust and credibility and be accessible. Some speakers may know a great deal about their topic, but the way they present themselves as separate from the audience may discourage attention to their speech. The attention statement should serve to create common ground with the audiences, drawing on common or familiar experiences to establish a relationship. You can do this, for example, by referring to the person who introduced you or the occasion for the speech, or use your attention statement or activity to establish common ground.

As fellow humans, we all have common experiences and stories to share, and your ability to tap into elements of common ground will help the audience become more engaged. You may find with this investment of energy and time that the audience becomes more active and less passive. They also may support you in your role as speaker, forgiving minor disfluencies or errors. Be careful to be genuine and authentic, as the audience will be able to ascertain false humility and you'll end up like the aloof or distant expert, listened to as a dispenser of information rather than as a speaker. This will negatively impact your ability to involve the audience and encourage active listening.

After establishing connections and a relationship with your audience, you will need to lead them clearly to your topic. This may involve outlining a logical sequence of events or main points, but it should also provide context for your speech. **Speech context** refers to topic area, content area, process, or place your speech will cover. By providing context, the audience can perceive where you are starting and where you are headed, allowing them to predict what comes next and to listen actively. In addition, by providing context in a successful transition from the attention statement or activity, you answer the questions all audience's ask themselves: "Why should I listen to this speaker and what's in it for me?" Give background on your topic, define a key term or phrase, or outline a concept, in effect creating context for the audience to grasp the area, purpose, and goal of your speech.

3. Body

As you leave your introduction you will move into the body of your speech. In this part of your speech, you will naturally turn to one of the eleven organizational structures. You will need to decide which structure, or combination of structures, to use and plan for them in your attention statement and introduction.

For example, let's say you are planning a speech to inform the audience about Area 51, a military installation outside Roswell, New Mexico, that is famous for its connection with unidentified flying objects (UFOs). You may choose to use both a time order structure as well as a spatial structure to cover your information. Your attention getter may involve a question like, "How many people believe in flying saucers from outer space?" You may then discuss how you became interested in the topic and, like many people, have noticed the increase in the coverage of them in the popular media. You might define UFOs and state that Area 51, the topic of your speech today, is an important part in the debate on flying saucers. You may then cover a brief history and then begin to illustrate key buildings in relation to one another, noting important controversies and reported events, with dates and facts, that relate to these structures. Your visual aids might include a map, a web site, or images that compliment your verbal message. Your combination of two organization structures can work to your advantage and gain audience attention, but it requires planning and preparation.

4. Conclusion

Your **conclusion** should provide the audience with a sense of closure by summarizing the main points and relating the points to the overall topic. In one sense, it is important to focus on your organizational structure again and to incorporate the main elements into your summary, reminding the audience what you covered. In another sense, it is important to not just state your list of main points again but to convey a sense that you have accomplished what you stated you would do in your introduction, allowing the audience to have psychological closure.

You may have had the experience of watching a television program only to have the end come with the "to be continued" message. Your sense of anticipation may help remind you to tune in next week, but then what happens when the channel fails to broadcast the second part of the program? You probably feel frustrated. This same experience is what you convey to your audience when you fail to leave time for a complete conclusion. A conclusion gives an important sense of closure to the audience and leads to your residual message.

5. Residual Message

One final element to include while drafting the outline of your speech is your residual message. The **residual message,** a message or thought that stays with your audience well after the speech, is an important part of your speech. Ask yourself, "What do I want the audience to remember?" "What information do you want to have the audience retain or act upon?" "What do you want the audience to do?" In answering these questions, from the consideration of your topic to the analysis of the audience, it is wise to keep the end goal in mind. Osborn and Osborn (1997, p. 388) articulate the idea when they state, "Even the best information is useless unless your listener's remember and use it." Steven Covey (1989) also underlines the importance of beginning with the end in mind. Make sure you repeat your main point and reinforce what you want to be the residual message, or the message that stays with your audience. You may choose to use a quote, make an appeal to the audience to consider an important point, or reference your attention statement in a new way for your residual message. Regardless of how you drive home your final thought, give consideration to how you make your central message stay with the audience.

Consider Visual Aids as You Plan Your Speech

By now you have gathered information and begun the process of outlining your speech. Before you complete your information gathering, make sure you have considered how you are going to show your audience what you are talking about. Visual aids will make all the difference in your speech, and planning their effective use while building your speech will not only save you time, it will help you create a more coordinated speech.

Here is a simple chart that can serve to help guide you as you plan how to discuss your main points and how to show, reinforce, and expand on your spoken words. Add as many rows and columns as you need, and the chart will help you keep track of how you will illustrate and reinforce each key point or concept.

Main Point	Discussion Points	Visual Aids
Roots of jazz	First recording	Picture of musicians

You may decide to use your pictures, video clips, and even sound files in a dynamic presentation to reinforce your main message. There are a number of software programs to help you accomplish the task, but be careful that you keep in mind that your goal is to reinforce, not overshadow, your main points. The visual aids should compliment, not overwhelm, your speech.

What the Audience Expects

On a final note, before you get your speech set firmly in your mind, consider that the audience has several expectations of you. No doubt you yourself have sat through a speech where you asked yourself, "Why should I listen?" or "What does this have to do with me?" These questions are normal and natural for audiences, but people seldom actually state these questions in so many words or say them out loud.

One central but often unspoken expectation of the audience is that the speaker will be ethical. Tyler (1978) discusses ethical communication and specifically indicates reciprocity as a key principle. **Reciprocity,** or a relationship of mutual exchange and interdependence, has four main components: mutuality, nonjudgmentalism, honesty, and respect. **Mutuality** means the speaker searches for common ground and understanding with his or her audience, establishing this space and building on it throughout the speech. This involves examining viewpoints other than your own and taking steps to ensure that the speech integrates an inclusive, accessible format rather than an ethnocentric one. **Nonjudgmentalism** underlines the need to be open minded, and an expression of one's willingness to examine diverse perspectives. The audience expects the speaker to state the truth as they perceive it, with supporting and clarifying information to support their position, speaking **honestly**. Finally, **respect** should be present throughout a speech, demonstrating the speaker's high esteem for the audience and individual members. Consider these expectations when designing your speech, and you will help address many of these natural expectations and more thoroughly engage your audience.

Summary

In this chapter we discussed how to choose a topic, define the specific purpose of your speech, learn more about the topic, and know your audience. As we discussed audience analysis, we examined both demographic and situational traits, how the audience needs visual aids. Finally, we focused on the need for organization and the eleven types of speech structures.

For More Information

For a comprehensive and concise guide to preparing for your speech, read

Jo Sprague and Douglas Stuart's *The Speaker's Handbook,* Forth Worth, TX: Harcourt College Publishers.

Sam Walch, at The Pennsylvania State University Department of Speech Communication, provides an excellent discussion of the importance of a residual message and how to formulate one at: http://www.personal.psu.edu/users/s/b/sbw3/100a/workbook/worksheet_residual_message.htm

Review Questions

1. Factual Questions
   a. What are the four speech purposes discussed in the chapter?
   b. What are three questions to help you focus on general-purpose and thesis statements?
   c. What are the eleven organizational structures for speeches?

2. Interpretative Questions
   a. When creating a speech, is it appropriate not to include certain information?
   b. How can a persuasive speech be ethical?
   c. How can a residual message impact an audience?

3. Evaluative Questions
   a. Which speech structure is best for a demonstration speech? A persuasive speech?
   b. To what degree do individual characteristics influence audience analysis?
   c. To what degree is repetition required to ensure message retention?

4. Application Questions
   a. Write a general-purpose statement and a thesis statement for a speech to inform. Now adapt these statements for a speech to persuade.
   b. Consider the elements of a speech to inform and adapt them for a speech to persuade? In what ways would you adjust key points or issues?
   c. Observe someone presenting a speech given the discussion in this chapter. What elements of their speech could you utilize in your own speech? What elements would you not want to use? Why? Compare with a classmate.

Works Cited

Ayres, J. & Miller, J. (1994). *Effective public speaking* (4th ed.). Madison, WI: Brown and Benchmark.

Barbero, Y. (1998). *Science, society & religion: The rule of threes.* Tucson, AZ: See Sharp Press. Also found at: http://www.yvesbarbero.com/threes.htm

Beebe, S. & Beebe, S. (1997). *Public speaking: An audience-centered approach* (3rd ed.). Boston: Allyn & Bacon.

Covey, S. (1989). *Seven habits for highly effective people.* New York: Simon and Schuster.

Faggella, K. & Horowitz, J. (1990). Different child, different style. *Instructor, September,* 1990.

Gardner, H. (1993). *Frames of mind: The theory of multiple intelligences.* New York: Basic Books.

Maslow, A. (1970). *Motivation and personality* (2nd ed., pp. 35–150). New York: Harper & Row.

Osborn, M. & Osborn, S. (1997). *Public speaking* (3rd ed.). New York: Houghton Mifflin.

Shutz, W. (1966). *The interpersonal underworld* (pp. 13–20). Palo Alto, CA: Science and Behavior Books.

Silver, H., Strong, R. & Perini, M. (1997). Integrating learning styles and multiple intelligence. *Educational Leadership, September,* 1997.

Tyler, V. (1978). Report of the working groups of the Second SCA Summer Conference on Intercultural Communication. In N. C. Asuncion-Lande (Ed.), *Ethical perspectives and critical issues in intercultural communication* (pp. 170–177). Falls Church, VA: SCA.

Walch, S. (1999). *The rule of threes.* The Pennsylvania State University Department of Speech Communication web site. Available at: http://www.personal.psu.edu/users/s/b/sbw3/100a/workbook/step6.htm

Speech Presentation

Chapter Objectives

After completing this chapter, you should be able to:

1. Articulate a clear goal for your speech or oral presentation.
2. Identify and describe four aspects of a good delivery of a speech or oral presentation.
3. Understand the difference between speech anxiety and communication apprehension.
4. Identify and describe three aspects that significantly contribute to the degree of speech anxiety.
5. Identify and describe five ways to cope with general anxiety.
6. Identify and describe three ways to handle specific speech anxiety.
7. Identify and describe aspects of voice, body, and movement that contribute to a positive delivery of your speech or oral presentation.
8. Identify and describe four presentation methods for delivery.
9. Describe the types of visual aids, their methods and materials, and how to prepare and use them effectively.

Introductory Exercise 11.1

Attend a presentation, conference, meeting, or similar situation where someone gives a speech or presentation. Take notes on what they talk about. Also take notes on how they say it, what you like or dislike about their delivery, and what you think you could use in your own speeches. Compare your results from the same or a different speech with a friend or classmate. Did you notice different aspects of the speech? What did you notice that was similar or the same?

226

Introductory Exercise 11.2

Watch a historical speech and repeat Introductory Exercise 11.1. Examples of speakers to consider are Martin Luther King, Jr, and John F. Kennedy, known for their ability to involve their audiences with issues such as civil rights, and more recent political speakers, such as Ronald Reagan, Bill Clinton, or Colin Powell. Again, compare your results. Are there any differences between your local speakers delivery style(s) and those speakers with more national experience?

Introductory Exercise 11.3

Based on what you learned in Introductory Exercises 11.1 and 11.2, create a list of common criteria to evaluate speakers. Be sure to include elements that capture what you thought worked and what did not work. After you complete this chapter, compare your list to the delivery aspects discussed. Did the lists match? Were there any differences? Compare your results with those of a friend or classmate.

In the last chapter we examined what you will say in your speech. Now let's examine how to say it. You may have heard before the statement by a speech coach to "Speak Naturally!" This is central to your ability to deliver your message in a coherent manner that your audience chooses to listen to and concludes with your getting your message across. In this chapter, we will examine the use of voice and body motions in the presentation of your speech. Keep in mind that although you will learn a great deal about delivery and become more aware of ways that you might improve, the key to your success is to improve while keeping it natural.

What Makes for a "Good" Delivery?

The term "good" in relation to delivery is a relative term. What may be good for one audience may not work at all with another. Your ability to adapt, however, is very important. Here are four key characteristics of a good delivery. Each characteristic applies to your particular choice of topic, the members of the audience, and the setting of your speech. How each characteristic should be implemented will call on your ability to understand the setting, get a feel for your audience, and adapt.

1. The Delivery Should Create Common Ground

When you are preparing to give a speech to an audience, you need to conduct an audience analysis. As outlined in the chapter on speech preparation, there are various traits and factors that influence the audience. It is in your and the audience's best interest to tailor your message to their individual needs and interests. Part of this includes (1) establishing your credibility with the audience and (2) reducing the psychological and physical distance between you and the audience. If you are going to give a speech on range management to a group of cattle ranchers and you wear a Wall Street power suit with a bright red tie, your appearance may reinforce your "otherness" or that you are an outsider.

Gudykunst and Kim (1997), two communication researchers, have examined this issue of in-group communication and communication with strangers in depth. They have found that this issue of "us and them" plays a significant role in communication, particularly in intercultural and international communication. We can learn from their efforts and apply the lessons to speech delivery. People are more likely to listen to people who they perceive are like them. By communicating through your words and actions that you have a lot in common with the audience, you help reduce the distance. See Intercultural Communication 11.1.

INTERCULTURAL COMMUNICATION 11.1 •
Body Movements

Did you learn to talk with your hands and find that even when you are talking on the phone you are motioning with your hands? Or do you keep your body motions to a minimum, and when you speak, your body motions are subtle but carry meaning? Italians often celebrate enthusiastic body motions, whereas the Chinese often reinforce a reserved posture, and nonverbal cues may carry significant meaning.

Body motions while giving a speech are important to establishing your credibility, illustrating your enthusiasm, holding the audience's interest, and reinforcing your message. If you are going to speak to a group that represents a single culture, it would be wise to interview a number of people from the culture to learn more about the cultural expectations of body motions. If, however, you are going to give a speech to a diverse North American audience, here are a few guidelines to effective body motions:

1. Stand and face the audience squarely. Show your interest by establishing and maintaining frequent eye contact. Nod your head to show you're listening. Keep your face relaxed, and smile when it is appropriate.
2. Assume an open posture. Keep your arms open and do not cross them. Do not put your hands in your pockets. Standing tall and walking with shoulders back shows your confidence. Specific movement of your arms can also communicate confidence. Watch your audience for clues that they are listening. Leaning forward, taking notes, and nodding can all indicate active listening and should encourage you as you speak.

In your range management speech, you may complete your audience analysis and find that Wrangler jeans are more popular than pinstripes suits. You may open your speech by discussing recent changes in range management and how you have seen these changes over time, making sure you highlight your long-term involvement and underline how your goals and those of the cattle ranchers are similar. This approach should be genuine and truthful. Audiences are quick to spot someone who is less than genuine, and doubts about credibility significantly impact their ability to actively listen. Another way to visualize common ground is to think about what you stand on and for. What are your foundations, roots, or guiding values and beliefs? What are your goals and what are you trying to achieve? Look for elements of both that you have in common with the audience and reinforce it in your delivery.

2. The Delivery Should Not Distract From the Message

Take a moment and turn on the radio. As the announcer speaks, how do they sound? Is their voice animated? Do they have a clear speaking voice with measured, even tones or a slightly exaggerated, overemphasized and quick speaking style? Many modern DJs use the second speaking style to help make their speech interesting and less monotonous or monotone. Radio competes with television for your attention, and the radio announcer wants your attention but lacks the visual channel. When you deliver your speech, you will not lack the visual channel and should not sound like it. Sighs, gasps, and overdramatic emphasis on less important words will only serve to distract your audience from the message. Presidential candidate Al Gore, a seasoned debater, will be long remembered for the sighs, gasps, shrugs of shoulders, and other aspects of his delivery in the first round of presidential debates. His message was significantly impacted, and even lost, because of the attention the audience paid to his delivery style. In your own speech, make sure your delivery compliments your message but does not overshadow or distract from it.

3. The Delivery Should Help the Audience Listen, Understand, Remember, and Act

After you establish common ground in your speech, how can you help the audience listen to your speech? One way is to be naturally and genuinely enthusiastic about your topic. If you are interested in your topic, you will naturally emphasize key words and phrases, helping your audience to listen. Take a breath and pause before a key point. Use your body language to reinforce your message. Together these elements will help your audience actively listen.

In addition to actively listening, your audience needs to understand your speech. Give context and background around your topic but do not get lost on a tangent and get "off message." Use what you learned about listening to help your audience grasp your message. Internal summaries help remind the audience about information you covered and lead into the next issue. Signposts, such as "Now let's consider (your next key point)" signal a change in your speech. Move with a purpose, and make sure your movements compliment your words.

Build into your speech ways for the audience to remember. Follow the rule of threes, and limit your information to no more than three main points. Remind them of the first point before you move to the second one, and remind them again of points one and two before transitioning to point three. Use pneumatic devices to help your audience remember the information. Let's say you are giving a speech to inform on the subject of the history of rhetoric. You want the audience to remember key historical figures, and you write on the board "SPAA." Then you proceed to discuss Socrates, Plato, Aristotle, and Alexander the Great, each the student of the former, referring in each transition to the acronym on the board. The use of the visual cue with repetition will help your audience recall your message.

Finally, make sure your speech provides for some way for the audience to act on your information. If your speech is about range management and you have successfully communicated a series of steps to maintain herd size while increasing range viability, the individual cattle rancher should leave your speech with at least one way he or she can act upon your information. You can consider the questions, "Why should I listen to you?" and "How does what you're saying serve my needs and goals?" and their possible answers as one way to focus on solution steps or ways the audience can act on your information.

4. The Delivery, and the Speech Itself, Should Be Flexible

If, after all your preparation and practice, audience analysis, and review and refinement of your speech you find that what you have prepared will not work as planned, adapt the plan. The first rule in adapting your speech is to keep positive and to keep smiling. Your enthusiasm will more than make up for any awkwardness that arises because of your last minute changes. The next is to focus on the key points you know and select those points to present and how to present them. Perhaps you will need more explanation of the point because your audience is much younger than your research indicated, and without extra context and background they might lose interest or fail to comprehend. Perhaps your time limit was changed at the last minute, and your ten-minute speech now has only five minutes or has been extended to twenty minutes. Use a new piece of paper, take what you know and had planned, and organize your new speech. If you get lost while delivering, just pause and say "excuse me," refer to your new plan, and get back on track. Your ability to adapt and to keep a positive attitude while adapting can have a significant impact on the success of your speech.

Speaking Effectively

According to Aristotle, the ability to speak effectively is called **rhetoric** (Covino & Jolliffe, 1995). In Aristotle's day, the ability to speak in public was valued, and the ability to speak persuasively was prized. Speaking effectively means that the speaker was able to capture and maintain the audience's attention, convey his or her message, and leave the audience with the residual message intact. Speaking persuasively adds, as we have seen previously, the element of motivation to change, adopt, or become involved in the speaker's proposal.

Speaking effectively and persuasively combines three key elements: ethos, pathos, and logos. **Ethos** involves the speaker's proof of character, presenting evidence of experience to establish credibility and competence. **Pathos** involves the speaker's passion, with appeals to common emotions to establish connections with the audience. **Logos** involves the speaker's use of logic to present a coherent view of the information or content based on facts, figures, or other objective information.

All speeches combine at some level all three elements. To gain your audience's attention and encourage them to become engaged in your topic, you need to address their interest in your credibility as a speaker. To create common ground and establish a relationship with the audience, rather than to be perceived as aloof or distant, your humanness needs to be underlined by displays or appeals to common emotions. For the audience to understand your point of view and the context of your speech, they need to see and hear information, facts, or evidence you gathered to arrive at that view.

Aristotle also discussed skill in rhetoric as the ability to see the available means of persuasion depending on the situation, context, or topic (Covino & Jolliffe, 1995). If you are going to persuade us to use safety belts, you may use a speech with a significant emphasis on ethos, or your own personal character. Your speech might feature a personal story in which you were involved in an accident and the role safety belts played in the extent of your injuries and the injuries of others. Spending the majority of the time in your speech on your story, with few appeals to emotion or facts, means your speech used ethos as the available means of persuasion. Perhaps the audience members are primarily your age or gender and can readily identify with you. This strategy may prove quite effective. If, however, you choose to use pathos as the available means of persuasion, then you may feature appeals to the emotions of fear, concern, or the need for safety. Graphic visual aids and vivid language may make your speech engaging and informative. Based on your audience analysis, if ethos is not the preferred means of persuasion, appeals to emotion can also be effective. Finally, if you look to statistics of deaths per year, differences in the extent of injuries depending on safety belt use, and cost to society each year, you are using logos as your means of persuasion. Aristotle preferred that all communication be conducted only through logic to encourage transparency and reduce manipulation, but he recognized that people also respond to character and emotion.

Element	Strategy	As a speaker, you should:
Ethos (Greek for *character*)	Ethos is the appeal based on the character of the speaker. An ethos-driven speech relies on the reputation of the speaker. Ethos refers to the trustworthiness or credibility of the speaker. Ethos is often communicated through the tone of voice, eye contact, and style of speaking. It can also be affected by the speaker's reputation apart from the speech, involving his or her expertise in their field, previous record, education, or integrity.	Establish your competence

Establish your trustworthiness

Establish your sense of common values |
| Pathos (Greek for *experience* or *suffering*) | Pathos is an appeal based on emotions. Advertisements, for example, are often pathos driven. Pathos involves an appeal to the audience's sympathies, imagination, and sense of common experience. An effective appeal to pathos causes an audience not just to respond emotionally but to actually identify with the speaker's point of view, seeing things through the speaker's eyes. | Establish your enthusiasm

Establish your concern

Use vivid language

Help the audience paint a mental picture of what it must be like |
| Logos (Greek for *word*) | Logos is an appeal based on logic or reason. Speeches involving scientific information or processes by companies, corporations, or universities are often logos driven. Logos involves the internal consistency of the message, or how well it fits together. How | Establish a logical sequence

Establish the credibility of your sources, appealing to authority |

clear is the main point or claim? Is
the information provided relevant
to the central claim? Does the
proposed solution follow logically
from the evidence provided?

Speech Anxiety

*The person who has confidence in themselves gains the confidence of
others.*

—Hasidic Saying

Now that we've discussed four key characteristics and three key elements
of a successful speech, and ended with what happens when the rules
change at the last minute, you may think to yourself, "I couldn't handle
that." You can handle that, especially if you can know what "that" is. Is
the idea of changing your speech hard in terms of content? If you know
your information and have prepared and practiced, the transition to a new
time limit won't be too bad. If it is not content, then is it delivery? Perhaps you are afraid that you will look unprofessional or "bad" because
you had to change your speech. We all experience nervousness, whether
we have to change our speech or not. **Speech anxiety,** the anxious feeling before speaking, is normal, and we will discuss ways to control your
feelings. **Communication apprehension,** however, is the most severe
form of speech anxiety (McCrosky, 1984; Seiler & Beall, 2000). People
who experience communication apprehension fear speaking in all situations, regardless whether it is interpersonal or public communication.

Joe Ayres and Tim Hopf (1993), communication researchers at
Washington State University, have studied communication apprehension
and speech anxiety extensively. Based on their research, in conjunction
with additional insight from Janice Miller, Ayres and Miller (1994) discuss
three aspects of speech anxiety, five ways to cope with general anxiety, and
three ways to handle specific speech anxiety.

Three aspects that significantly contribute to the degree of speech anxiety include:

1. Novelty   The degree to which something is new and
                           unfamiliar influences the extent of speech anxiety.
                           How often do you give speeches? Most people give
                           speeches infrequently, with a lot of time between
                           each speech. Even seasoned speakers come up
                           against new situations that are unfamiliar.

2. Conspicuousness   Standing out from the audience makes the speaker
                           feel conspicuous or self-conscious. This self-

awareness is only enhanced by the fact that everyone's attention is focused on the speaker.

3. Audience characteristics

When a speaker is faced with a large audience, he or she is more likely to feel more fearful (Ayres, 1990). Other factors may include status, prior knowledge, and degree of familiarity with audience members.

Five ways to cope with general anxiety:

1. Be prepared

The single most important way to cope with anxiety is to prepare. If you are prepared, know your material, and practice, you will feel more confident in your material.

2. Plan to use movement

Anxious speakers sometimes have nervous energy before the speech. Plan to use this energy in a positive way, using movement and showing your enthusiasm in the introduction of the speech.

3. Be flexible

Flexibility, like adaptability, is important. Speakers need to know their material well enough that they can adapt to "what if's."

4. Take a public-speaking course

Students typically report much lower levels of speech anxiety at the end of the course (Thompson, 1967). By giving a series of speeches with the guidance of a speech coach or instructor, students become more comfortable with the formats, organizing and presenting information.

5. Seek professional help

Finally, speech anxiety can for some speakers be serious. There are a number of programs at leading universities that treat this fear.

Here are three ways to handle specific speech anxiety:

1. Performance visualization

Drawing from the concept of self-fulfilling prophecy, this technique requires the speaker to visualize a positive outcome, step by step, increasing the likelihood of success (Ayres & Miller, 1994).

2. Rational-emotive therapy (RET)

The technique has an assumption that people have an irrational fear of public speaking (the whole audience has to like me, they'll think I'm stupid, or everything must go perfectly). By pointing out these irrational thoughts and restating them as rational ones (not everyone has to like me, they will give me the benefit of the doubt, no speech is perfect), the speaker's anxiety lessens (Ellis, 1962).

3. Cognitive restructuring

Like RET above, cognitive restructuring involves irrational thinking but focuses instead on developing coping statements. Through education, skills acquisition, and practice, speakers improve and their anxiety lessens (Glaser, 1981).

The best speakers know enough to be scared. Stage fright is the sweat of perfection. The only difference between the pros and the novices is that the pros have trained the butterflies to fly in formation.
— Edward R. Murrow

Voice

Your voice is one variable of a speech you can control. It makes sense to practice and use it to your advantage to get your message across effectively. Let's examine eight distinct aspects of your voice to focus on while remembering that variety and variation are necessary. Focusing too much on one aspect may "wear out" that aspect, making it monotonous and repetitive, and negatively impact the message.

Volume, just like the volume button on a remote control, refers to how loud your voice is during the speech. How loud is too loud? You need to speak loud enough that the audience can hear you without overpowering them. Look to the audience for signs, or simply ask, "Can everyone hear me?" Another aspect of your voice you'll want to consider is pitch. **Pitch** refers to the highs and lows of your voice. Some variation is important while speaking, but too wide a variation or a higher than your normal voice pitch may signal your stress and anxiety to the audience. **Rate** refers to your rate of speech. Are you a fast talker? A slow talker? Regional differences in the United States or speaking English as a second language may impact this aspect of voice. Make sure you watch your audience for clues that you are speaking too fast and they can't keep up, or too slow and they are losing interest. **Pauses** are what lie between words, phrases, and sentences. Silence and strategic pauses not only allow you to take a breath, they add emphasis to the words that follow and signal the audience to a change or transition.

Pausing with "umms," "ahhs," "you knows," "likes," and similar filler words are called vocalized pauses and can be distracting. Pausing too often or at the wrong places can sound awkward or unnatural. When you ask the audience members a question, give a moment for them to consider the question. Not pausing long enough creates the sensation that you are hurrying through the speech. **Fluency** refers to how smooth you sound, and awkward pauses or stumbling over hard to pronounce words and phrases disrupts the fluidity of your speech. Again, the goal is to speak naturally, but pay attention to where you place pauses, and make sure they make sense.

Articulation and **enunciation** are two sides of the same vocal aspect. Articulation means the degree to which you speak with clarity individual sounds within words. Do you drop the "g" off of "ing" words, as in "I was runnin' fast." This would be considered a lack of articulation. Enunciation is the degree to which you speak each word clearly and distinctly. For example, do you say "gonna" instead of "going to?" **Pronunciation** is the socially acceptable way a word is said. People from England, Boston, and Ohio, all pronounce the word "can't" differently. U.S. professional announcers for the most part are trained in standard American English, which features a mid-American style of pronunciation that is more universally understood.

Body

Your body language and how you choose to use it can have a significant impact on our speech. Have you ever watched a speech or presentation where the speaker hides behind the podium or lectern? Did their lack of accessibility influence your perception of them? Did it impact your desire to listen? Closed motions like crossed arms, stiff posture, and hands clenched to the podium all communicate nervousness and defensiveness clearly, whether the speaker wanted to or not. Audiences respond more to open, dynamic speakers who use their bodies to effectively communicate their messages.

Your body can be an effective tool. First, let's begin with the age-old expression, "You never get a second chance to make a first impression." When your audience first sees you, just like in a job interview, they begin to make judgments and predictions about you. If you are well dressed and every crease is ironed, people may notice your attention to detail. Your holey jeans, torn T-shirt, and baseball cap send a different message. Your **appearance** can affect your credibility, and as a speaker attempting to create common ground and reduce the distance between the audience and yourself, you want your appearance to help establish your credibility.

Movement is important in your speech, but it should not be left to chance. Although you should strive for being natural, you do not want to naturally shuffle your feet, pace, or rock back-and-forth through your

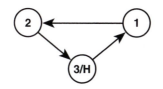

FIGURE 11.1   *Speaker's Triangle*

entire speech. These behaviors can all distract your audience from your message. In the classical speech, positions on the stage serve to guide both the speaker and the audience through transitions. The speaker's triangle (see Figure 11.1) shows where the speaker starts in the introduction, moves to points one and two, and then returns to the original position to conclude. This technique can be effective to help you remember each point and to help yourself break down your speech into manageable parts. It also gives purpose to your movement and helps you move through your speech.

Part of you body movements involve using your hands and arms, called **gestures,** during your speech. Aside from putting your hands in your pockets during a speech, you have to do something with them. For many this presents a challenge. Gestures provide one way to channel your nervous energy into a positive activity that benefits your speech and gives you something to do with your hands.

Watch people in conversation sometime. Do they use their hands to express themselves? Do you think *they* think about how they use their hands? Most people don't, and their arm and hand gestures come naturally as part of their expression. To some extent this holds true for professional speakers. They want to come across comfortable and natural, and their use of arms and hands contributes to their presentation. Professional speakers, however, also recognize that a well-chosen gesture can help make a point memorable or can lead the audience to the next step. As professional speakers lead up to a point, you may see them raise their hand slightly, perhaps waist high. This gesture is commonly referred to as an **anticipation step.** The gesture shows the audience your anticipation of an upcoming point. Following the anticipation step comes the **implementation step.** This step involves using your arms and hands above your waist, perhaps taking your anticipation step with your right hand at waist level pointing outward, and raising it up with your palm forward, as in the gesture "to stop." This gesture communicates to your audience your message and compliments your words. After your implementation step, you slowly lower your hand down past your waistline and away from your body, letting go of the gesture. This final step is called the **relaxation step,** where your letting-go motion compliments your residual message.

We have now discussed your overall body movements, use of arms and hands to make gestures, and it is time to turn our attention to **facial gestures** and expressions. Facial gestures contribute to your message and can either reinforce or contradict your message. If you state a serious statement with a smile, people may not understand the incongruity between your verbal and nonverbal messages. If, however, your smile and enthusiasm are in line with your verbal message, the audience will be better able to "read" your face and use the cues to interpret your spoken message. As in other body movements, your facial gestures should come naturally, reflecting the tone and emotion of your verbal communication.

As you may imagine, the single most important facial gesture (in the United States) is eye contact (Seiler & Beall, 2000). **Eye contact,** which refers to the speaker's gaze that engages the audience members, can vary in degree and length and in many cases is culturally influenced, both in the speaker's expectations and the audience member's notion of what is appropriate. Avoid looking over people's heads, or staring at a point on the wall. The audience will find this unnerving and will not feel as connected, or receptive, to your message. Move your eyes gradually and naturally, looking for faces that look interested and engaged in your message. Be careful not to focus in on only one or two audience members, but instead try to give as much eye contact as possible across the audience. Make sure you establish eye contact with individual audience members throughout your speech, and keep it natural.

Now that we have examined the use of voice and body in speech presentations, let's look at four distinct presentational methods.

Presentational Methods

There are four standard presentational methods: impromptu, manuscript, extemporaneous, and memorization.

1. Impromptu   A speech given without notes or preparation.
2. Manuscript   A speech given from a written script, using exact words.
3. Extemporaneous A speech given with a lot of preparation but the delivery is conversational and notes are rarely used.
4. Memorized   A speech given from memory, requiring extensive practice and preparation.

These four presentational methods have strengths and weaknesses. **Impromptu** speeches can seem informal and allow for creativity, but they do not allow for extensive preparation or practice. **Manuscript** speeches allow you to choose your words carefully beforehand, but in your delivery, reading rather than speaking and lack of eye contact are two significant risks. You may also lose your place while looking up at the audience and have a hard time finding it again when you glance back down at the manuscript.

Extemporaneous style is audience centered and involves a more relaxed style, which allows the speaker to close distance with the audience. The appearance of a speech "on the spur of the moment" does not reveal all the research, preparation, and practice required. This method of presentation is quite common and very useful in a variety of professions but does require significant initial preparation work. A **memorized** speech may appear flawless but in its structure lies its weakness—the audience cannot ask questions in the middle of the speech, and if the speaker gets off track, he or she may find regaining focus difficult. See Computer-Mediated Communication 11.1.

Practice and Preparation

When considering your speech delivery, it is important to consider voice, body movements and gestures, and which presentational method to use. Once you have chosen a style, you need to consider how you are going to show your audience what you are talking about. Have you ever asked for driving directions and not understood someone's response? Did they talk about "right on 42nd Street" or "right at Sam's Grocery Store, the new one"? Chances are that unless you know the town well or have a map

COMPUTER-MEDIATED COMMUNICATION 11.1 •
Presentational Methods

There are a number of excellent sites available online to assist you with your presentational methods.

Dave Patterson of the Computer Science Division, University of California–Berkley, wrote an essay entitled *How to Give a Bad Talk* (1983). His essay, modeled after the Ten Commandments, listed ten ways to ensure failure. Can you guess what is the one way that always ensures a bad talk? Never practice. Mark Hill, also of UC at Berkley, also wrote an essay entitled *Oral Presentation Advice* (1997), which features a comprehensive summary of various presentational methods. Both essays can be found at: http://www.cs.wisc.edu/~markhill/conference-talk.html

Finally, the Digital Desert Library at New Mexico State University features a web site entitled Presentation Methods and Ideas that is full of useful ideas at: http://horizon.nmsu.edu/ddl/presentation2.html

handy, the visual cue of grocery store might be just the information you need to know where to turn.

Your audience experiences the same frustration, or sense of accomplishment, when they get lost or find their way during your speech. Consider how you can express yourself visually, providing common references, illustrations, and images that lead the audience to understand your point or issue.

Visual aids:

1. Make your speech more interesting.
2. Enhance your credibility as a speaker.
3. Serve as guides to transitions, helping the audience stay on track.
4. Communicate complex or intriguing information in a short period of time.
5. Reinforce your verbal message.
6. Help the audience use and retain the information.

Types of Visual Aids

As you begin your speech with an introduction, you may choose to highlight the way you will be showing the audience what you are talking about. Let's say you are doing a speech about a new test required by the state in which you live for high school seniors to graduate and receive their diploma. You may, in your introduction, state that you will be discussing the history and development of the test, current content areas of questions on the test, and results of the test at local, county, and state levels.

After your introduction, you may choose to use a **chart** or **diagram** to show a timeline of events to date, from the first meeting about the proposed test to its first implementation. This timeline may work for you, but let's say you would like to get into the actual decision-making process that motivated leading educators to create the test requirement. You may decide to use **decision trees** showing the variables in place at the beginning of the discussion about tests and how each decision led to the next, which brings us to where we are today.

To compliment this comprehensive guide and help make a transition to current content areas of questions, you may use a **bar** or **pie graph** to show the percentage of seniors below the national average in reading, writing, or mathematics. If you have a computer program to assist you, you may use a **topographical map** showing the state in three dimensions, and the hills and valleys may reflect test scores rather than geographical features like mountains. Then you may show a comparable graph illustrating the distribution of test questions, their degree of difficulty, or approximate grade-level correlation.

Finally, you may move to the issue of results, and present the audience with an old-fashioned dunce cap and a large light bulb, asking which they prefer. The **object** may be just the visual aid you need to make your point and reinforce the residual message. Additional visual aids can include, but are not limited to, sound and music, video, and even yourself. If your speech is about the importance of stretching before exercising, your demonstration may just be the best visual aid.

Methods and Materials

When it comes time to use your visual aids, you will want to give some thought to how to portray your chart, graph, or object. The **chalk** or **white board** is one standard way of presenting visual aids. Your instructor may write key words or diagrams on the boards while discussing a textbook chapter. **Flip charts** on a pedestal can also serve to show a series of steps or break down a chart into its components. **Posterboard** is one common way of organizing your visual aids before a speech. It is portable, relatively inexpensive, and allows you a large "blank page" in which to express yourself. **Handouts** may also serve to communicate complex information to the audience, but be careful never to break **Speech Rule #1.**

> Speech Rule #1. Never give handouts to the audience at the beginning of your speech. You cannot compete with paper. People read at their own pace. People want to ask questions from what they are reading, and if everyone is on a different paragraph or section, jumping back and forth to answer questions will take you off balance in your speech. People will "listen" to what they are reading and not you, the speaker. If handouts are needed or required, give them out at the end of your speech.

Transparencies and **slides** have largely been replaced by computer-generated slide show programs like PowerPoint by Microsoft. This program and others like it can be very helpful in presenting visual information, but because computers and projector sometimes break down and fail to work as planned, packing transparencies is always a good idea. You may arrive at your destination, find the equipment is no longer available, or out for service, and your transparencies will allow you to stay on track for your speech.

Video can also be an effective visual aid but, like computer programs, can sometime fail you at the last minute. In addition, because video can captivate the audience, take care that the video selection contributes to your speech but doesn't leave the audience wishing you had left the video on just a little longer instead of resuming your speech.

Preparing Visual Aids

There are four general guidelines to follow when preparing visual aids. Make your visual aids:

1. BIG   The audience needs to be able to see it from the back.

2. CLEAR   The audience needs to be able to "get it" the first time they see it.

3. SIMPLE   The audience needs to have visual aids that simplify concepts.

4. CONSISTENT The audience needs consistency across all of the visual aids.

   Get started early. Make sure you use a large enough font or image and that you actually test it before the speech. Ask a friend to stand at the back of the room and read or interpret your visual aid. Allow time for revision based on what you learn.

Using Visual Aids

There are three general guidelines to follow when using visual aids. Make sure you:

1. Make a clear connection between your words and the visual aid for the audience.

2. Do not distract the audience with your visual aid, blocking their view of you or adjusting the visual aid repeatedly while trying to speak.

3. Do not talk to the whiteboard, the video, or other visual aids. Speak to the audience.

   Becoming proficient at using visual aids takes time and practice. The more you practice before your speech, the more comfortable you will be with your visual aids and the role they serve in illustrating your message. Taking care to give thought as to where to place visual aids before speaking will help, but when it comes time to actually give your speech, make sure you reassess your plans and ensure that they work for the audience as it really is. Speaking to a visual aid (or reading it to the audience) is not an effective strategy. Know your material well enough that you refer to the visual aid, not rely on it.

What wisdom can you find that is greater than kindness?

—Jean-Jacques Rousseau

Incorporating Ethics into Your Communication

On a final note, in this text you learned about the important and dynamic process of communication. Together we have seen how communication with others impacts our self-concept and how that in turn impacts our expectations of ourselves. We have also seen how communicating effectively can improve interpersonal relationships and making our lives together more fulfilling. We discussed communication across cultures and how your own background and range of experiences contributes to your communication with others. In terms of mass communication, we examined how messages are created and controlled and discussed ways to be a critical media consumer. Finally, we discussed this powerful force called communication in public-speaking situations.

Oral communication can move communities and cultures and change history. It can also motivate you to take a stand, consider an argument, or purchase a product. The degree to which you consider both the common good and fundamental principles you hold to be true when crafting your message directly relates to how your message will impact others. Every action has an ethical aspect to it, and it is important to consider this in the act of communication.

Ethics refers to a set of principles or rules for correct conduct. Ethics in communication means considering the good of everyone as well as basic principles when choosing to communicate. Whether you look to consequences, duty, or actions themselves to establish whether a choice is moral, you need to look at with whom you communicate and your responsibility to them. The audience is made up of individuals, each important in their role as an audience member, but also as a mother, a daughter, a father, or a son to someone. Consider to yourself how you would like to have your mother, father, sister, or brother treated by another, and this will help guide your actions with others. We may share different customs, cultures, and languages around the world, but everyone wants to be treated with respect.

Consider the golden rule, in all its many forms, when you communicate. The golden rule incorporates human kindness, cooperation, and reciprocity across cultures, languages, backgrounds, and interests. In the basic principles of communication, we discussed how communication is irreversible. Regardless of where you travel and with whom you communicate, remember how you want to be treated and express it in your communication with others.

The Golden Rule	"Do unto others as you would have them do unto you."
Bahá'í	*"Blessed is he who preferreth his brother before himself."* - Baha'u'llah, Tablets of Baha'u'llah, 71
Christianity	*"All things whatsoever ye would that men should do to you, do ye even so to them."* - Matthew 7:12
Buddhism	*"Hurt not others in ways that you yourself would find hurtful."* - Udana-Varga, 5:18
Confucianism	*"Do not unto others what you would not have them do unto you."* - Analects 15:23
Hinduism	*"This is the sum of duty: do naught unto others which would cause you pain if done to you."* - Mahabharata 5:1517
Taoism	*"Regard your neighbor's gain as your own gain, and your neighboar's loss as your own loss."* - T'ai Shang Kan Ying P'ien
Islam	*"No one of you is a believer until he desires for his brother that which he desires for himself."* - Sunnah
Judaism	*"What is hateful to you, do not to your fellow man. That is the law: all the rest is commentary."* - Talmud, Shabbat 31, a
Native American	*"Respect for all life is the foundation."* - The Great Law of Peace
Jainism	*"In happiness and suffering, in joy and grief, we should regard all creatures as we regard our own self."* - Lord Mahavira, 24th Tirthankara

Summary

In this chapter we discussed four important characteristics of a good delivery and three key elements according to Aristotle, examined the difference between communication apprehension and speech anxiety, and outlined several strategies to reduce speaker apprehension. We examined the use of voice, body, and visual aids in the delivery of a speech. Finally, we discussed general principles about the preparation and use of visual aids during a speech and the importance of ethics in communication.

> *To effectively communicate, we must realize that we are all different in the way we perceive the world and use this understanding as a guide to our communication with others.*
>
> —Anthony Robbins

For More Information _____

To learn more about the use of visual aids, read "eHow to Use Visual Aids During a Speech" by Sharon Rose Beaulaurier on Encarta eHow at:
http://encarta.ehow.com/eHow/eHow/0,1053,3477,FF.html

Review Questions _____

1. Factual Questions
    a. What is the difference between communication apprehension and speech anxiety?
    b. What are four key characteristics of a good delivery?
    c. What are eight distinct aspects of your voice to focus on?

2. Interpretative Questions
    a. Should additional characteristics of a good speech be considered? Describe them.
    b. What does the term fluidity mean? What is correct pronounciation?
    c. Can you think of an example for each of the four presentational methods? Which do your prefer and for what purpose?

3. Evaluative Questions
    a. Do you think credibility impacts the audience's ability to listen? If yes, how? If no, why not?
    b. Do you think use of voice is a talent, something you are born with, or a skill, something you can learn?
    c. Do you think any of the visual aids discussed can actually decrease the audience's ability to understand your key points?

4. Application Questions
    a. Create a list of questions to assess what an audience needs to understand a speaker and their message. Survey an equal number of men and women. Compare your results.
    b. Create a list of visual aids you notice during your day. Note which are helpful and which are not and why.
    c. Record yourself giving a speech (audio only) and see when you, as the audience member, would like to see a point or issue illustrated with a visual aid.

Works Cited _____

Ayres, J. (1990). Situational factors and audience anxiety. *Communication Education, 39:* 283–291.

Ayres, J. & Hopf, T. (1993). *Coping with speech anxiety.* Norwood, NJ: Ablex Publishing.

Ayres, J. & Miller, J. (1994). *Effective public speaking* (4th ed.). Madison, WI: Brown and Benchmark.

Covino, W. A. & Jolliffe D. A. (1995). *Rhetoric: Concepts, definitions, boundaries.* Boston: Allyn & Bacon.

Ellis, A. (1962). *Reason and emotion in psychotherapy.* New York: Stuart Publishers.

Glaser, S. (1981). Oral communication apprehension and avoidance: The current status of treatment research. *Communication Education, 30,* 321–341.

Gudykunst, W. & Kim, Y. (1997). *Communicating with strangers: An approach to intercultural communication* (3rd ed.). New York: McGraw-Hill.

McCrosky, J. (1984). The communication apprehension perspective. In J. A. Daly & J. C. McCroskey (Eds.), *Avoiding communication: shyness, reticence, and communication apprehension.* Beverly Hills, CA: Sage.

Seiler, W. & Beall, M. (2000). *Communication: Making connections* (4th ed.). Boston: Allyn & Bacon.

Thompson, W. (1967). *Quantitative research in public address and communication* (pp. 175–176). New York: Random House.

Index